D0462312

The American Woman 1992–93

Edited by Paula Ries and Anne J. Stone for the Women's Research & Education Institute Betty Dooley, Executive Director

W · W · NORTON & COMPANY

NEW YORK · LONDON

Women
and
Politics

The American Woman
1992–93
A Status Report

Printed in the United States of America

First Edition

The text of this book is composed in Goudy Old Style, with the display set in Bodoni Bold Condensed. Composition and manufacturing by the Haddon Craftsmen, Inc.

ISBN: 0–393–03110–1
ISBN: 0–393–30871–5 (pbk)

W.W. Norton & Company, Inc., 500 Fifth Avenue, New York, N.Y. 10110
W.W. Norton & Company Ltd., 10 Coptic Street, London WC1A 1PU

1 2 3 4 5 6 7 8 9 0

Contents

List of Tables and Figures

American Women Today: A Statistical Portrait
Section 1: Population

Section 2: Health

Section 3: Family and Household Structure

10 List of Tables and Figures

Section 4: Child Care and Support

Section 5: Education

Section 6: Employment

Section 7: Earnings and Benefits

Section 8: Income and Assets

Section 9: Politics

Section 10: International Comparisons

Editors' Notes

The American Woman 1992–93, which is the fourth volume in WREI's series of reports on the status of U.S. women, differs considerably in some respects from the earlier volumes. From the outset, *The American Woman* was conceived as an evolving publication, and the staff at WREI has always been interested in feedback—critical as well complimentary—from people who use the book. Before beginning work on the fourth volume, WREI held a series of focus groups where readers who use *The American Woman* were asked to tell us candidly what they had found most useful—and least useful—about the series. The participants in these focus groups included researchers, congressional staff, and others involved in policymaking, as well as representatives from women's organizations, labor unions, and the corporate world. From these extremely fruitful sessions, as well as from suggestions offered by the book advisory committee, the new *The American Woman 1992–93* emerged.

There are two major departures from the earlier volumes. The first is that, whereas each of the first three volumes contained many chapters by contributing authors that covered a wide, and rather eclectic, range of topics, this volume has only four chapters by outside authors, and each explores a particular facet of—and brings a particular perspective to—a single topic: women and politics.

The second change involves the statistical tables and fig-

ures, which in previous volumes were in the appendix, and
are now central to *The American Woman 1992–93*. There are
about four times as many tables and charts as before and they
are accompanied by much more extensive interpretive text.
This change has allowed us not only to provide a greater
variety of data related to such basic areas as employment and
earnings, but also to introduce new areas, including international comparisons. The statistical information has been organized by topic area into sections, each of which begins with
highlights of what we see as notable, encouraging, or dis-
couraging, and guides the reader to specific tables or figures.
Thus, for example, a congressional staffer or reporter who
needs to know the racial composition of the nation's college
student population can quickly turn to the education statistics to find the information.

Because this volume of *The American Woman* is scheduled
for publication in the spring of an important national election year, women and politics seemed an appropriate focus.
We are extremely fortunate to have four fine chapters on this
topic. While each stands alone, having its own perspective on
the subject and addressing a different angle, we were struck—
as we think the reader will be—by how well they complement
each other.

"In Review," which in this volume covers 24 months
(from the beginning of July 1989 through June 1991) is generally organized as in previous volumes—that is, in a calendar
format. It highlights "firsts" and other significant accomplish-
ments of women, as well as noteworthy social and economic
developments and major judicial decisions affecting females.
However, in a minor departure from past practice, we have
brought together information on two topics that have re-

ceived a great deal of media coverage—(1) women in the military, and (2) state laws enacted as a result of the Supreme Court's decision in *Webster v. Reproductive Health Services*. Each of these subjects has been given its own "box."

"In Review," explores briefly some of the issues that may concern women in a political context. We notice, for example, how often events involving some conflict between "fetal protection" and women's rights cropped up in a context other than abortion—and, of course, the controversy over the issue of abortion rights, itself, remained heated over the entire period. By no means everything "In Review" is about conflict or controversy, however. Two especially heartening items concern women who have achieved distinction in science—one of them a retired scientist, Gertrude Elion, who at age 70 was the first woman ever to be elected to the Inventors Hall of Fame; the other is 17-year-old, Ashley Reiter, who won first prize in the Westinghouse Science talent search.

As was the case in the earlier volumes, a section of this book is devoted to the Congressional Caucus for Women's Issues, a bipartisan group of members of Congress who work together to advance equity for women.

We cannot close this note without mentioning our great debt to two individuals. The first is WREI's executive director, Betty Dooley, who has furnished the moral backing, and raised the financial support, that made it possible for us to devote all our energies to this book. The second is Sara Rix, the editor of the first three volumes of *The American Woman*, which provided a solid foundation for building the fourth. We thank Sara for sharing what she learned from producing three volumes in the series, for encouraging us to try a new format for this volume, and for the many other ways in which she has helped us in preparing *The American Woman 1992–93*. Most of all, we want to express our admiration for the high standard of critical analysis and attention to detail that she set for the series.

PAULA RIES
ANNE J. STONE

Acknowledgments

THIS IS THE FOURTH VOLUME IN *The American Woman* series prepared by the Women's Research and Education Institute (WREI). With the very first volume, *The American Woman 1987–88*, this series of periodical reports on the status of women established itself as an invaluable and comprehensive source of up-to-date information and thoughtful analysis for policymakers, the media, and the general public.

The American Woman series was launched with a generous grant from the Ford Foundation, supplemented by contributions from other donors. WREI is especially grateful to the Charles H. Revson Foundation, the AT&T Foundation, RJR Nabisco, Chevron USA, Inc., the Chrysler Corporation Fund, and Sears, Roebuck and Company for helping to make the preparation of this fourth volume possible. We would also like to acknowledge the support of the American Express Company; American Income Life Insurance Co.; ARCO; Ford Motor Company; Guinness America, Inc.; International Brotherhood of Teamsters; Johnson & Johnson; Martin Marietta Corporation; Pfizer Inc.; Sara Lee Corporation; and Sea-Land Services, Inc.

No book of this kind could be published without the assistance and encouragement of scores of individuals, many of whom have donated time and expertise. In WREI's own "family," Jean Stapleton, president of WREI's board of directors, has been an enthusiastic and tireless spokeswoman for every volume in the series. Indeed, the WREI staff is grateful to the entire board, and particularly to the members of its executive committee—Jean Stapleton, Dorothy Gregg, Matina Horner, Juanita Kreps, and Paquita Vivó—for their belief in the book and for their encouragement and moral support.

A superb advisory committee, many of whose members have served since *The American Woman* series was first conceived, has been generous with wisdom, expertise, and encouragement. For their help with this fourth volume in the series, we want especially to thank Brenda Pillors, Ann Schmidt, Sara E. Rix, Irene Natividad, Beverly Guy-Sheftell, Sarah Pritchard, Ronnie Steinberg, Margaret C. Simms, Mariam K. Chamberlain, Jane Chapman, Harriette McAdoo, and Ida G. Ruben. Sara Rix, who edited the first three volumes in *The American Woman* series and who generously agreed to provide continued guidance as a member of the advisory committee, deserves special mention—her suggestions for *The American Woman 1992–93* were invaluable.

WREI is indebted, also, to Mary Ellen Capek, of the National Council for Research on Women, and to Jill Miller of the Displaced Homemakers Network.

WREI cannot adequately express its appreciation to the many people who provided information or material for inclusion in *The American Woman 1992–93*, and in many cases gave generously of their advice and expertise as well. We are especially grateful to Howard Hayghe and John Stinson of the Bureau of Labor Statistics, Lucy Baruch of the Center for the American Woman and Politics, Cynthia Harrison of the Federal Judicial Center, Phillip Lattimore III of the National Center for State Courts, Laura Lorenzen of the Congressional Caucus for Women's Issues, Terry Sollom of the Alan Guttmacher Institute, and Rebecca Tillet of the National

Women's Political Caucus. Thanks, too, to Alison Bernstein of Princeton University and June Zeitlin of the Ford Foundation for their willingness to provide guidance.

Judith Dollenmeyer, Allison Porter, and Kitty Stone made critical writing and editorial contributions to this volume. Pamela Briggs ably assisted with the statistical work and Roberto Celi helped with proof reading. Mary Cunnane, our editor at W. W. Norton, and her assistant, Rebecca Castillo, have been staunch sources of advice and encouragement.

Every member of WREI's own staff played a role in producing *The American Woman 1992–93*. The hardworking core editorial team, led by Paula Ries and co-editor Anne Stone and assisted by Nancy Peplinsky, devoted a phenomenal amount of their time, effort, and critical intelligence to this book. Three volunteer WREI interns—Emily Gould, Annelisa Hedgecock, and Susan Entman—were invaluable, and without their energy and enterprise there would be no "In Review" section. Carolyn Becraft, WREI's expert on women in the military, also contributed to this section. Terry Walker and Alison Dineen not only helped in many ways with the preparation of this volume, but worked tirelessly on promoting and disseminating earlier volumes in the series.

Finally, I want to emphasize the fact that neither the funders, nor any of the advisors, reviewers, or independent editors are responsible for any errors or misstatements that may appear in the book, nor do the opinions expressed herein necessarily represent the opinions of anyone other than the authors of the chapters.

BETTY PARSONS DOOLEY
Executive Director
Women's Research and Education Institute

Introduction

JEAN STAPLETON

MOST OF US BELIEVE that greater freedom, so long as it does not infringe on others, is a worthy goal. The peoples of Eastern Europe and the Soviet Union today are only the most recent groups to wrestle with the often-difficult consequences of that concept of freedom. This book is a report on how American women are faring in pursuit of the same vision of a larger, freer, more open life—politically, economically, and socially.

Let me venture for a moment into dangerous territory, thorny with thought-stopping labels. I'd like to capture the attitude that energizes themes in this book. Although in 1988 both presidential candidates shunned "the L word" as a kind of scarlet letter, the American journalist Dorothy Thompson in 1938 dared to use the word in offering a serviceable, lower-case definition of the dream of freedom, beyond a party or gender label:

To be a liberal means to believe in human freedom. It means to believe in human beings. It means to champion that form of social and political order which releases the greatest amount of human energy; [and] permits [the] greatest liberty for individuals and groups, in planning and living their lives; cherishes freedom of speech, freedom of conscience and freedom of action, limited by only one thing: the protection of the freedom of others. (Kurth, 1990)

The fourth volume in *The American Woman* series assesses where women are now on the road to a life of greater opportunity and political and economic parity. Are American women closer to their goals? The picture painted by the four essays that follow is multicolored and many layered, replete with lights and shadows. A statistical section gives the picture analytic perspective and a comparative international dimension. Overall, Dickens's line is apt, "This is the best of times and the worst of times for women."

Political Highlights

Our vehicle is politics. The first four chapters in this book focus on women in politics through different lenses. They reflect the persistent questions: "Do females in politics matter? Does their presence bring measurable gain on issues women care about?" The answer is clearly "Yes." Or "Yes, But." Most of the authors acknowledge that until women's underrepresentation is remedied, and half of the nation finds her voice in high policy councils, no complete answer is possible.

Four essays open the book. First, Celia Morris conducts lively interviews with a handful of notable females serving as local, state, or national officials and legislators in "Changing the Rules and the Roles: Five Women in Public Office." Governor Ann Richards of Texas, Senator Nancy Kassebaum of Kansas, Representative Maxine Waters of Los Angeles, and Mayor Carrie Saxon Perry of Hartford, Connecticut are "members of a bridge generation raised with assumptions about women's roles that reach back in Western society to the 18th century and the beginning of the Industrial Revolution." Technology and economics, notes Morris, have transformed the United States and women's roles in this country. To the old Latin tag that times change, and we change with them, should possibly be added "but slowly." Where females in politics are concerned, attitudes of those in power (mostly male) are changing only gradually.

These women officials are master practitioners of psychological judo. They wittily play off conventional attitudes and use apparent conformity—plus well-chosen moments of non-conformity—to win unconventional progress for women. One key to their success is having keen senses of humor and excellent antennae. The staff of U.S. Speaker of the House Tom Foley was therefore "startled, but not surprised" when freshman Congresswoman Maxine Waters bucked custom by walking into his office saying, "I need one hot minute with the Speaker!"

Lena Guerrero, at 32 the first woman member of the powerful Texas Railroad Commission, is the new generation after the "bridge" females. Like them, she took male mentors' advice but walked a woman's way. One Hispanic leader who counseled her captured the generational difference: "We've popped the [door] open. Now they invite us to the table. Your generation of leadership—men and women—is going to be required to know parliamentary procedure, to know how to read budgets, and to eat your lunch at the negotiating table. . . . Your job is to be *substantively* good!"

In "Women of Color and the Campaign Trail," Irene Natividad surveys the political road for the African American, Hispanic American, Native American, and Asian American woman. The United States is now experiencing a wave of immigration resulting in a third of the country's population growth in the 1980s coming from new arrivals, mostly from Asia and Latin America. "Given demographers' projections that minorities could be the majority of the population in some important states by the next century, and taking into account the increased presence of women as a whole in the political arena—both as candidates and voters," she writes, ". . . many more of our nation's leaders will be women of color." Barriers blocking access to politics for these females include lack of funds, low credibility, unconventional images and accents, cultural resistance from men of color, and accepted norms of appropriate female behavior.

Paths into politics vary among different groups of women of color. For African American females, experience as community leaders, church leaders, and "as leaders of families often bereft of men," Natividad says, builds credibility. The largest number of Hispanic American women officeholders are on school boards; for them, the political path leads through the PTA and school-centered activism. The empowerment of Native American females has occurred primarily within their tribal organizations, as in the 1987 election of Wilma Mankiller as the first woman head of the Cherokee Nation.

Barriers differ among the groups. One Native American woman leader points out that "[Our] bid for mainstream political power has had to take a back seat to [our] community's struggle to gain official recognition from the United States." The relatively tiny number of Asian American females in politics today reflects in many instances their status as recent arrivals, as well as strong cultural norms against roles outside the family. Margaret Chin, a 1991 New York City Council candidate, gives her mother's view of Chin's political work: "A daughter doesn't go out and mind other people's business."

In "Do Women Officeholders Make a Difference?" Ruth Mandel and Debra Dodson address the key issues more directly, offering the results of a systematic large-scale survey by the Center for the American Woman and Politics (CAWP) of the policy and legislative effects of females in elected office.

"The best of times, the worst of times" coloration is evident in their findings. In 1991, women hold about 18 percent of elected statewide and state legislative offices, more than four times women's representation a generation ago. "On the other hand," they write, "almost three-quarters of a century after winning the right to vote, women still are far from achieving parity among officeholders at any level of government." The ratio of men to women in Congress is 17 to one; in state legislatures, four to one.

Why should we care? Mandel and Dodson believe, in line with their findings of solid policy gains for females when women do hold office, that our systematic underrepresentation "symbolizes the failure of American society to provide equality of opportunity for all citizens. [And] half the nation's talent remains largely untapped . . ."

The message Mandel and Dodson send is clear: females of all ideological perspectives are making a difference in public policy for women. The data they present are impressive. CAWP studies in 1977, 1981, and 1988, together with related findings, show a consistent gender gap, or difference in attitudes, between female and male elected officials, and "women were more likely to have feminist and liberal views than their male counterparts within the same political parties and in the same self-identified political position on the spectrum of political ideology (i.e., conservative, moderate, and liberal)." Supporting women candidates, they conclude, pays off in the increasing commitment to human needs and well-being while widening the perspective of lawmakers on economic and security priorities.

Campaign pollsters and consultants Celinda Lake and Vince Breglio agree that the "gender gap" is a reality in both the voting booth and the policymaking process. In "Different

Voices, Different Views: The Politics of Gender," they lead us to the edge of the gender gap and point out its scenic features. Not only ideological perspective but party identification reflects a difference: men prefer the Republican label, women the Democratic—although women are "only slightly more likely than men to identify themselves as liberals." In both parties, young (under 45) and working females tend to support women candidates—so much for the canard that feminism is going gray.

Issues of war and peace have been the source of the greatest historical differences between men's and women's political attitudes, at least from the time of the Korean War. (Ironically, today this shows up as more distrust of Soviet President Gorbachev and the Soviet Union on the part of women.)

Particularly on economic issues, since the early 1980s females have been more pessimistic than males about America's direction. This continuing trend began to show up at the ballot box in the polls after the 1983 recession, say Lake and Breglio.

Surprisingly, perhaps, "women's issues (women's rights and abortion) have been less a factor in the gender gap than differences in perspectives on issues like the economy and priorities for the budget." Males and females support abortion in roughly equal numbers, but "women are more likely to consider this issue central to their voting decisions and to be active in either pro-choice or pro-life politics."

Trends to Watch

Our volume's statistical chapters look at population demographics first—health, the structure of families and households, and child care. Then the economic status of American women is examined through the numbers on employment, income, benefits, and poverty. Education and politics have their own sections.

A new feature in this year's edition of *The American Woman* is a set of international comparisons that offer a look at where American females are in relation to women of other nations.

The lights and shadows of American women's situation in 1991 appear in the statistics. Let me mention a few of them:

Good News: In 1991, nearly one out of every five statewide elected officials and legislators, and 17 percent of all elected mayors, were women.

Bad News: Only six percent of voting members of the U.S. House and Senate were female.

Good News (and Bad News): Infant mortality rates were at an all-time low, nine per 1,000 live births. However, in 1990, black babies were twice as likely as white babies to die in their first year.

Good News: Birth rates of teenage girls 18 and 19 years old have decreased 29 percent since 1970.

Bad News: Between 1973 and 1988, the incidence of breast cancer among women increased 25 percent.

Good News (and Bad News): Almost six out of 10 eligible mothers were awarded some form of child support in 1987, although white females were much more likely than either black or Hispanic females to be granted such awards.

Good News: In 1989, three-quarters of all Americans of both sexes completed at least four years of high school and women have earned over half of all bachelor's and masters degrees awarded in American colleges.

Good News: Female labor force participation was at an all-time high. In 1990, nearly six out of every 10 women were working or looking for work.

Good News: The number of businesses owned by females soared between 1977 and 1987—30 percent of U.S. businesses were owned by women in 1987.

Bad news: In spite of inroads females have made into traditionally male occupations, most jobs continued to be segregated by gender and in 1990, close to half of all employed women worked in relatively low-paying service and administrative support occupations such as health aides and secretaries.

Good News (Or Is It?): American women are now earning 72 cents for every dollar earned by men, up from 64 cents in 1980. However, this is as much a result of declines in males' wages as increases in females' wages.

Bad News: Female workers were less likely than male workers to have pension plans through their employers or union.

Bad News: The option of taking maternity or paternity leave was not the norm for full-time workers in American firms.

Good News (and Bad News): In 1989 the median annual income of a female college graduate exceeded that of a male high school graduate for the first time—by $100. However, this was as much because his income decreased as because her's increased.

Bad News: The face of poverty is much more youthful than it used to be. In 1989, one in five children lived in poverty. Among the elderly (age 65 and older), women were twice as likely as men to be poor.

Looking Ahead

So the 1990s begin for American women as the best of times, yet also the worst of times. Whether the picture is hopeful or shadowed is ambiguous, depending in part on the borders where a woman stands—borders of income, race, occupation, class, family responsibility, and nationality.

One thing is sure: putting more females into office does matter. And not just on "women's issues," although most issues have a dimension particular to females that needs attention. For instance, in health research recent assertions that the differential effects of disease on women have not been adequately investigated are now compounded by allegations that women with heart disease do not receive as aggressive a treatment as do men. With clouds over the Supreme Court and not much sign that a kinder, gentler national family policy will soon appear, women need to pay close attention to legislative politics. In the longer term, true choices for women—between workplaces and home, for example—will be narrowed to some degree by public policy. To increase the freedom women enjoy, we must be sure that they are represented adequately in policy debates.

Keeping fresh a dream of freedom for women, and for all people, will be a critical source of energy. The vital questions for American females are also posed for women in other nations, some of which have better answers than we've found. American women need to begin reaching across borders for answers and, perhaps, problem-solving alliances.

The American Woman 1992–93 again shows that women have been moving on stage from their traditional places in the audience, or in the wings as sweating stagehands. In coming years, we will see fewer women in supporting parts and cameos of the public drama, and more in principal roles.

In Review:
July 1989–June 1991[1]

1989

July 3 / The U.S. Supreme Court hands down its ruling in *Webster v. Reproductive Health Services* (see the box, "In the Wake of *Webster*," pages 42–43).

July 11 / In a column in today's issue of the *Des Moines* (Iowa) *Register*, editor Geneva Overholser tackles the controversial question of whether the media should publish the names of rape victims. Noting that it is her paper's policy not to publish this information, Ms. Overholser goes on to explain why the policy troubles her: "I believe that we will not break down the stigma [associated with being a victim of rape] until more and more women take public stands. . . . Rape is an American shame. Our society needs to see that and attend to it, not hide it or hush it up." She urges women "who have suffered this awful crime and attendant injustice to speak out."

July 11 / The Chrysler Corporation, in an agreement with the National Association for the Advancement of Colored People, pledges to double (to 20 percent) the number of women and minorities in management positions.

July 13 / Jennifer Johnson, who used drugs while she was pregnant, is convicted in Florida of delivering drugs to a minor—a felony—on the grounds that she delivered drugs to

---

[1]Emily Gould, Annelisa Hedgecock, and Susan Entman compiled most of "In Review." Carolyn Becraft also contributed to it.

her fetus through the umbilical cord. This is the first time that a law intended for drug traffickers has been used in this way.

July 27 / Delegates to the 125th national convention of the Elks Club vote down a resolution to strike the word "male" from the group's membership requirements.

August 1 / Gwendolyn King is appointed Social Security commissioner. Ms. King is the first black to head the federal government's largest domestic program.

August 9 / According to today's *New York Times*, a study done for the National Collegiate Athletic Association found that female and male basketball players spend the same amount of time at their sport, but the women attend class more regularly, study more, and get higher grades than the men.

August 18 / *The National Report on Work and Family*, published today, describes a Mobil Oil Corporation study of the effect employees' family lives have on their careers. According to the Mobil study, a higher percentage of men (27 percent) than of women (19 percent) refuse to relocate and employees who are spouses in dual-career couples are less likely to relocate than others. Explanations given by both men and women for not wanting to relocate include spousal employment and family reasons, such as nearby relatives and child care support networks.

August 22 / The National Commission on Working Women releases *Unequal Picture: Black, Hispanic, Asian and Native American Characters on Television*. The report says that almost three-fourths of all minority females on TV are cast in light-weight "sitcoms," which rarely represent the realities of life for a minority woman. In addition, only two percent of all producers working on shows with minority characters are minority women.

August 29 / Ileana Ros-Lehtinen (R-FL) is elected to the U.S. House of Representatives to succeed the late Claude Pepper. She is the first Cuban American ever elected to Congress.

September 7 / Julia Chang Bloch is sworn in as U.S. ambassador to Nepal. She is the first American ambassador of Asian descent.

September 11 / In a joint effort, seven large New York employers begin a program to provide emergency child care to their workers who live in New York City and northern New Jersey. The employers will pay most or all of the cost of at-home care for children 13 and under for up to three consecutive days. The care will be provided by two licensed home health care agencies.

September 26 / In a 7–4 ruling, the U.S. Court of Appeals for the Seventh Circuit holds that it is not a violation of Title VII of the Civil Rights Act of 1964 (which prohibits employment discrimination on the basis of sex) for employers to ban all fertile women from jobs that pose a potential risk to a fetus, even if the women say they are not pregnant or have no intention of getting pregnant. The case at issue (in *UAW and Local 322 Allied Industrial Workers of America v. Johnson Controls*) involved a company's policy of excluding fertile women from jobs where workers are exposed to high concentrations of lead. Today's ruling causes dismay among women's equity advocates and labor unions, and may be appealed to the U.S. Supreme Court.

September 27 / The French researcher who developed RU-486, commonly referred to as an abortion pill because it prevents a fertilized egg from implanting and can dislodge an implanted egg in the early stages of pregnancy, receives the Albert Lasker Clinical Medical Research Award, one of the most prestigious medical prizes in the United States. In addition to its value as a safe and effective abortifacient in the first trimester, RU-486 may be effective in other ways, such as fighting breast cancer.

September 30 / Effective today, the spouses of nursing home residents whose bills are paid by Medicaid will no longer face the threat of impoverishment. Until now, the law required that virtually all of a nursing home resident's income and assets be exhausted before Medicaid would help. This has meant deprivation, especially for women whose husbands are in nursing homes, because the bulk of couples' assets and income have typically been in the husbands' name. From now on, the spouse who is at home must be allowed to keep the house, a car, at least $815 a month of the couple's combined income, and $12,000 of their total assets.

October 2 / The U.S. Public Health Service, claiming that many tests performed on healthy pregnant women are expensive, time-consuming, and provide no real benefit, issues a report recommending that women whose fetuses are at no apparent risk be given less prenatal care.

October 5 / Florida's Supreme Court, striking down a state law requiring parental consent for minors' abortions, rules unanimously that the state constitution's privacy amendment protects the right to abortion for minors as well as adults because it provides the right of privacy for "every natural person."

October 12 / As part of the Douglass Project for Rutgers Women in Math and Science, a program designed to address the national shortage of female scientists and engineers, New Jersey's Douglass College dedicates a dormitory designed for 110 women studying science.

October 13 / *Ms.* suspends publication. The magazine's

failure to turn a profit is attributed largely to the difficulty it has had in attracting advertisers.

October 17 / Antonia Novello, a pediatrician born in Puerto Rico, is appointed U.S. Surgeon General. She is the first woman, as well as the first person of Hispanic origin, to hold the position.

October 18 / The Child Care Employee Project releases a study finding that child care workers are paid 27 percent less now than in 1977, and that the turnover rate for employees at child care centers rose from 17 percent in 1977 to 41 percent in 1988.

October 21 / President Bush vetoes legislation that would have allowed the use of federal Medicaid funds to pay for abortions in cases of rape or incest.

November 8 / *The Boston Globe* reports that the Massachusetts treatment program for women who are drug or alcohol abusers has become so overburdened that some women have been put in a state prison, where they receive little or no treatment. Most of these women, who have not been convicted of any crime, are crack cocaine abusers who were committed involuntarily under a state law allowing judges to commit substance abusers to a 30-day treatment program if they pose a threat to themselves or others.

November 8 / By a vote of 89 to 8, the Senate approves compromise legislation that would raise the minimum wage to $3.80 an hour in 1990, and to $4.25 in 1991, with a lower "training wage" for workers ages 16 through 19 in their first jobs.

November 14 / Representatives Nancy Johnson (CT), Lynn Martin (IL), Claudine Schneider (RI), and Olympia Snowe (ME), Republican congresswomen who support abortion rights, meet with President Bush to urge him to change

IN THE WAKE

The very last entry in "In Review" in the previous volume of *The American Woman* (1990–91) was for July 3, 1989, when the U.S. Supreme Court upheld the right of a state to impose significant restrictions on abortion. Both pro-choice and anti-abortion activists saw the 5–4 decision, in *Webster v. Reproductive Health Services*, as inviting all-out challenges to the 1973 Supreme Court decision in *Roe v. Wade* that guaranteed abortion rights, as well as opening the door to more state restrictions of the kind the Court allowed in *Webster*.

Indeed, after the *Webster* ruling, bills that sought either to outlaw abortion, or to restrict it drastically, were introduced at an accelerating pace in state legislatures across the country, with the expectation that, if enacted, one of them would ultimately furnish the vehicle for testing the constitutional right to abortion before a Supreme Court very different from the *Roe* decision Court. At the same time, there was an increase in the introduction of bills that sought to make abortion legal under a particular state's own laws, so that abortion rights would be guaranteed in that state even if *Roe* were to be overturned.

The major enactments at the state level through June 30, 1991 that could be said to be direct "products" of the *Webster* decision are summarized here. Parental consent and/or notification laws are not included among them; however, as of May 31, 1991, 18 states had such laws in force, or soon to take effect. Ten require parental consent, seven require notification, one requires either consent or counseling. All but one provide for a judicial bypass. In addition, two states require that a minor get counseling before having an abortion.

1989

November 17 / Pennsylvania Governor Casey signs a law with tight restrictions on abortion, including: requiring a married woman to sign a statement that she has notified her husband of her intention to get an abortion; requiring a woman seeking an abortion to be given a state-prescribed lecture about the dangers of abortion; requiring a 24-hour waiting period; outlawing "sex-selection" abortions; banning abortion after 24 weeks of pregnancy except when pregnancy would cause extreme "irreversible" physical damage to the woman or danger to her life; and prohibiting most abortions in public hospitals. (Some of these provisions were later enjoined in court; the last three are in force.)

OF *WEBSTER*

1990

March 19 / Guam Governor Ada signs a law making the performance of an abortion a felony and soliciting or having an abortion a misdemeanor, except when pregnancy would endanger the woman's life or gravely impair her health. (The law was later enjoined.)

April 30 / Connecticut Governor O'Neill signs a law guaranteeing abortion rights in that state as under *Roe v. Wade*, except that a minor under age 16 must get counseling before having an abortion.

1991

January 25 / Utah Governor Bangerter signs a law making the performance of an abortion a felony, punishable by a heavy fine and up to five years in prison, except in cases of life endangerment, grave damage to the woman's health, rape and incest that have been reported to the authorities, and severe fetal deformity. (The law was later enjoined, pending resolution of a court challenge.)

February 28 / Maryland Governor Schaefer signs a measure making abortion rights, as presently guaranteed by the federal Constitution under *Roe v. Wade*, part of the state's law. However, unlike *Roe*, Maryland's new law requires the notification of one parent of a minor under 18, although there is a physician-bypass provision. The law also includes a provision allowing a voter referendum.

June 18 / Louisiana's legislature overrides Governor Roemer's veto and enacts a law making the performance of an abortion a criminal offense, subject to heavy penalties, with exceptions in cases where the woman's life is threatened, and very narrow exceptions in cases of rape or incest. (Last year, Roemer was twice able to make his vetoes of similar legislation stick.) Anti-abortion groups reportedly believe that a court challenge to the Louisiana law will offer the best opportunity yet to persuade the Supreme Court to overturn the 1973 decision in *Roe v. Wade*. (Lawsuits were later filed in both state and federal courts to prevent the Louisiana law from taking effect, as scheduled, in September 1991.)

WREI thanks the Alan Guttmacher Institute (AGI) for providing the information used in this section. Readers interested in detailed information on state legislation related to abortion rights and many other reproductive and maternal health issues should contact the AGI.

his mind and support permitting Medicaid to cover abortions in cases of rape or incest.

November 16 / Because of conflicting views in Congress over how to structure federal assistance for child care, several key members of the House say they will not try to complete a landmark child care bill this year, and child care legislation is reportedly not on the Senate leadership's current list of legislation to be considered before adjournment. However, many lawmakers said that child care would be a top priority in the next session, and that they were optimistic that legislation would be approved quickly once Congress reconvened.

November 17 / According to Census Bureau statistics reported in today's *Wall Street Journal*, 52 percent of managers under age 35 are women. However, the statistics also showed that college-educated managerial and professional women had median earnings of $25,400 in 1988, while their male counterparts earned $32,100.

November 29 / The Women's Rights Project of the American Civil Liberties Union and the New York Civil Liberties Union file a class-action suit against three hospitals and a drug-treatment center in New York City, challenging their policies of excluding pregnant women from drug and alcohol treatment programs.

December 1 / Rosabeth Moss Kanter, a professor at the Harvard Business School, takes over the top editorial job at the *Harvard Business Review*. Ms. Kanter is the first woman ever to hold this post.

December 4 / Upholding a consent decree established in June 1988, a federal appeals court rejects a union claim that San Francisco's agreement to hire and promote women and members of minority groups violates the rights of white men.

December 4 / A prosecutor in Massachusetts drops a

charge of motor vehicle homicide against a woman who gave birth to a still-born baby the day after she was involved in a drunk-driving accident. The prosecutor explains that there are "serious and unresolved" questions about what caused the fetus's death. (Under a 1984 ruling by the Massachusetts Supreme Court, a fetus is a "person" for purposes of the motor vehicle homicide law.) The case caused concern among pro-choice advocates, who feared that a conviction could eventually lead to women being held liable for many actions concerning their fetuses, including abortion.

December 7 / A U.S. Labor Department rule allowing work at home in five apparel-related industries is upheld by a federal district judge, despite claims by the International Ladies' Garment Workers' Union and others that the regulation would, among other things, lead to the exploitation of tens of thousands of workers, primarily immigrant women.

December 20 / The U.S. Conference of Mayors releases its annual report on homelessness and hunger. The survey, involving 27 cities, says that requests for emergency shelter are up 25 percent from 1988, and that requests for food are up 19 percent, with two-thirds of those requesting food being children or parents. The study also says that, on average, 36 percent of the homeless are families with children and 14 percent are single women.

December 29 / Eve Atkinson is named athletic director of Lafayette College, becoming the first woman to head a combined men's and women's athletic program at an NCAA Division I institution with a I-AA football program.

1990

January 1 / The Johns Hopkins Medical Institutions and six other medical centers begin recruiting participants for a major four-year study of heart disease in post-menopausal women. Previous research on heart disease conducted at these institutions has focused entirely on men. The research seeks to determine whether the administration of certain hormone drugs can help reduce heart disease in post-menopausal women.

January 4 / New Jersey Governor Jim Florio signs a family leave law that will require employers to give their employees up to 12 weeks to care for a newborn or adopted child, or for an ill or injured immediate family member. Although the leave will be unpaid, workers will still receive health insurance and benefits, and will be given their former jobs, or equivalents, upon their return.

January 7 / Drug treatment is scarcer than ever for women, reports Susan Diesenhouse in an article in today's *New York Times*. "Federal officials agree that there is a particular shortage of [drug] treatment programs for women who are pregnant or have children."

January 9 / The U.S. Supreme Court, ruling unanimously in *University of Pennsylvania v. EEOC*, holds that universities charged with discriminating in faculty tenure decisions must make the relevant confidential personnel files available to federal investigators looking into complaints of discrimination. The case arose from a complaint by Rosalie Tung, who charged that she was denied tenure by the university because of discrimination on account of her race, sex, and national origin.

January 11 / Today's issue of the *New England Journal of*

Medicine reports that women become intoxicated more quickly than men because their stomachs contain smaller amounts of an enzyme that breaks down alcohol before it reaches the bloodstream. As a result, one drink for a woman of average size has the same effect as two drinks for a man of average size.

January 19 / Mayor Kathryn Whitmire names Elizabeth M. Watson chief of police of Houston, Texas. Ms. Watson will be the first woman to head the police force of any of the country's 20 largest cities.

January 20 / The space orbiter Columbia lands at Edwards Air Force Base, nearly 11 days after launch—the longest space shuttle mission so far. Mission specialist Bonnie Dunbar, one of two women on the crew, has now logged more hours in orbit (430 hours) than any other American woman.

January 21 / A new exhibit, A Woman's Place is in the Patent Office, opens at the U.S. Patent and Trademark Office in Washington, D.C. Only three percent of all U.S. patents ever awarded have gone to women, but their share of new patents is over five percent.

January 25 / A new study published today in the *New England Journal of Medicine* reports that a woman's risk of heart attack is tripled by smoking, and that the more she smokes the greater the risk. However, the good news is that even a heavy, long-time smoker can reduce the risk by quitting; by about three years after she stops, her risk of heart disease is no greater than if she had never smoked.

February 1 / Kimberly Hardy, a Michigan woman, is ordered to stand trial for delivering cocaine to a minor. The charge: that she delivered the drug to her newborn baby via the umbilical cord in the minutes before the cord was cut.

February 2 / A judge in Wyoming dismisses a charge of

felony child abuse against a pregnant woman who drank alcohol, ruling that the state failed to produce probable cause that the fetus had been harmed.

February 7 / A bipartisan coalition of U.S. senators and representatives introduces the Civil Rights Act of 1990. The bill is designed primarily to restore the scope and effectiveness of federal civil rights laws that were severely cut back by six 1989 Supreme Court decisions. The bill also seeks to correct some other inequities in antidiscrimination laws. One such inequity is that a victim of intentional race discrimination is entitled to financial damages but a victim of intentional sex discrimination is not. Senator James Jeffords (R-VT), one of the bill's sponsors, says the new legislation is "a direct result of and response to [the Court's] effort to roll back the hard fought gains in equality for minorities and women won over the past twenty-five years."

February 12 / A study of women and minorities in law firms, published today in the *National Law Journal*, finds some progress for women but none for minorities. The number and percentage of women among partners and associates in law firms grew steadily in the 1980s, but the record was dismal with respect to the hiring and promotion of blacks, Hispanics, Asians, and Native Americans.

February 14 / The United States trails far behind many other countries in making new forms of birth control available, according to a report released today by the National Research Council and the Institute of Medicine. Asserting that up to two million unintended pregnancies result annually from contraceptive failure, the report estimates that more and better birth control options could cut the number of abortions in the United States by between one-third and one-half.

February 15 / Citing government statistics showing that moonlighting—holding more than one paying job—is becoming as commonplace among women as it has been among men, *The New York Times* publishes a long article about women workers who moonlight. A Bureau of Labor Statistics workforce survey in May 1989 found 3.1 million women working two or more jobs—nearly five times the number in 1970.

February 21 / *The Washington Post* reports on findings by researchers at the Wisconsin Institute for Research on Poverty that the average amount of child-support awards to women age 18 and over declined by nearly one-fourth (adjusted for inflation) between 1978 and 1985, and that most of the decline was due to the fact that women's earnings increased markedly relative to men's earnings during that period. Most states take the custodial parent's income into account when determining what the noncustodial parent should pay.

February 25 / Releasing its annual scorecard on women holding appointed state cabinet posts, the National Women's Political Caucus (NWPC) deplores the fact that there were fewer women in such posts in 1989 (136) than there had been the year before (149). Maryland's Governor William Donald Schaefer gets the highest score; his cabinet was nearly 39 percent female in 1989.

February 25 / The first of five articles by Jane Schorer chronicling the abduction and rape of Nancy Ziegenmayer, and Ms. Ziegenmayer's subsequent experiences with the criminal justice system, is published on the front page of the *Des Moines* (Iowa) *Register*. Ms. Ziegenmayer volunteered to tell her story, and her name, after reading Geneva Overholser's column in the *Register* (see July 11, 1989).

February 26 / Every tax dollar spent on providing birth control to women who might not otherwise have access to contraception saves the taxpayers well over $4, according to a study discussed in today's *New York Times*. The study, published in the January/February issue of *Family Planning and Perspectives*, bases its figures on an estimate of the number of unwanted births to low-income women that would occur in the absence of publicly funded contraceptive services, and the likely costs to the government of providing medical care, welfare, and other services to these women and their babies.

March 1 / Karen Ignagni and Peg Seminario assume their duties as directors of two newly created departments of the AFL-CIO. Ms. Ignagni heads the Employee Benefits Department, and Ms. Seminario heads the Department of Occupational Safety and Health. Only one other woman has headed a department of the AFL-CIO.

March 1 / The U.S. Justice Department files suit against Virginia Military Institute (VMI), an all-male institution that receives more than 40 percent of its support from Virginia taxpayers, charging that VMI violates the Civil Rights Act of 1964 and the 14th Amendment's equal protection clause because it bars women.

March 8 / French researchers, reporting in today's issue of the *New England Journal of Medicine*, say the abortion pill RU-486 is as safe and effective as a surgical abortion. A much less expensive alternative to surgical abortion, RU-486 is not available in the United States, and its French manufacturer (Roussel-Uclaf) has not sought permission to test the drug in this country, reportedly because anti-abortion groups here have vowed to boycott any company that sells it.

March 8 / A woman who is past 30 when she has her first child is no more likely than a first-time mother under 30 to have a premature birth or to have the baby die soon after birth, according to a new study described in today's *New England Journal of Medicine*. First-time mothers over 30 are, however, more likely than their younger counterparts to have complications during pregnancy and labor.

March 12 / At a hearing on discrimination in the construction field in New York City, female construction workers testify about constant sexual harassment on the job, and female and minority workers report encountering pervasive sex and/or race bias in hiring and promotion decisions.

March 13 / Ann Richards wins the Texas Democratic gubernatorial primary.

March 14 / A report released today by the National Academy of Sciences finds the quality of child care services in the United States inadequate and urges the government to allocate between five and 10 billion dollars more a year to upgrade it. A critical problem, according to the report, is high staff turnover and insufficient ratios of child care workers to children. The report recommends establishing national standards for the minimum ratios at various age levels, as well as the maximum size of a group or class, and also recommends that the federal government require employers to offer a year of unpaid, but job-protected, leave to the parents of new babies.

March 14 / California's attorney general proposes that the state allow testing and licensing of RU-486, which, he says, is a "safer, more private alternative to surgical abortion."

March 17 / The National Coalition of Hispanic Health and Human Services Organizations (COSSMHO) reports that the majority of poor Hispanics who lack employer-provided health insurance coverage are not covered by Medicaid

either. The problem stems from Medicaid eligibility requirements, which in most states are based on eligibility for AFDC
or SSI and thus shut out many of the working poor. According to COSSMHO, two-thirds of poor Hispanics work, but
only 13 percent of these workers have health insurance
through their jobs.

March 18 / Compared to children in 11 other industrialized countries, American children are more likely to be
poor, to live in a single-parent family, and to be killed before
the age of 25, according to a Census Bureau report released
today. The report looks at 57 social, economic, and health
indicators for American children versus children in Australia,
Great Britain, Canada, France, Hungary, Italy, Japan, Nor-
way, the Soviet Union, Sweden, and West Germany.

March 22 / Even well-educated young women typically
ignore the risk of getting AIDS and other sexually transmitted diseases, if a study published in today's *New England Journal of Medicine* is any guide. Researchers who surveyed Brown
University women in 1975, 1986, and 1989 about their sexual
activity found that the women surveyed in 1989 had about
the same number of sexual partners, and engaged in the same
variety of sexual behaviors, as their counterparts in 1975.
Only one-fourth of the women surveyed in 1989 used condoms as their usual method of birth control; still, this was an
improvement over 1975, when the proportion was six percent.

March 29 / Obesity is almost as dangerous for a
woman's heart as smoking, according to a study reported
today in the *New England Journal of Medicine*. Researchers
found that mildly to moderately overweight women had almost twice the rate of heart disease as the leanest women.

March 30 / Governor Cecil Andrus of Idaho vetoes a

bill that would have prohibited abortions in the state except in cases of rape, incest, "profound" fetal deformity, or when the woman's life or physical health is threatened. He also signs the repeal of a trigger law that would have made abortion illegal in Idaho if the Supreme Court should ever overturn *Roe v. Wade*.

April 1 / As of today, Medicaid must cover prenatal and early childhood health care for about a million lower-income women and children who did not qualify for it previously because their family incomes were too high. Under the Omnibus Budget Reconciliation Act of 1989, states are now required to extend Medicaid coverage to pregnant women and children under six if their family income is no more than 133 percent of the federal poverty level.

April 5 / U.S. Roman Catholic bishops announce that they have hired Hill & Knowlton, a large public relations firm, to conduct a nationwide, multi-million dollar campaign to persuade Catholics and non-Catholics to oppose abortion.

April 6 / A review of the major, methodologically sound studies of U.S. women who have obtained legal abortions in the first trimester indicated that having an abortion rarely causes long-term psychological problems. The analysis, published in today's issue of *Science* magazine, was done by a panel of scholars commissioned by the American Psychological Association.

April 9 / The U.S. Equal Employment Opportunity Commission files a class-action lawsuit against American Airlines, charging that the carrier's weight limits for its flight attendants discriminate against female attendants, and especially against those over age 40. The Association of Professional Flight Attendants, with a 90-percent female membership, has also filed suit against American over this issue.

April 10 / According to a report issued today by the National Research Council, unless current trends are reversed, by the year 2000 there will not be enough American workers qualified to fill the U.S. jobs requiring a mathematical background.

April 11 / "Lessons," an education column in today's *New York Times*, reports on a study of classroom interaction at Wheaton College, a liberal arts institution in Norton, Massachusetts. Reportedly, Catherine Krupnick, a researcher at the Harvard University Graduate School of Education who analyzed thousands of hours of videotape filmed in Wheaton classrooms, found that faculty members consistently took male students more seriously than females, and permitted males to dominate discussions far out of proportion to their numbers. These findings are especially disturbing in light of the fact that Wheaton, until two years ago an all-female institution, considers "gender-balanced education" an important goal.

April 16 / A commission that studied how Florida's justice system treats women has found pervasive gender bias, reports today's *Wall Street Journal*, which notes some of the commission's findings: women lose out financially in divorce cases; women serve more time in prison than men do for the same offenses; women's prisons have fewer innovative programs and facilities than men's prisons; and female lawyers are treated as inferiors by many lawyers and judges in the courtroom. Lynn Hecht Schafran, an advisor on the Florida study, is reported as saying that similar studies of other states' legal systems have yielded similar results.

April 23 / Derrick Bell, Harvard Law School's first black professor, announces that he has requested a leave of absence without pay from the law school until it appoints a black woman to a tenured position on its faculty. Of Harvard Law School's 60 tenured professors, five are women (none black) and three are black men.

April 27 / In a new book, *Drawing the Line*, published today by the Urban Institute, economist Patricia Ruggles calls for revising the federal poverty formula to reflect the changes in the overall standard of living and in patterns of consumer spending that have occurred since the existing formula was developed. Ms. Ruggles argues that a standard of living considered decent 35 years ago is no longer viewed as such by the average person, and that a society's concept of who is poor is based on the overall degree of prosperity, not just on the minimum needed for physical survival.

April 29 / The Girls Clubs of America becomes Girls, Inc. The name change reflects the organization's shift to a more educational focus.

May 1 / Experienced professional and managerial women who leave big corporations do so because they see their opportunities to advance as limited, not because of a lack of family-friendly benefits, according to a study released today by the Delaware-based research firm Wick and Company. The study was based on interviews with 50 women, about half of whom were mothers, who had left Fortune 500 companies after five or more years of employment.

May 3 / President Bush comments on a dispute at Wellesley College about the college's invitation to Barbara Bush to serve as its commencement speaker. According to *The Washington Post*, the president said, "I think that these young women can have a lot to learn from Barbara Bush and from her unselfishness and from her advocacy of literacy and of being a good mother and a lot of other things." A petition signed by 150 Wellesley students protested the selection of

Mrs. Bush because "[t]o honor [her] as a commencement speaker is to honor a woman who has gained recognition through the achievements of her husband, which contravenes what we have been taught over the last four years at Wellesley."

May 9 / The Older Women's League (OWL), releasing a report about biases against women in the Social Security and private pension systems, urges Congress to give some form of Social Security credit to women who stay home to care for children or disabled family members.

May 10 / The U.S. House of Representatives passes the Family and Medical Leave Act by a vote of 237 to 187. The full Senate has not yet acted on its version of the bill.

May 14 / A federal district judge in Washington, D.C., orders Price Waterhouse to make Ann B. Hopkins a partner in the firm, on the grounds that she was originally denied a partnership because of illegal sex stereotyping. The decision followed the U.S. Supreme Court ruling last year in *Price Waterhouse v. Hopkins*, which held that if a woman charging sex discrimination under Title VII of the Civil Rights Act of 1964 presents direct evidence that illegal sex stereotyping was a motivating factor in denying her the promotion, the burden is on the employer to prove that the promotion would have been denied even if sex stereotyping had not been a factor. Today's decision is the first in the country in which a court has awarded partnership in a professional firm as a remedy for discrimination based on sex or race.

May 14 / Bernice King, daughter of the Reverend Martin Luther King, Jr., and the only one of his children to enter the ministry, receives a master's degree in divinity from Emory University in Georgia. Ms. King also has a law degree.

May 15 / *The New York Times* reports on findings, published in this month's issue of *Demography*, that married people typically live much longer than unmarried people. Princeton University researchers, who analyzed 50 years of data from 16 industrial countries, found that married men live twice as long as their unmarried counterparts and married women live one and a half times as long as their unmarried counterparts.

May 17 / The Manpower Demonstration Research Corporation (MDRC) releases a study concluding that, although workfare can save states significant amounts of money, it may not improve welfare recipients' incomes and living standards. According to the MDRC study, welfare mothers gained only $8 to $30 a year in net income under workfare programs.

May 18 / In response to an angry but nonviolent student strike that shut down the college for two weeks, Mills College officials reverse their May 3 decision to enroll male undergraduates, hoping that recruiting and fundraising will enable the college to remain financially secure without opening admission to men.

May 21 / The U.S. Supreme Court lets stand a lower court order that permanently bars anti-abortion demonstrators from blocking access to abortion facilities and imposes fines on demonstrators who refuse to obey the court order.

May 22 / The General Accounting Office releases a study of health care costs showing that during the 1980s, the portion of health care costs paid by individuals increased while the portion paid by business and government declined. This represented the reversal of a trend that dated back to the 1960s.

May 22 / U.S. Energy Secretary James D. Watkins announces initiatives and new government programs designed to enhance "scientific literacy," especially among women and minorities. The focus of the programs is on establishing a partnership between education and national laboratories that will provide students with hands-on experience in the labs and scientists with first-hand experience teaching in the schools.

May 29 / The U.S. Supreme Court agrees to hear *Rust v. Sullivan*, in which it will decide whether it is constitutional for federal regulations to prohibit federally funded family planning clinics for low-income women from providing clients with any information about abortion. The plaintiffs in the case argue that the regulations, adopted during the Reagan administration, not only burden women's constitutional right to abortion but also infringe on physicians' and women's right to free speech.

May 31 / The National Displaced Homemakers Network reports that one in three of the nation's 15.6 million displaced homemakers—women who stayed at home to raise families but lost the support of their husbands through divorce, desertion, or death—lives below the poverty line.

June 1 / Florida Governor Robert Martinez signs into law a measure that bars rape defendants' lawyers from introducing evidence about the clothing the victim was wearing. The measure was introduced by State Representative Elaine Gordon after a man was acquitted of rape because jurors thought that the way the victim was dressed might have brought on the attack. (The man acquitted in this case was subsequently found guilty in another rape case.)

June 2 / The National Governors' Association releases a study finding that more than two-thirds of the states have taken steps to reduce the incidence of teenage pregnancy and to enhance the lives of teenage mothers and their children.

June 5 / Dianne Feinstein, former mayor of San Francisco, wins the California Democratic gubernatorial primary, becoming the first woman to win a major party nomination for governor in the state.

June 11 / According to an analysis released today by the House Ways and Means Committee, the average inflation-adjusted income of the highest-paid female earner in each household rose 28.2 percent between 1979 and 1987. For the poorest two-fifths of families, the decline in the male's earnings decreased more than the female's increased, resulting in a decline in total family income.

June 13 / Bernadette Locke is named assistant men's basketball coach for the University of Kentucky, making her the first female assistant coach in an NCAA Division I men's basketball program.

June 14 / The Senate approves the Family and Medical Leave Act, which would require businesses with 50 or more employees to grant workers up to three months of unpaid leave at the time of the birth or adoption of a child or when a member of their immediate family falls ill.

June 18 / The U.S. Supreme Court upholds a lower court decision granting unconditional tenure to Julia Prewitt Brown, a professor of English at Boston University who was denied a permanent teaching post because of her sex.

June 18 / The General Accounting Office (GAO) reports that the National Institutes of Health (NIH) are failing to follow their own policy of actively including women subjects in medical research studies. Several important NIH studies have excluded women, according to a GAO analysis that was conducted at the request of U.S. Representatives Patricia Schroeder (D-CO), Olympia Snowe (R-ME), and Henry A. Waxman (D-CA).

June 25 / The U.S. Supreme Court hands down decisions in two cases involving state laws requiring parental notification before an abortion is performed on an unemancipated minor. In *Hodgson v. State of Minnesota*, the Court holds that it is constitutional for a state to require the notification of both biological parents of a minor, as long as a judicial bypass is available, and to mandate a 48-hour waiting period. In *Ohio v. Akron Center for Reproductive Health*, the Court holds that a state may require that one parent be notified, but declines to rule on whether a judicial bypass is necessary in order for a one-parent notification requirement to pass constitutional muster. (The Ohio statute at issue in the case includes a bypass provision.)

June 28 / From Parlor to Politics, an exhibit commemorating women's political contributions, opens today at the National Museum of American History. The exhibit focuses on such developments as the temperance movement, women's suffrage, the home economics movement, and labor reforms.

June 28 / The American Medical Association winds up its annual convention, during which it adopted a resolution "support[ing] legal availability of RU-486 for appropriate research and its indicated clinical practice."

June 30 / President Bush vetoes the Family and Medical Leave Act.

June 30 / Congress gives final approval to a bill that would restore allotments for many of the poor women and children who have been cut from the government nutrition program WIC. The measure will permit states to make up for the shortage in 1990 funds by borrowing against the appropriation for fiscal year 1991.

June 30 / Some 2,000 delegates to the National Organization for Women (NOW) Conference meet this weekend in

San Francisco to celebrate a record number of women running for political office. NOW President Molly Yard announces the appointment of a 40-member commission to study the possibility of starting a new political party.

June 31 / This is a nonexistent day for a non-event sponsored by the Women's Ordination Conference. After years of angrily protesting the refusal of the Catholic Church to ordain women as priests, the group is trying a humorous approach—soliciting contributions from its supporters with an invitation not to attend the "First Annual Non-Ordination of Women."

July 3 / The New Jersey Supreme Court orders the last two remaining male-only undergraduate clubs at Princeton University to begin admitting women.

July 5 / After hearing the recommendations of an interagency group that it commissioned to rethink the nation's antipoverty efforts, the Bush administration announces that the group's recommendations are too expensive and politically controversial. Administration officials explain that they will try to make current programs work better.

July 11 / A study by the Centers for Disease Control published today in the *Journal of the American Medical Association* discusses the alarmingly high rate of AIDS in women, and points to the implications for the rising caseload of AIDS babies. According to the study, AIDS is rising rapidly as a cause of death among women of childbearing age (15 to 44), and is the leading killer of black women in that age group in New York and New Jersey.

July 12 / A new breakthrough is reported in the fight against osteoporosis, a debilitating bone disorder that afflicts one-half of American women over the age of 50. A study described in today's issue of the *New England Journal of Medi-*

cine found that etidronate, a relatively inexpensive and easily obtainable drug, may be effective in reversing osteoporosis.

July 18 / By a vote of 65 to 34, the Senate passes the Civil Rights Act of 1990, after having adopted several modifications to the bill. The bill approved today would allow employers to defend themselves in so-called disparate impact cases—cases where there is no evidence of intentional discrimination—by showing that their hiring practices bear a "substantial and demonstrable relationship to effective job performance." The bill also includes language stating that it cannot be "construed to require an employer to adopt hiring or promotion quotas." President Bush has threatened to veto the bill, charging that it will force employers to adopt quotas.

July 19 / *The Washington Post* reports on the dispute between Representative Mary Rose Oakar (D-OH) and the General Accounting Office (GAO) over the GAO's failure to follow through with Oakar's 1989 request for a study of the apparent lack of pay equity in the federal government.

July 20 / Supreme Court Justice William J. Brennan, Jr. announces his retirement. A champion of civil liberties, he did much to advance women's rights. In an important employment discrimination decision (*Frontiero v. Richardson*, 1973), Justice Brennan wrote: "Our nation has had a long and unfortunate history of sex discrimination . . . rationalized by an attitude of 'romantic paternalism' which, in practical effect, put women not on a pedestal, but in a cage." Among the many landmark decisions that Justice Brennan helped to shape was *Roe v. Wade*.

July 25 / The U.S. State Department signs a consent decree settling a 14-year-old sex discrimination suit. The department is reported to have agreed, among other things, to give some women Foreign Service officers priority for prestigious assignments or honors they were denied because they were female and to allow 14 women who had been tracked into consular, administrative, and economic jobs to move into the more prestigious political track. Twenty-two women who had been denied superior honor awards for work that met the department's standards for such awards will each receive $180—the only monetary compensation involved in the settlement.

July 25 / The House fails to override President Bush's veto of the Family and Medical Leave Act. The vote fell 53 short of the two-thirds needed to override.

July 26 / *The New York Times* reports on a study finding that menopause does not cause stress or depression in most healthy women and that it may even improve mental health for some. The study findings were published in the June issue of the *Journal of Consulting and Clinical Psychology*.

July 26 / The Congressional Caucus for Women's Issues introduces the Women's Health Equity Act, a legislative package designed to address a range of women's health problems. The proposals include allocating more than $50 million for additional research, expanding Medicare coverage, and establishing federal centers to study contraception and infertility.

July 27 / Republicans for Choice have a press conference to discuss their efforts to change the Republican Party's strong anti-abortion platform.

July 30 / *Ms.* magazine reappears on the newsstands. The resurrected magazine contains no advertising; its founder, Gloria Steinem, and its editor-in-chief, Robin Morgan, are hoping *Ms.* can flourish largely on the basis of a loyal subscription base.

July 30 / U.S. Secretary of Labor Elizabeth Dole is devising a "glass ceiling" initiative to try to speed up the promotion of women and minority members to top posts, according to today's *New York Times*.

August 1 / The General Electric Foundation announces that it has established a program designed to attract more women, blacks, Native Americans, and Hispanic people to teaching careers in engineering, the physical sciences, and business. The foundation will make a series of grants to the nation's colleges and universities for undergraduate research, fellowships, forgivable loans, and faculty grants.

August 1 / The Screen Actors Guild holds its first National Women's Conference. Actress Meryl Streep addresses the group and expresses concern about the declining number of strong female characters on screen.

August 2 / The Senate Judiciary Committee adopts a resolution warning judicial nominees that membership in clubs that discriminate on the basis of sex or race is "inappropriate" and "conflicts with the appearance of impartiality" required of members of the bench. The resolution applies to membership in clubs where "contacts valuable for business purposes, employment and professional advancement are formed."

August 3 / The House of Representatives approves, by 272 to 154, its version of the Civil Rights Act of 1990. It is virtually identical to the bill passed by the Senate in July.

August 8 / The House of Delegates of the American Bar Association (ABA) votes to rescind the abortion-rights position it approved only last February. The vote changes the ABA's official position from pro-choice to neutral.

August 13 / White males still hold more than 95 percent of the top management jobs at the country's largest corporations, according to a study released today by the University of

California at Los Angeles Graduate School of Management and Korn/Ferry, a corporate recruiting firm.

August 22 / A study published today in the *Journal of the American Medical Association* found that girls are just as likely as boys to have dyslexia. Researchers found that schools in the study identified dyslexia in more than four times as many second-grade boys as girls, when there were actually equal numbers of boys and girls with the disorder.

August 28 / B'nai B'rith International votes to admit women as full members. The 147-year-old fraternal order of Jewish men passed the measure unanimously, replacing the word "men" with "persons" in a section of the group's constitution. Delegates to the group's convention also approved a plan to allow B'nai B'rith Women to continue as a self-governing, affiliate organization pursuing an independent agenda—with female members only.

September 3 / According to a congressional report released today, the Federal Reserve Board is overwhelmingly dominated by white men. The study, conducted for House Banking Committee Chairman Henry B. Gonzalez, found only two nonwhites and three women among the 72 directors of regional Federal Reserve banks.

September 7 / In a brief filed with the Supreme Court in connection with *Rust v. Sullivan* (see May 29, 1990), the U.S. Justice Department reiterates the Bush administration's position that the Court's 1973 decision in *Roe v. Wade* legalizing abortion should be overturned.

September 10 / The rate at which women were appointed heads of the nation's colleges and universities increased during the late 1980s, according to data published in today's *Journal of Higher Education and National Affairs*. Although between 1984 and 1987, the number of female academic CEOs increased only from 286 to 296, it was up to 328 by 1989.

September 10 / In a meeting with members of the Congressional Caucus for Women's Issues, officials of the National Institutes of Health announce plans to create a new Office of Research on Women's Health at NIH. The purpose is to ensure the adequate representation of women subjects in clinical research and to target research areas of particular concern to women.

September 12 / Jack Kemp, U.S. Secretary of Housing and Urban Development, submits to Congress a report on the 1988 Fair Housing Amendments that outlawed housing discrimination against families with children and handicapped persons. According to the report, complaints of discrimination against families have accounted for more than half of all housing discrimination complaints since the law took effect.

September 13 / U.S. Roman Catholic bishops indefinitely postpone voting on the final draft of a papal letter that would set official church policy on issues of concern to women—from abortion to sexual discrimination to ordination. Both liberals and conservatives have rejected this draft as an unacceptable compromise between traditional church teachings and strong affirmations of women's equality.

September 17 / Several New England Patriots players subject *Boston Herald* sportswriter Lisa Olson to crude sexual harassment and lewd behavior while she is interviewing another player in the Patriots' locker room.

September 18 / Testifying at a Senate confirmation hearing on Supreme Court nominee David H. Souter, representatives of women's rights and abortion rights groups urge the Senate to reject Mr. Souter due to his lack of a clear record on women's issues. Objectors express concern about Mr. Souter's refusal to answer questions on abortion rights and air misgivings about where he stands on key aspects of constitutional law dealing with race and sex discrimination and church-state separation.

September 18 / The Women's Research and Education Institute (WREI) presents its second annual American Woman award to Johnnetta Cole, president of Spelman College.

September 19 / *The New York Times* reports that the executive council of the Cantors' Assembly has voted 29 to one to admit women. The Assembly is associated with the Conservative movement of Judaism.

September 24 / In a study released today, the Center for Population Options estimates that teenage pregnancy costs the federal government $22 billion per year in welfare outlays. The study says that about one-third of all families that started with a teenage birth have ended up on public assistance.

September 25 / A House-Senate conference committee agrees on a compromise version of the Civil Rights Act of 1990. To the dismay of women's advocates, the compromise calls for a $150,000 cap on the amount of punitive damages a victim of intentional sex discrimination in employment could collect. (There is no cap on the damages allowed by existing law for victims of intentional race discrimination, and no cap has been proposed.)

September 27 / A new translation of the Bible that uses contemporary language, eliminates many male-centered terms, and is sensitive to issues of race and homosexuality is introduced today for use in the nation's major Protestant churches.

October 1 / The U.S. Department of Agriculture releases to Congress a study of the WIC program which supports earlier findings that the government's special nutrition program for low-income women, infants, and children sharply reduces later Medicaid health outlays and results in improved birthweights.

October 2 / The Senate votes 90 to 9 to confirm David H. Souter to succeed retired Justice William J. Brennan, Jr. on the U.S. Supreme Court.

October 5 / The University of Wisconsin releases research showing that workers whose performance was tracked by computers suffered more job stress than those under human supervision. According to the study, which was commissioned by the Communications Workers of America, electronically monitored workers reported twice as many wrist pains as, and 20 percent more neck pains than, those who were not electronically monitored.

October 7 / The U.S. Justice Department reports that the number of inmates in state and federal prisons rose by nearly 43,000 in the first half of 1990. Although men remain the majority, the number of female inmates is increasing at a faster rate than that of men.

October 11 / In a study published in today's *New England Journal of Medicine*, a National Institutes of Health research team compares the pregnancies of medical school residents and physicians' wives. The findings contradict conventional wisdom: difficulties with pregnancy were no greater for the medical residents, even though they were working under significantly more stressful and more physically demanding conditions.

October 17 / The House approves the compromise version of the Civil Rights Act of 1990 by a vote of 273–154—a margin short of what would be needed to override a presidential veto. (The Senate approved the measure yesterday, also by a majority that was less than veto-proof.)

October 22 / President Bush vetoes the Civil Rights Act.

October 24 / Elizabeth Dole announces that she is resigning as U.S. Secretary of Labor to become president of the American Red Cross.

October 25 / President Bush's veto of the Civil Rights Act is upheld when a vote in the Senate to override it falls one vote short of the 67 required.

October 27 / Climaxing an often contentious effort that began in 1988, both Houses of Congress give final approval to a major child care assistance bill, a package targeted primarily at low- and moderate-income families and budgeted at $22.5 billion over five years. Tax credits account for the bulk of that sum ($18.3 billion): the bill expands the existing Earned Income Tax Credit for working lower-income families with children, allowing an extra credit for infants under age one, and creates a new health insurance credit for families with children. The bill provides $4.25 billion in grants to states, largely to help them subsidize child care for low- and lower-income families.

November 6 / Women governors are elected in three states—Joan Finney (Democrat) in Kansas, Barbara Roberts (Democrat) in Oregon, and Ann Richards (Democrat) in Texas. Dianne Feinstein loses the California governor's race to Pete Wilson.

November 8 / Sexual activity on the part of teenage girls increased sharply throughout the 1980s, with the largest increase among girls who are white or from higher-income families, according to an Alan Guttmacher Institute study released today.

November 11 / The International Women's Media Foundation presents its first Courage in Journalism awards. Of the five recipients, one is a U.S. woman—Caryle Murphy of *The Washington Post*. The only American journalist known to have been in Kuwait from the start of Saddam Hussein's invasion, Ms. Murphy is honored for her reporting from Kuwait City during the first 25 days of Iraqi occupation.

November 13 / Martha S. Pope is named Sergeant-at-Arms of the U.S. Senate, the first woman ever to hold that position. Ms. Pope will be responsible for ensuring security in the Senate chamber, as well as for overseeing the Senate's communications and press facilities and its post office.

November 14 / A study released today by Women in Film and the National Commission on Working Women reports that network television continues to give women fewer leading roles, both on and off the screen, than it gives men. According to the study, "[w]omen are often still depicted as half-clad and half-witted and needing to be rescued by quick thinking, fully clothed men."

November 15 / A federal appeals panel overturns a Montana man's rape conviction on the grounds that "Women Against Rape" buttons worn by courtroom spectators may have denied the man a fair trial by "convey[ing] an implied message encouraging the jury to find the man guilty."

November 15 / As part of a program to help women get access to skilled trade jobs in manufacturing and construction, the U.S. Department of Labor announces plans to step up an anti-sex discrimination enforcement effort at its Bureau of Apprenticeship and Training.

November 15 / The Reverend Joan Brown Campbell is elected the general secretary of the National Council of Churches. Mrs. Campbell is the second woman to head the nation's largest ecumenical body.

November 20 / Russell Reynolds Associates, a management recruiting firm, releases a study finding that more corporate women than men show leadership traits. Using the Burke
Leadership model, the study categorized as "leader-style"
those executives displaying predominantly visionary, change-
agent, charismatic, and strategic traits. The study found that
women executives in both line and staff positions were more
likely than their male counterparts to display these traits.

November 24 / Calling the September 17 sexual harassment of Boston Herald sportswriter Lisa Olson a "serious
incident in the [New England Patriots'] locker room," the
commissioner of the National Football League announces
that he is fining the three players involved (one for $12,500,
two for $5,000) and the team itself ($25,000). The team is also
ordered to pay $25,000 to supplement the materials it uses to
instruct players on "responsible dealings with the media."

November 27 / *The Washington Post* reports on Small
Business Administration administrator Susan Engeleiter's re-
action to a new Parker Brothers board game, "Careers for
Girls," which offers only six "careers" to choose from: super
mom, schoolteacher, rock star, fashion designer, college graduate, and animal doctor. Ms. Engeleiter is quoted as saying,
"If the Parker 'Brothers' were the Parker 'Sisters' this game
would never have passed 'Go'."

November 27 / The National Organization for Women
(NOW) calls for an immediate withdrawal of the U.S. troops
from the Persian Gulf, comparing the way Saudi Arabia and
Kuwait treat women with South Africa's racial apartheid policy.

November 28 / The George Washington University
Medical Center settles out of court today with the American
Civil Liberties Union on a policy to ensure that the decisions
on how to treat severely ill pregnant women and their fetuses

will be made by the women, their families, and their doctors, and not by the courts. The settlement ends a lawsuit brought by the parents of Angela Carder, a cancer victim who died after undergoing a caesarian section ordered by a judge in the interest of saving the fetus. The patient, her family, and her doctors were opposed to the operation. This agreement sets an important precedent in the conflict between maternal and fetal rights.

December 2 / Welfare rolls increased in 49 of the states in the past year, according to an Associated Press survey that appeared in *The Washington Post* today. Among the reasons cited were regional recessions, changes in immigration laws, federal mandates making it easier for pregnant women to qualify for Medicaid, and "one-stop" benefit programs that make more benefits available at one time to recipients.

December 4 / Ann Hopkins makes the news again when the U.S. Court of Appeals for the District of Columbia upholds a lower court's ruling that the accounting firm Price Waterhouse must admit her as a partner (see May 14, 1990).

December 10 / Federal health officials give final approval to Norplant, the first major new birth control option for American women since the 1960s. Norplant uses the same synthetic hormones as the pill, but the hormones are delivered for up to five years in a steady trickle by six matchstick-sized pellets implanted under the skin of a woman's upper arm. While the new contraceptive is praised as a breakthrough for women, civil libertarians are concerned about its potential for being used coercively.

December 11 / The IBM Corporation announces that it will spend $3 million next year to build five child care centers near its offices and plants around the country.

December 14 / President Bush nominates Lynn Martin, a former Republican congresswoman from Illinois, to succeed Elizabeth Dole as U.S. Secretary of Labor.

December 21 / Ohio Governor Richard Celeste grants clemency to 25 women who had been convicted of killing or assaulting husbands who had physically abused them. Because of an Ohio law that has since been changed, the women were barred from presenting expert testimony at their trials about their abusive relationships.

1991

January 1 / The Civil Rights Act of 1991 (H.R.1) is introduced in the House. Unlike the final version of the Civil Rights Act of 1990 that was approved by Congress, the 1991 act would allow workers who are victims of intentional sex discrimination to sue for damages without a cap on the amount.

January 2 / A California judge orders a woman convicted of beating her children to have a Norplant contraceptive device implanted in her arm for three years as a condition of her probation. This marks the first time a judge has ordered a woman to use the device.

January 4 / Sandra Gardebring is sworn in as the fourth woman justice on the Minnesota Supreme Court, making Minnesota the only state to have a female majority on its highest court.

January 9 / The American Association of University Women (AAUW) makes public a study finding that girls are twice as likely as boys to lose their self-esteem as they enter adolescence. Surveying youngsters ages 9 to 15 in 12 locations across the country, researchers found that by the time they

WOMEN IN

American women in the military made history between mid-1989 and mid-1991. They, and developments affecting them, are featured here.

1989

August 9 / Kristin Baker is selected Brigade Commander and First Captain of the Corps of Cadets at the U.S. Military Academy at West Point. She is the first woman ever to hold that position.

December 20 / Army Capt. Linda Bray is the first U.S. military woman to lead troops in combat. Bray is one of some 800 U.S. servicewomen involved in the Panama invasion.

1990

January 25 / A *New York Times*/CBS News Poll indicates that seven out of 10 Americans say women in the Armed Forces should be allowed to serve in combat units if they want to.

February 9 / The Army reports that helicopter pilots Lt. Lisa Kutschera and Warrant Off. Debra Mann came under heavy fire while ferrying troops into combat in Panama. (They subsequently become the first women to receive the Air Medal with "V" for valor.)

April 22 / The Army rejects a recommendation by the Defense Advisory Committee on Women in the Services (DACOWITS) that women be allowed in selected combat jobs on an experimental basis.

June 8 / The Navy announces that Cdr. Rosemary Mariner will become the first woman to command a Navy jet aircraft squadron.

July 16 / Air Force Maj. Eileen Collins, the first female selected to be a NASA space-shuttle pilot, reports to NASA for training.

August 7 / Women are among American military personnel deployed to Saudi Arabia in response to Iraqi aggression against Kuwait.

September 1 / Col. Marcelite Harris becomes the first black Air Force woman promoted to the rank of Brigadier General.

September 11 / A Defense Department study reports that 64 percent of military women were sexually harassed on the job.

December 7 / Lt. Col. Marne Peterson becomes the first woman to assume command of an Air Force flying squadron.

December 28 / Lt. Cdr. Darlene Iskra takes command of the salvage vessel USS *Opportune*, becoming the first female to command a Navy ship subject to long assignments at sea.

THE MILITARY

1991

January 15 / The United States and its allies begin the aerial phase of the Persian Gulf War. Over 35,000 U.S. military women, including many reservists, are now serving in the combat theater.

February 19 / The House Armed Services Committee holds hearings on the children of military personnel sent to the Gulf. The Defense Department estimates that in about 17,500 families children were separated from their only parent or both parents by the war.

February 26 / A Scud missile hits a U.S. Army barracks in Saudi Arabia, killing 28 soldiers, including three women (Spec. 4 Christine Mayes, Spec. 4 Beverly Clark, and Pvt. Adrienne Mitchell).

March 1 / Army Maj. Marie Rossi and three members of her crew are killed when their Chinook helicopter crashes in Saudi Arabia. Rossi was commanding officer of B Company, 18th Aviation Brigade.

March 6 / Iraq releases 25 prisoners of war, including two Army women (Maj. Rhonda Cornum and Spec. 4 Melissa Rathbun-Nealy).

March 28 / A WREI fact sheet reports that 11 servicewomen lost their lives during the Gulf War. Five were killed in action.

April 4 / The Navy releases a report admitting that sexual harassment is a pervasive problem for Navy women and that "inconsistent and ambiguous" assignment policies hobble the careers of many women.

April 24 / DACOWITS votes to recommend the repeal of Air Force and Navy combat exclusion laws.

April 25 / The U.S. Naval Academy announces that Juliane Gallina has been appointed Midshipman Captain. She is the first woman to be given command of the Brigade of Midshipmen.

April 25 / Secretary of Defense Cheney suggests that he favors expanding women's roles in the military but stops short of recommending dropping the bans on combat roles for women.

May 22 / The House of Representatives passes a bill allowing the assignment of female Air Force and Navy pilots to combat missions.

June 18 / The military service chiefs tell a Senate Armed Services subcommittee that they oppose repealing combat exclusion laws.

June 20 / Secretary of Defense Cheney backs away from his previous statements supporting lifting restrictions on assignments for military women, indicating the issue is for Congress to decide. (See page 84.)

are in high school, only 29 percent of girls say they are happy with themselves, compared to 46 percent of boys.

January 13 / *The Washington Post* reports on a study by a California researcher who found that women bring a new and successful management technique to the workplace. Judy B. Rosener, a professor at the University of California at Irvine, calls the technique "transformational leadership" because it is interactive and consists of relying on personal characteristics like charisma, interpersonal skills, hard work, or personal contacts for success. Ms. Rosener's study was published in the November/December issue of the *Harvard Business Review*.

January 13 / The U.S. Justice Department's Bureau of Justice Statistics releases a study showing that female victims of violent crime are six times more likely than male victims to have been attacked by someone they know.

January 14 / Senator Joseph Biden (D-DE) introduces the Violence Against Women Act (S.15). The bill would double federal penalties for rape, authorize $300 million for local law enforcement efforts to combat sex crime, and define rape as a "hate" crime, thereby allowing victims to bring civil rights suits against their assailants.

January 18 / Lois Robinson, a welder in a Florida shipyard, wins a ground-breaking court ruling that posting pictures of nude and partly nude women in the workplace is a form of sexual harassment. According to the federal district judge who issued the ruling, Jacksonville Shipyards Inc., where Ms. Robinson works, maintained a "boys club atmosphere with an unrelenting visual assault on the sensibilities of female workers." The judge orders the shipyard to institute a comprehensive sexual harassment policy written by the NOW Legal Defense and Education Fund, which brought suit on behalf of Ms. Robinson.

January 22 / By letting a New Jersey Supreme Court ruling stand, the U.S. Supreme Court forces the last remaining all-male eating club at Princeton University to admit women as members.

January 31 / A Kansas state senator proposes a bill under which the state would pay $500 to any welfare mother who uses the contraceptive implant Norplant.

February 1 / In a case involving a women-only health club in the Chicago area, a federal judge rules that the club's policy of refusing to hire men is discriminatory under Title VII of the Civil Rights Act of 1964, which prohibits employment discrimination on the basis of sex.

February 4 / A Michigan circuit court judge dismisses a drug charge against an attorney alleged to have passed cocaine to her newborn baby by using the drug while pregnant. According to the judge, the prosecution violated both the woman's right to privacy and her constitutional right of due process because she was not notified that the law could apply to her.

February 7 / Wisconsin Governor Tommy Thompson proposes a welfare experiment that would financially reward teenaged mothers on AFDC who marry, and penalize single mothers of any age who have more children while receiving AFDC benefits.

February 12 / The Stride Rite Corporation, which was the first corporation to open an on-site child care center (in 1971), officially opens its innovative Intergenerational Day Care Center in Cambridge, Massachusetts, the company's headquarters. The center, which will accommodate 55 children from 18 months to six years old, and 24 older adults, will be open to people in the community as well as to relatives of Stride Rite employees.

February 19 / Maryland Governor William Donald Schaefer commutes the prison sentences of eight women whose attacks—some fatal—on husbands or boyfriends were, he believed, triggered by repeated physical abuse.

February 27 / In an attempt to stem the spread of AIDS, the New York City Board of Education approves a plan to make condoms available on request to the city's 250,000 high school students. Students will be able to request condoms from school or neighborhood volunteers without parental consent and without mandatory counseling.

March 1 / The Bush administration proposes an alternative to the Civil Rights Act of 1991 but supporters of the latter charge that the administration's bill places overly restrictive limits on monetary damages for workers victimized by intentional discrimination, and gives too much leeway to employers. The president's bill would allow employers to defend themselves successfully in disparate impact suits if they could prove that their hiring and promotion practices had "a manifest relationship to the employment in question" or serve an employer's "legitimate business goal." Civil rights advocates say these are much weaker standards than the standard—substantial relationship to successful job performance—embodied in the congressional measure.

March 4 / Congresswoman Patricia Schroeder (D-CO) announces that she will become the new chair of the House Select Committee on Children, Youth, and Families.

March 4 / Ashley Reiter, a 17-year-old high school senior from North Carolina, wins the $40,000 first-place scholarship in the 50th annual Westinghouse Science Talent Search for her entry of a project in fractal geometry.

March 5 / The Marriott Corporation releases the terms of its settlement in a class-action sex discrimination suit. Marriott has agreed to adopt specific goals for promoting women to managerial and supervisory jobs in the food and beverage division of its hotel chain for the next three and a half years.

March 6 / Testifying before the House Budget Committee, the chairmen and CEOs of some of the nation's biggest corporations, including AT&T, Prudential Insurance, Bell-South, Honeywell, and Sky Chefs Inc., call for a near doubling of the Supplemental Food Program for Women, Infants, and Children (WIC).

March 11 / Gloria Molina takes office as a member of the Los Angeles County Board of Supervisors. She is not only the first woman but the first Hispanic ever to win election to this powerful board.

March 12 / The Minnesota Court of Appeals rules that Diane McCourtney, a woman who lost her job last year because she had frequently stayed home to care for her sick baby, is entitled to unemployment benefits. The state argued that by electing to stay home with her sick child rather than going to work, McCourtney was guilty of misconduct and was therefore ineligible for unemployment benefits, which are available only to those who lose their jobs through no fault of their own. The court, however, found that Ms. McCourtney's absences did not amount to misconduct under the law. "Each of her absences was excused and was due to circumstances beyond her control," the court said, and she "made substantial efforts to find care for her child so she could work."

March 16 / U.S. skaters Kristi Yamaguchi, Tonya Harding, and Nancy Kerrigan place one, two, and three at the world women's figure skating championships in Munich, Germany. Never before have three skaters from a single country swept the event.

March 20 / The House Committee on Education and

Labor approves the Family and Medical Leave Act of 1991 by voice vote. This year's bill is virtually identical to the bill approved by Congress last year and vetoed by President Bush on June 30, 1990.

March 20 / The U.S. Supreme Court reverses the appellate court's ruling in the *Johnson Controls* case (see September 26, 1990). The High Court holds that employers cannot exclude fertile women from jobs that pose reproductive hazards, classifying "fetal protection" policies as illegal sex discrimination. According to today's decision, authored by Justice Blackmun, "[w]omen as capable of doing their jobs as their male counterparts may not be forced to choose between having a child and having a job."

March 21 / The Senate Judiciary Committee releases a study finding that the rate of nationwide sexual assaults is now increasing four times faster than the overall crime rate.

March 26 / The U.S. Supreme Court rules that, as written, Title VII of the Civil Rights Act of 1964 does not extend its antidiscrimination protections to Americans working for American firms operating overseas. The case involved a complaint of discrimination on the basis of religion and national origin.

April 2 / A Michigan appeals court rules that Kimberly Hardy should not stand trial on charges of delivering cocaine to her fetus through the umbilical cord (see February 1, 1990). The American Civil Liberties Union brought the appeal on behalf of Hardy. Today's is the highest-level ruling yet on the question of whether a mother's drug use during pregnancy should be a criminal matter.

April 3 / Up to 80,000 U.S. women of child-bearing age may be infected with the virus that causes AIDS, according to a study published in today's issue of the *Journal of the American Medical Association*.

April 5 / U.S. Secretary of Health and Human Services Louis W. Sullivan announces that, despite some modest recent gains, the government's record in collecting child support remains "abysmal."

April 9 / This year's Pulitzer Prizes are announced today, and 11 women—a record number—are among the winners. The women are Mona Van Duyn, for Poetry; Jane Schorer, for Public Service (see February 25, 1990); Shulamit Ran, for Music; Laurel Thatcher Ulrich, for History; Natalie Angier, for Beat Reporting; Caryle Murphy, for International Reporting (see November 11, 1990); Susan M. Headden, co-recipient for Investigative Reporting; Susan C. Faludi, for Explanatory Reporting; Sheryl James, for Feature Writing; and Marjie Lundstrom and Rochelle Sharpe, for National Reporting.

April 10 / Patricia F. Saiki is sworn in as head of the Small Business Administration, the federal agency created to help entrepreneurs form successful small enterprises. Ms. Saiki, a former Republican congresswoman from Hawaii, is the first Asian American to hold this post.

April 12 / The undergraduate members of Skull and Bones, a Yale secret society (and one of the last all-male clubs at Yale), vote to admit women. Dismayed alumni "Bonesmen" react by locking the undergraduates out of the club's meeting hall. President Bush is one of the prominent Yale graduates who are known to be members of Skull and Bones.

April 17 / Republican National Committee Chairman Clayton Yeutter says he hopes his party retains the strict anti-abortion plank in its platform.

April 18 / A Florida appeals court upholds the conviction of Jennifer Johnson, who was found guilty of delivering cocaine to her newborn baby through the umbilical cord (see July 13, 1990).

April 23 / The U.S. Supreme Court upholds National

Labor Relations Board regulations that make it easier for unions to organize hospital workers. The American Hospital Association sought to overturn the regulations.

April 23 / The United States has achieved modest improvement in its infant mortality rate by relying on high-cost medical technology rather than on low-cost expansion of prenatal care for pregnant women, according to a report issued today by the National Commission to Prevent Infant Mortality.

April 24 / The Senate Committee on Labor and Human Resources approves the Family and Medical Leave Act of 1991 by a vote of 12 to 5.

April 30 / The Bush administration proposes major changes in federal pension laws in an effort to extend some form of private retirement benefits to an additional 42 million workers, and to make the first step toward portable pensions. According to U.S. Labor Secretary Lynn Martin, these pension proposals would be particularly helpful to women, who tend to be out of the labor force more than men.

April 30 / The National Academy of Sciences announces the election of 60 new members. Only six are women.

April 30 / The Census Bureau reports that the average American household last year was smaller than it had ever been (2.63 persons), and that one-quarter of all U.S. households consist of people living alone. Officials attribute the trends in household size to various factors, such as more elderly widows, lower birthrates, and the delaying of marriage.

May 2 / Three members of La Mujer Obrera and four garment workers begin a hunger strike in support of the International Ladies' Garment Workers' Union (ILGWU) strike that began recently at four apparel factories in El Paso, Texas. La Mujer Obrera (The Working Woman) is a group of Hispanic garment factory workers, most of whom speak little or no English, who have organized and are working with the ILGWU for the purpose of improving working conditions in garment "sweatshops."

May 4 / Fort Worth, Texas, elects its first female mayor, Kay Granger.

May 8 / The House Armed Services Committee agrees to an amendment, sponsored by Representatives Beverly Byron (D-MD) and Patricia Schroeder (D-CO), to repeal the prohibitions against allowing women pilots in the Air Force and Navy to fly combat missions (see also the box, "Women in the Military," on page 75).

May 10 / Teresa Fischette, a ticket-counter agent who was dismissed from Continental Airlines because she refused to wear makeup, announces that she will fight to regain her job.

May 15 / *The Random House Webster's College Dictionary* is published today. Random House claims that sexist language has been eliminated from the definitions in the dictionary, which also contains guidelines that warn when a word might give offense.

May 16 / The New Hampshire state legislature enacts a resolution offering the state as the nation's first clinical testing site for the French abortion pill RU-486.

May 17 / Gertrude Belle Elion is inducted into the National Inventors Hall of Fame in Akron, Ohio. She is the first woman to take her place alongside such innovators as Alexander Graham Bell and Thomas A. Edison. Ms. Elion won a Nobel Prize in 1988 for pioneering DNA research that led to the development of drugs to combat leukemia, septic shock, and tissue rejection in patients undergoing kidney transplants.

May 19 / *The New York Times* reports today that 19.4

percent of all President Bush's appointments have been women, the most of any president. However, there are no more women in senior staff or cabinet positions in the Bush administration than in the Reagan administration, according to the *Times*, and the president's innermost circle of advisors is entirely male. The only woman among the 15 officials on the White House senior staff is Edith Holiday, who is secretary of the Cabinet.

May 20 / Sarah Williamson takes office as the first female mayor of Boys Town, a Nebraska institution that was founded 74 years ago for troubled boys and was first opened to girls in 1979.

May 20 / Democratic leaders unveil a compromise civil rights bill in hopes that the changes will attract enough conservative votes to withstand an almost certain veto from President Bush. The new bill expressly forbids the use of quotas in the workplace and includes a $150,000 cap on punitive damages in intentional discrimination cases brought by women and people with disabilities.

May 22 / Legislation that includes a provision to allow female Air Force and Navy pilots to be assigned to fly combat missions passes the full House of Representatives. The provision is part of the defense authorization bill, which the Senate is expected to take up in July.[2]

May 22 / A report released today by the Families and Work Institute shows that state laws requiring employers to

[2]"In Review" in this volume of *The American Woman* has a cut-off date of June 30, 1991. However, the editors want readers to know that on July 31, 1991, as this book was going to press, the U.S. Senate also approved legislation repealing the prohibitions against allowing women Air Force and Navy pilots to fly combat missions. The measure, which was an amendment to the defense authorization bill, was introduced on the floor of the Senate by Senators William V. Roth, Jr. (R-DE) and Edward Kennedy (D-MA).

provide job-protected unpaid leave for new parents have proven relatively easy and inexpensive to implement. Researchers who surveyed thousands of employers in Minnesota, Wisconsin, Rhode Island, and Oregon found that only nine percent of respondents reported that compliance with the law was difficult.

May 23 / The U.S. Supreme Court, ruling in *Rust v. Sullivan* (see May 29, 1990), upholds federal regulations prohibiting employees in federally funded family planning clinics for low-income women from providing clients with information about abortion. Under the regulations approved by the Court, clinic personnel—including physicians—are forbidden either to offer any information about abortion as an option or to refer a woman elsewhere for this information. A woman who asks about abortion may be told only that "the project does not consider abortion an appropriate method of family planning." Justice David Souter was one of the five justices voting to uphold the restrictive regulations. Justice Sandra Day O'Connor was one of the four justices dissenting.

May 24 / Dr. Frances Conley, a 50-year-old tenured professor at Stanford Medical School and one of the nation's first (and few) female neurosurgeons, announces that she is resigning, effective September 1, in protest at the prevalence of sexual harassment in the profession. Dr. Conley explains that she was for years the object of demeaning comments and unwelcome advances, and that she feels very guilty for having put up with it for so long.

June 1 / The U.S. Department of Education publishes *Women at Thirtysomething: Paradoxes of Attainment*, which is based on analyses of statistics from the National Longitudinal Survey of the High School Class of 1972. The report describes the educational careers and labor market experiences of the members of that class from the time they left high school through age 32 and finds that although the women's educational achievements were superior to the men's, their rewards in the marketplace were fewer. For example, in only seven of 33 major occupations did women achieve pay equity with their male classmates.

June 1 / President Bush tells West Point's graduating class that he opposes the congressional Civil Rights Act because, he says, employers would be forced to adopt hiring and promotion quotas to protect themselves from job-discrimination lawsuits. (An interesting sidelight: today's graduation brings to 1,000 the total number of women who have graduated from West Point since Congress ordered it to admit women. The first class to include women was the class of 1980.)

June 3 / The U.S. Supreme Court lets stand a federal policy that denies U.S. Agency for International Development (AID) family planning grants to any overseas organization that spends money—even money that is privately raised and kept separate from public money—on activities relating to abortion, including providing information about abortion.

June 3 / Reflecting the effort that the California Institute of Technology (Caltech) has been making to attract women, Caltech—regarded as the premier science and technology institution in the West—announces that the number of women who have accepted admission has increased for the third straight year. Females will account for more than a third of the class of 1995.

June 5 / The Episcopal bishop of Washington, D.C. ordains Elizabeth Carl, an openly lesbian woman, into the priesthood.

June 5 / The House passes a modified version of the

Civil Rights Act of 1991 by a vote of 273–158, a majority 17 votes short of the number that would be needed to override a veto. As approved by the House, the legislation would expressly bar employers from establishing hiring or promotion quotas based on race, color, religion, sex, or national origin, and would forbid "race norming" of test scores. The bill also includes a provision capping at $150,000 the amount of punitive damages that would be allowed for employees who are the victims of intentional discrimination under Title VII of the Civil Rights Act of 1964 (the law that prohibits discrimination on account of sex, disability, or religion). Arguing that it was inequitable, especially to women, Representatives Patricia Schroeder (D-CO), Patsy Mink (D-HI), and Barbara Kennelly (D-CT) led an unsuccessful effort to delete the cap. Only victims of intentional race discrimination are allowed punitive damages (not capped) under existing federal laws.

June 7 / The General Federation of Women's Clubs, the world's largest and oldest women's volunteer service organization, begins its centennial convention with a symposium, Forum for the Future: Agenda for Women in the 21st Century. Moderated by Dr. Joyce Brothers, the symposium brings together experts in health, education, and the environment.

June 7 / Federal public health officials announce that they are considering changing the definition of AIDS to include all HIV-infected persons who show serious signs of a depressed immune system. The existing definition, which largely reflects how AIDS manifests itself in male homosexuals, makes it difficult for many infected people, including many women, to qualify for benefits.

June 8 / By a vote of 412 to 40, the General Assembly of the American Presbyterian Church approves a historical statement of faith, in the form of an 80-line prayer, that

makes sexual equity and environmental concerns part of the
official canon of the church.

June 9 / *You Just Don't Understand: Women and Men in
Conversation* reaches the top of *The New York Times* paper-
back nonfiction best-seller list. In the book, author Deborah
Tannen, who teaches at the Georgetown University School of
Languages and Linguistics, likens communication between
men and women to cross-cultural communication, saying that
women speak and hear a language of connection and intimacy and men a language of status and dependence. Tannen
says these patterns are developed in childhood—girls use talk
as a way to maintain intimacy and boys use it as a way of
negotiating status.

June 10 / According to today's *Washington Post*, the
alumni board of Skull and Bones, the (possibly no longer so)
secret society at Yale, has voted to allow women to be members. The board's decision reportedly must be ratified by a
vote of the membership.

June 11 / Speaking to the National Association of Temporary Services, a trade association for temporary employment agencies, the head of the Equal Employment Opportunity Commission says that discrimination complaints against
employment agencies have risen by 20 percent over the past
year. EEOC chairman Evan Kemp cites this as the primary
reason why the EEOC has agreed to accept complaints from
civil rights groups that use "testers"—individuals sent out to
detect job bias against minorities or women.

June 13 / According to a Census Bureau report released
today, even a modestly priced home was too expensive for 48
percent of the nation's households in 1988, and 15 percent
could not afford to buy a home even at the lowest prices. A
co-author of the study reportedly explained that lower inter-

est rates did almost nothing to improve renters' prospects of buying homes because "[t]hey just flat don't have the money."

June 15 / According to today's *New York Times*, state child-support enforcement agencies around the country have become far more aggressive and more successful at collecting child support. New mechanisms are reportedly in place for garnisheeing the wages of parents who owe child-support payments, and most states have started issuing "Most Wanted" lists, or staging round-ups to arrest parents who are delinquent.

June 17 / The Families United for Senior Action Foundation charges that more than half of the low-income elderly who are entitled to exemptions from Medicare premiums and to reimbursements for certain other Medicare costs are not getting these benefits. The Social Security Administration admits there is a problem, but says it has been unable to identify eligible recipients, who must meet specific income and asset standards. Members of Congress urge more outreach.

June 17 / A federal judge rules that Virginia Military Institute (VMI) can continue as a male-only institution, even though it is partially supported by the taxpayers (see March 1, 1990). During the course of the trial, the judge heard testimony by a Harvard University sociologist who, according to news reports, "agreed with VMI's contention that its program of intense exercise, hazing, and psychological indoctrination would be diluted by including women."

June 21 / The United Nations publishes *The World's Women 1970–1990*. According to U.N. Secretary General Javier Perez de Cuellar, the U.N. report finds that while there have been recent gains, the majority of the world's women still lag far behind men in power, wealth, and opportunity.

June 24 / An attorney representing Margo Mankes, a Miami third-grade girl who was refused admission to a Cub Scouts summer camp, files a sex discrimination lawsuit against the Cub Scouts.

June 24 / Dr. Bernadine P. Healy is officially sworn in as director of the National Institutes of Health. Dr. Healy, a cardiologist and former president of the American Heart Association, is the first woman ever to lead NIH.

June 25 / Sharon Pratt Dixon and Ruth Wright Hayre are among the nine women honored today by the National Coalition of 100 Black Women with the Coalition's Candace Awards for outstanding achievement. Ms. Dixon is the first female mayor of Washington D.C.; Dr. Hayre is the first woman and the first black to be elected president of the Philadelphia Board of Education.

June 27 / The U.S. House of Representatives overwhelmingly approves an appropriations bill that includes a provision to allow federally funded family planning clinics to provide abortion counseling. The measure would reverse the effect of the Supreme Court ruling in *Rust v. Sullivan* (see May 23, 1991), which abortion-rights advocates call "a gag rule." Those who oppose allowing federally funded family planning clinics to give clients any information on abortion reportedly are counting on President Bush to veto the House-passed measure, which is expected to pass the Senate as well.

June 27 / Justice Thurgood Marshall, the only black Supreme Court justice in the nation's history, announces his retirement, saying that his advancing age and medical condition have made it impossible for him to meet the "strenuous demands of court work." Although not entirely unexpected, Marshall's retirement within a year after Justice Brennan's resignation is dismaying to women's equity and pro-choice groups. Justice Marshall, like Justice Brennan, has been a staunch advocate of civil rights and abortion rights.

June 30 / Senator John Danforth (R-MO), who has been trying for many weeks to work out a compromise on the civil rights bill with the White House, says on "Meet the Press" that Bush administration aides are trying to enable employers to impose "extraneous" job qualifications that have nothing to do with ability to do the job but could be used to screen out women, blacks, and other minorities.

Women
and
Politics

ONE Changing the Rules and the Roles: Five Women in Public Office

CELIA MORRIS

In 1978, when Nancy Landon Kassebaum was elected to the U.S. Senate, the *London Daily Mail* was flabbergasted: "A woman has been elected to the Senate—not from a trendy East Coast or West Coast state, but from conservative Kansas, where a man's a man and a woman's his cook!" In 1990, when Governor-elect Ann Richards appointed 32-year-old Lena Guerrero to the Texas Railroad Commission, the first woman to sit on the three-member commission that for decades had indirectly controlled the world price of oil, her aunt burst into tears: the railroad was no place for a lady! (Guerrero cautioned her mother not to tell her aunt that the appointment had something to do with politics, lest she find that reality even more dire.) At a time when every woman who thrives in American politics still has her own specially-woven story to tell, some threads are shared—and the ability to surprise, even to shock, is one of them.

Nothing more vividly demonstrates the power of ideas over human experience than the extraordinary tenacity of the idea of "woman's place." "In my generation," says Kassebaum, who is 59, "you were more or less expected to pursue

Lena Guerrero *Credit: Senate Media Services*

a certain path." After graduating from the University of Kansas, Nancy Landon wanted to go to New York and find a job, but her father said "Absolutely not!" Alf Landon, sometime governor of Kansas and Republican nominee for president of the United States in 1936, "couldn't understand why I'd want to work anyway."

That set of assumptions about woman's place did not die with the social and economic changes that have undermined it. In 1990 when she ran for governor, for instance, Ann Richards had not only been state treasurer of Texas for two terms, but had done her job so well she had saved the taxpayers $2 billion in nontax revenue. Nevertheless, she was told more than once that she should stay home with her children. "Well, my children left years ago," Richards, who is 57, points

Nancy Kassebaum *Credit: U.S. Senate Photo*

out. (Three of her four children, along with her son-in-law, were key members of her campaign staff.) She adds philosophically: "That will always be said, but it's beginning to die out."

Richards, Kassebaum, Congresswoman Maxine Waters of California's 29th District, and Mayor Carrie Saxon Perry of Hartford, Connecticut, are members of a bridge generation of women—raised with assumptions about women's roles that reach back in Western societies to the 18th century and the beginning of the Industrial Revolution. During their life-

Ann Richards

times, economics and technology have transformed the
United States of America and women's roles in it. And very
gradually, attitudes are changing as well.

Like most middle- and upper-middle-class white women
in the late 1950s and early 1960s, Richards and Kassebaum
obeyed the cultural imperative to stay home and raise their
children. (Both had four, and some have speculated that a
woman with the energy and drive to do that successfully can
do anything.)

Like many black women of their generation, Maxine Wa-

Carrie Saxon Perry *Credit: Riley Johnson*

ters and Carrie Saxon Perry had paid jobs. Waters started out
as a Head Start aide before working up to assistant teacher
and then to supervising volunteer services. She managed a
variety of political campaigns and acted as chief deputy to a
Los Angeles city councilman before running in 1976 for the
California Assembly. Holding the seat she won then through
six more elections, in 1990 she moved on to Congress. Carrie
Perry, for her part, was a social worker for the state of Connecticut, an administrator with an anti-poverty agency, and
executive director of a group home for adolescent women
before running for the Connecticut Assembly. Women of the

Maxine Waters *Credit: Nareshimah Osei*

next generation, whatever their color, are likely to have a wider range of choices still—and a more complex set of imperatives.

Just after the 1990 election, the results of a Texas Poll

prompted the announcement that "anti-woman politics will not play in Texas in the future." On this issue, at least, the young were not of the same mind as their parents. While four out of 10 Texans over age 62 believed that "women should stay home and take care of the house, and leave running the government to men," only nine percent of those under age 30 agreed with that statement. While 53 percent of the people over 62 believed that "men are better emotionally suited for politics than women," only 30 percent of those under 30 agreed.

But nobody is sure yet what kinds of women can be elected to public office. Must they be ladies? Must they be dour? Must they be sexless? Must they be proper, blameless, and old? The possibilities vary, of course, depending on the office, although a nursing mother is probably ruled out from the beginning. So is a working prostitute, a bag lady, a mystic, a poet, or a saint—as much because she would not want the job as that the public would not feel comfortable with her or confident in her executive powers.[1]

After that, the answers we give lose their edge of certainty. Campaign consultants make fortunes advising women candidates on what will and will not play with a demanding public, but since most campaign consultants now are men, they speak a somewhat different language than their clients. And they are often wrong.

Who would ever have guessed, for instance, that a small brown woman with a ponytail that falls past her shoulder blades—a woman who wears large hats, possibly even to sleep—would be mayor of Hartford, Connecticut? Hartford is

---

[1] Just as this book went to press, we were informed that nursing mothers have joined the political workforce, which tells you how fast times are changing. However, we have as yet received no reports of poets or saints.

the home of Mark Twain, Harriet Beecher Stowe, and Wallace Stevens, and although they were all people of large imaginations, it is hard to imagine them imagining Carrie Saxon Perry. Certainly "the bishops" who ran Hartford for decades—the kings of insurance and banking—never imagined her.

"The bishops" practiced what was called "The Hartford Process." The chief executive officers of the leading businesses in the city, they met together to run the municipal show. They were "hands-on," as Perry puts it: "They met with community people, but they were the drivers . . . they didn't listen." It's a familiar scenario, and one repeated all through the country, from the East Coast to the West Coast and the North to the South. Although "the bishops" invested a great deal of time and money in their city, the inevitable happened: their high-handedness finally caught up with them when "a memo was leaked and it all fell apart. The bishops never came back."

Since the 1980 census, Hartford has lost almost 19 percent of its white citizens while gaining 18 percent more blacks, almost 140 percent more Asians, and nearly 59 percent more Hispanics. Nostalgia lingers for a process that was orderly and dependable, but Perry tells those who long for the good old days: "It's not coming back. They were too small a group with too wide a bottom. The numbers of women and minorities make ours a new order."

So the mayor of a city that "the bishops" once governed now sits in that august office in her trademark wide-brimmed hat. She grins with obvious pleasure when a class of emotionally disturbed children walks in to see the lady who runs the shop. She hugs them one by one, asks some questions, and shows them the council chambers. Around her are pictures of her heroes: Zora Neale Hurston, Jesse Jackson, Martin Luther King, Jr., Septima Clark, Rosa Parks. And no doubt for laughs as well as to demonstrate that she is a canny politician, there is a picture of her and her mother with President Ronald Reagan. No: though they had done a good job in their fashion, "the bishops" would not be coming back to the mayor's office in Hartford.

The junior U.S. senator from Kansas may not be so nearly like a pixie or a druid as Carrie Perry, though she is even smaller. But despite her state's heritage of strong women pioneers, who would ever have thought that Nancy Landon Kassebaum, a softspoken mother of four on the edge of divorce in 1978, whose highest elective post had been to the school board of a rural district, could have led a field of nine in the Republican primary? Who would ever have thought that then, in the general election, she could have beaten a former congressman who had come very close to defeating Kansas's favorite son, Senator Robert Dole, only four years earlier?

Certainly not her famous father, Alf Landon, a politician who had the distinct misfortune in 1936 to run against Franklin Roosevelt for the presidency of the United States. Probably because he loved his third child and youngest daughter and did not want to see her suffer, as he had, the pangs of ignominious defeat, Alf Landon argued against her running for the U.S. Senate.

And then there's Texas, which sets the national norm for the macho style: the Marlboro man lives in the Texas Panhandle, and Larry McMurtry, who wrote the granddaddy western of them all, *Lonesome Dove*, grew up in those flat lands where the cowboy myth reigns supreme. But people who were appalled when Ann Richards, at the 1988 Democratic National Convention, had the temerity to mock the vice president of the United States by saying George Bush "was born with a silver foot in his mouth" had heard nothing yet! To nail the cowboy, Richards said he was the guy who kissed the horse instead of the girl before he rode off into the sunset. A woman like that is outright dangerous, and the idea that she could be elected governor struck many Texans mute with amazement.

Texas had had a woman governor before, but she was not what a modern-day feminist would call a "role model." Miriam ("Ma") Ferguson (1924–26 and 1932–34), was a surrogate for her husband, "Farmer Jim," better known as "Pa," who had resigned the governorship in 1917 to escape being impeached. Ma Ferguson's campaign slogan was "Two Governors for the Price of One." Her bumper stickers read "Me for Ma!" (to which her opponents came back with "Too Much Pa!"). She was anti-suffrage, and her major contribution to the state folklore was a comment disparaging bilingual education: "If English was good enough for Jesus Christ, it is good enough for the children of Texas." (Although historian David G. McComb suggests that this story is probably apocryphal, Ann Richards never tires of quoting it and appears indifferent to Dr. McComb's judgment.)

To be sure, Texas boasts more than 100 women mayors. In fact, four of its largest cities now have women mayors—prompting observers to speculate that running a town or city has become an extension into the public realm of domestic housekeeping. But the percentage of women in the Texas legislature is far below what it is in states like Minnesota or Oregon, and the only woman ever to represent Texas in the

Congress of the United States was Barbara Jordan in the late 1960s and 1970s. So when Ann Richards announced in June 1989 that she was running for governor, no one, including Richards, knew whether a wise-cracking, tart-tongued divorcee who lived in Travis County, the San Francisco of Texas, had a chance to win the hearts and minds of enough Texans to put her in the governor's mansion.

In the past quarter century, the roles of women have changed more rapidly and dramatically than ever before in world history, and since all the old certainties have been called into question, styles of behavior among political women range from the deferential modes of the past to the more egalitarian manners of the young. In the hands of shrewd women for millennia, deference has been not only the prescribed mode but a clever tool, and it has had its uses. As Virginia Woolf puts it in *A Room of One's Own*: "Women have served all these centuries as looking-glasses possessing the magic and delicious power of reflecting the figure of man at twice its natural size. Without that power probably the earth would still be swamp and jungle."

Now, in certain communities, the old style can mask the new ways, or vice versa. Among Hispanics, for instance, the ancient idea of woman's place still holds extraordinary power, even when it is at odds with the reality. As Lena Guerrero puts it, seven of the nine children in her family are women, "and you're not going to meet one woman in my family who isn't a lot like me, who isn't tough and straight-forward and piercing in her commitment to get things done. My two brothers are very laid-back." This pattern, she claims, is found in many Hispanic families, and she tells the story that whenever she and her husband leave Austin and drive down into Hispanic South Texas, about the time they get to Falfurrias (some 80 miles from the Mexican border), he says, "I love this place: this is where men rule!" Guerrero comments wryly: "He has to wait till Falfurrias to say this, and even then it isn't true." Her father, if asked who wore the pants in the family, would say, "I do, but your mother tells me which pair to wear." Guerrero's father has been dead for 20 years, and when her mother hears her tell that story, she says, "I washed them. I had every right to tell him which ones to wear!"

The myth of woman's place has never required women to be weak-willed or stupid, of course. It has only required that they be circumspect at best, or devious and manipulative at worst. Carrie Saxon Perry explains that in the black church, which is at the political center of the black community, the minister is a "very strong father figure." He brooks no debate and seldom even discussion. Women, on the other hand, "control the church, but they don't do it up front. They're manipulative: they do all the work, all the organizing, all the raising of the money. But in many instances they become very sheepish. . . ." As Ann Richards observes, "women who are really strong in whatever they do. . . . [often] get around men and they just turn into these coy, eyelash-batting fools. And you want to say 'What is going on here? I just saw you cut that guy off at the knees in a committee meeting. And here you are carrying on a conversation and you'd think it was Mata Hari!' "

A strong woman in public office so unnerves many people that they can be relentlessly curious and often ill-mannered. A white minister on a television program asked Carrie Perry abruptly, "Are you gay?" to which she replied, "No, I'm black." The more conspicuous you are, Perry finds, the harder people fight you. And since they will remain curious and rude until women officeholders are nearly as common as men, a sense of humor should top the list of qualities required for the job.

Women who are part of that bridge generation and have succeeded in politics have had an experience uncommon in world history: they have lived two fundamentally different lives. And those we interviewed have loved it. Beginning her fourth term in the U.S. Senate, Kassebaum says, "I look back and am *amazed* that I did it. It's been a wonderful experience." Kirk Adams echoes the comments of many Ann Richards-watchers when he says of his mother-in-law, "She's having the time of her life!"

The cost is high: they have had to sacrifice their privacy. Maxine Waters tries to be philosophical: "If you're a firefighter, fires break out at night, and 24 hours a day." Carrie Saxon Perry, however, says, "if I'd known it was like going into a nunnery, I might have thought harder about doing it. You take the oath of chastity because you have absolutely no personal life. You take the oath of poverty because the jobs don't pay." (She didn't mention obedience, since any woman amenable to that one would never go into politics in the first place.) Perry, who, like Richards and Kassebaum, is divorced, explains that her busy schedule has run off a lot of men: "It's hard for anybody to deal with you. You can moderate, but you can't ever moderate down to nine-to-five." A certain wistfulness remains: "Just this Christmas it seemed like every man I've ever known called. I wondered if I was dying. They couldn't stand my running around, but they'd [remember our fine times and] say 'You are a good person.' " Still, Perry's job is so all-consuming that she has no time even to shop and her mother claims her refrigerator has an echo in it. "But right now," she adds, "there's nothing I'd rather do."

Although the rumors of high life that swirl around certain prominent political men seem to have little or no effect on their margins of victory, a single affair for their female colleagues could be politically fatal. As Perry says, "There's no such word as 'man-izer.' You couldn't get away with it. Never!" In her autobiography, *Straight from the Heart*, Richards writes that she could not be much fun to date because she is always working the crowd. Kassebaum laments the incessant demands on her time: "For women it's certainly not easy. It can be very hard on one's personal life." As a consequence she rejects most official functions at night, preferring "to go home and put my feet up, put my blue jeans on, and get out in the garden."

Maxine Waters is the only one of our four in the bridge generation who married again after being divorced, and she recognized early on that she must "reconcile the need for personal time and public life." She and her second husband, whom she married after being elected to the California Assembly, have had to sit down and "work on it all the time." Fortunately, her husband, an independent soul who at least theoretically knew what he was getting into, "likes what I do [and] is very supportive."

Still, these women lived fully and richly for decades with all the privacy they chose to enjoy. Kassebaum, Richards, Waters, and Perry raised their children before getting into public life, and Kassebaum, for one, says she could "never have mixed politics and raising a family." Convinced that "being a homemaker requires just as much ingenuity and creativity as being a television producer," Kassebaum sees that the community activities for which she volunteered were a good preparation for politics. Nor has she any regrets: "I completely enjoyed raising my family and taking part in a rural school district. You were always going to some game or event. I wouldn't have missed those days for anything."

Richards, in her autobiography, describes the challenge vividly: "Keeping a household fairly clean and attractive and decorated, putting good food on the table, getting children delivered to the various places they need to be, fighting the battle of the PTA or the school board, being involved peripherally in political races, volunteering at school, being room mother—I mean, you have here a tossed salad that's bigger than most bowls."

Social and economic changes over the past three decades have left most families dependent on two incomes, and the rate of divorce is so high that women have to be prepared to support themselves and their children. Because most women consequently now work, even when their children are young, volunteer activities have for the most part gone by the board, and as Kassebaum puts it, "our children miss that, especially when they were raised in a home where community activities were important."

And the decisions political women have to make remain very difficult, especially for the young. Lena Guerrero has a three-year-old son, and when asked to name the hardest decision she has had to make in the course of her career in politics, she replies, "probably to stay in it. Because it is such a sacrifice!" So public and demanding is her life that her toughest decision, which she revisits periodically, is "whether this is the way I want this three-year-old to grow up, whether to keep trying the personal relationship of a marriage this way."

Although Guerrero has never known the privacy as an adult that women a generation older took for granted, so far she has decided that even though the things she has given up are fine things, her commitment to public service makes hers "a good balance." To be one of the three people who together regulate the state's energy and transportation industries is no mean challenge: the Texas Railroad Commission is responsible for conserving the state's crucial oil resources as well as for ensuring that hamlets like Dime Box get transportation services as good as Dallas's. Still, Guerrero expects her commitment to public life to be harder to maintain when her son is on Little League teams and hopes his mom will come to see him play. "Giving up so much of my private time is tough," she admits. She and her husband "talk about it a lot. The expectations, the role, the visibility . . . it's like being in a fishbowl." Despite the sacrifices, Guerrero says "I love public service. I can see myself being in it 30 years. Or helping others to be in it 30 years without being directly involved myself. Because I don't think I'm the only woman in government who will contribute. . . ."

The role that women's groups have played in the success of these five women's careers is almost as varied as the women themselves. Maxine Waters is on the board of virtually every pro-choice organization on the books—the National Abortion Rights Action League, the California Abortion Rights Action League, Voters for Choice—and although groups like the National Council of Negro Women, the National Organization for Women, and the Women's Political Caucus had little money to give Waters in 1976, they threw themselves from the beginning into her races for the California Assembly. She is "so steeped in women's issues" and so well-connected with their organizations that she can always count on their playing a major role in her political life.

In 1987, when Carrie Saxon Perry became the 60th

mayor of Hartford, she also became the first black woman elected mayor of a major city in the East. (In 1990, Sharon Pratt Dixon of Washington, D.C. became the second.) Perry has depended on organizations like the Coalition of 100 Black Women for their political networking and their canvassing, bell-ringing enthusiasm, although, as she observes, "they're not as vibrant as they were when I started out."

For Lena Guerrero, the Texas Women's Political Caucus was not only a support group and an introduction to far-flung parts of her state, but a source of income. In 1980, at the age of 21, Guerrero was chosen to be its executive director, and three years later she became state chair. For all her adult life, the caucus has been a resource.

When Guerrero decided at 25 to run for the legislature, she also turned to the Mexican-American Business and Professional Women, the only Hispanic women's organization in Travis County. This group contained the core of politically active women in her district but had no structure or money to speak of. (The former they gradually developed; raising the latter turned out to be less difficult than Guerrero expected, and she finally pulled in $150,000.) She and her supporters borrowed a typewriter, and one day a woman named Mrs. Rodriguez knocked on Guerrero's door and volunteered to do the typing: "She said something had called her to that office!"

To Nancy Kassebaum, on the other hand, women's groups have mattered scarcely at all. In 1978, when she first ran for the Senate, she opposed the extension of the Equal Rights Amendment on the grounds that "like anything else, there was a finite time you had to pass it." Consequently, both the National Women's Political Caucus and the National Organization for Women endorsed her male opponent. The Women's Campaign Fund sent money, but her principal network of support came from men and women who had graduated, as she had, from the University of Kansas: "There were people I could call in nearly every community I went into whom I knew from the university, or that somebody I knew would know."

Certain women, however, played a major role in encouraging Kassebaum to run, the chief among them being her mother and her former mother-in-law, though "neither had any real interest in politics." And three close female friends in Wichita, convinced that "it was a good time for a woman to run," spent every day helping with the campaign. In a state with a population of only two and a half million, this kind of informal support can make the winning difference, and Kassebaum has the luxury of saying "I wasn't part of an old-boy network, nor would I be part of an old-girl network. . . . I'm a senator from Kansas." Nevertheless, she has spoken at conventions of the National Women's Political Caucus and the Business and Professional Women, and has a good rapport with members of those organizations.

In Texas, with a population of 17 million, networks are critical to the success of anyone running statewide, and Ann Richards has been at the center of progressive women's organizing there since the early 1970s. The core of women who have been key to her political career first came together in 1972, when Sarah Weddington ran for a seat in the state legislature, and many of the women who worked in that campaign went on to found the Texas Women's Political Caucus and then to work in Richards's 1975 campaign for Travis County Commissioner.

At least as important as political groups to the evolution of Richards's career has been the Foundation for Women's

Resources, a nonprofit organization that she founded with a handful of others as a mechanism to raise money for an assortment of projects. One project was Leadership Texas, which introduces promising women throughout the state to each other and to the realities of modern-day Texas. Another was the Women in Texas History project, which identified women of grit and distinction, most of them forgotten, and assembled artifacts like the MixMaster with which Bette Graham devised the formula for Liquid Paper, which simplified secretaries' lives. The Women in Texas History exhibit opened at the Institute of Texan Cultures in San Antonio, where Richards said, "I started this project for my daughters and discovered along the way that it was for me." She subsequently introduced a traveling version of that exhibit all over the state, and it became an effective means to introduce Richards herself to a far-flung potential constituency.

Like all women, these five have taken their mentors where they could find them, and since, as Kassebaum puts it, politics has "never been an arena that's very accepting of women," most of their mentors have been men. Kassebaum's is an extreme version of the familiar story.

Because her father was governor and deeply involved in the Republican party, Kassebaum grew up in politics. Unlike her mother, who didn't like the "rough and tumble," she enjoyed it and was in no way mystified by its workings. Although polls and focus groups make it clear that older people, and especially older women, tend to be problematic for women candidates, in 1978 Kassebaum found that she got "the most support from older women and the least from my own peer group"—a fact she attributes to her father. "I had a name that was identifiable and ties to people in the state. I told my dad that he'd outlived his enemies." When she got to the Senate, she was the only woman there, and during her tenure, there has never been more than one other female senator. Politically speaking, Nancy Kassebaum has always lived in a world of men.

When Carrie Saxon Perry arrived in the Connecticut Assembly as a representative from Hartford, her first mentors were two men in the Democratic leadership. Ideologically speaking, they were diametrically opposed to Perry. "We never voted the same way on anything," she remembers, but when she was appointed assistant majority leader "by some kind of fluke" as a mere freshman, they took her under their wing. She was "short and black and a woman," which made her "sort of dear." Her mentors taught her procedure and "were fair with me—and straight," but most important, they taught her, "Don't ever settle for bullshit!"

Perry would eventually have the chance to admire and emulate Unita Blackwell, mayor of Mayersville, Mississippi. Despite the fact that her town has only 300 people, Blackwell was elected president of the National Association of Black Mayors—the first woman president of an organization in which she outranks men like Coleman Young of Detroit and David Dinkins of New York City. Perry describes her in terms she would clearly be delighted to have used for herself: "She maximizes people underestimating her! And she still has the capacity for wonder." Blackwell, Perry marvels, has used her presidency to go all over the world. Her contacts are so widespread that the CEO of American Express asked her to introduce him to one of the leading banks in Hong Kong. When they heard about that request, as Perry tells the story, the men among the black mayors asked "What did you get?" while the women responded: "Go ahead girl! That's power. The Man had to come to you!" Blackwell answered the men wryly by counseling patience: "There are such things as deposits, you know."

Since Ann Richards was the first woman to be elected to statewide office in Texas in 50 years, she, too, had perforce to learn much of her trade from men. "While I was growing up," she says, "I can't say I ever thought of any woman in politics as being ideal." She admired Eleanor Roosevelt, who came to a naval base during World War II where Richards's father was stationed and made sure that her photograph was taken with black enlisted men. "I was stunned by that," Richards remembers, "and I've often thought how heroic and brave that was." To a white girl from a town outside Waco, Texas, Mrs. Roosevelt's metaphorical embrace of black people was equivalent to a revolutionary act, and Richards credits her "significance in molding the thinking of this country." Among contemporary politicians, she considers none more worthy of emulation than Barbara Jordan.

Nevertheless, Richards's colleagues, for the most part, have been men, and she has shaped her political style accordingly. Ten days before the 1990 gubernatorial election, the *Los Angeles Times Magazine* ran a cover story about her and her Republican opponent Clayton Williams titled "The Cowboy and the Good Ol' Girl." When asked to define a "good ol' girl," Richards suggests a woman who is canny and has a self-deprecating sense of humor. And because a primary requirement for good ol' girls is that they "appreciate and enjoy" good ol' boys, Richards has made it a point to be friends with men. As she said at a dove shoot on the eve of the traditional Labor Day kickoff for the 1990 general election, men and women are brought up doing different kinds of things, and they don't get to know each other very well. Occasions like the dove shoot bring them together in different ways and help them become friends. "It's a new experience for [men]," she says, to think of women as real friends rather than as sexual partners: "You have to consciously work at that."

Maxine Waters, on the other hand, has a style that grew out of being the fifth of 12 children. "We were not taught diplomacy as much as how to fend for ourselves," Waters recalls, before modifying slightly: "To *defend* ourselves is really what it was. You had to make sure you shared in the opportunity, be it dinner or something going on in the family or the neighborhood." Undaunted by the unflattering adjectives she has attracted, Waters recognizes that the woman she is evolved naturally from the girl she was in St. Louis: "I didn't know [what I was doing] was 'assertive' behavior. I didn't know that was 'aggressive' behavior. I didn't know women weren't supposed to act like that."

Bill Boyarsky, a columnist on the *Los Angeles Times*, called Maxine Waters "the conscience" of the current Speaker of the California Assembly and, accordingly, rued the day that Waters was elected to Congress. "She'll just chew you out if she thinks you're wrong," Boyarsky says: "I know, because she's done it to me." To be the conscience of any Speaker is a hefty job, but when the Speaker is Willie Brown—a man so brilliant and irreverent that he dominates every conversation, and so quick on the draw that virtually every politician in California is wary of him—the job becomes very nearly herculean.

Waters laughs at the notion that she kept Willie Brown in line, but she doesn't take exception to Boyarsky's description of her style. "I have not attempted to be liked by my male colleagues or to pamper them," she says, "I have not tried to be *male* enough for them to like me. I simply am what I am; I care about what I care about. *I'm me!* So I've had fights and I've had good moments." People work best together when they respect each other, Waters insists, and since she tries to be fair, she expects fairness in return. When she doesn't get it, "I let 'em know. I'm not going to practice disguising my feelings. I'm not socialized in being subtle: I just say it!"

Unlike Willie Brown, Thomas S. Foley, the Speaker of the U.S. House of Representatives, is a decorous, understated man. The Congress's rituals derive from the 18th century, and its rhetorical traditions run to the baroque. Foley's legislative assistant, Melinda Lucke, was therefore startled, but not surprised, when the new member from Los Angeles, whose reputation had preceded her, walked saucily into his office and said, "I need one hot minute with the Speaker!"

"This place is so steeped in custom and tradition that [the members] don't really do the work people expect them to do," Waters says with exasperation. As a freshman member on a Veterans' Affairs subcommittee, Waters was told that the chairman, G.V. "Sonny" Montgomery from the Mississippi Delta, did not look kindly on amendments to his legislation. Congresswoman Waters was not impressed. "They said 'That's the way he operates.' I said, 'These people are elected to serve, and if they've got something to offer, they should be allowed to offer it.'" She had something to offer—an amendment that would allow veterans to hire private legal counsel and have their attorneys' fees paid by the government—and when the pro forma call for amendments came, she offered hers. "This is not a good time for people who purport to support their government to oppose helping veterans return to their jobs," Waters observes cannily, and after some modest finagling, she got a unanimous vote in support of her amendment. "I respect custom and tradition that gets the job done," Waters insists, but "if it thwarts the process or throws up obstacles to your being able to represent your district, I'm not going to go along with it."

Younger political women are more likely to have had female models and teachers in the ways of politics—many of them the women of that key transitional generation. Among those whom Ann Richards has mentored, Lena Guerrero has already become something of a star in her own right. She was Richards's political director in her campaign for the Democratic gubernatorial nomination, and Richards's initial act as governor-elect was to appoint Guerrero to the Texas Railroad Commission.

Since Guerrero is a full generation younger than the other women we interviewed, she could be expected to have had a somewhat different experience, and indeed, like so many Texan women her age, she was inspired by Barbara Jordan. Guerrero was 13 when Jordan struck her imagination, along with the nation's, during the televised Watergate impeachment hearings. "I thought 'that is *exactly* what I want to do.' " Guerrero remembers: "I read everything that anybody wrote about that woman. I cut out newspaper articles. I wanted to be a member of Congress, and I never thought what that meant for an Hispanic woman. After all, she [Jordan] was black!"

In 1976, while Jordan gave her keynote address to the Democratic National Convention, Guerrero "watched her like I was delivering it. Most people don't remember that she co-keynoted it with John Glenn. He was so boring—she *was* the keynote. 'What's new? What's different?' [Jordan intoned:] 'Barbara Jordan is keynoting this Convention!' It was so great!"

Guerrero credits the Sisters of Mercy who ran the school she attended with her strong belief in conscience, which is at the root of her pro-choice position on abortion—an irony the nuns might not appreciate. "I was educated by nuns," Guerrero recalls, who "were extremely independent, bright, conscientious, demanding women. They taught me to think. They taught me that someday I was going to be judged for *my* actions—not somebody else's." And she learned her basic leadership skills in the Catholic Church: in the late 1960s, when boys still monopolized virtually all the helping roles in the Church, she was actually an altar girl. "My church was two blocks from my house," Guerrero remembers, "and I did a lot of helping around the back and during the service. But I also led in the choir. Mexican boys don't sing in the choir! They grow up to be famous singers, but they don't sing in the choir!"

Nonetheless, Guerrero's first explicitly political mentoring came from a man, Gus Garcia, the first Hispanic to be president of the Austin school board and a principal plaintiff in the suit that finally broke down Texas school segregation for Mexican American children. When Guerrero was a student at the University of Texas at Austin, Garcia took her aside and told her "something extremely visionary." His generation of Hispanic leaders in Austin, he told her, had "spent the better part of the last 15 years in a movement that has taught us basically where the hinges on the door are. We've popped the damn thing open. Now they invite us to the table. Your generation of leadership—men and women—is going to be required to know parliamentary procedure, to know how to read budgets, and to eat your lunch at the negotiating table." When you find a door that's closed, he insisted, "you call me, because we'll knock that sucker right down! We know how to do that. But that's not your job. Your job is to be *substantively* good!" Garcia made her focus on what she might do, according to Guerrero, and it was at his prompting that she mastered *Robert's Rules of Order*.

Will women in politics do things differently from men? The question is tantalizing—even haunting—but for the moment we have no sure answer. In a world in which almost all the rules have changed, and the information is as yet sparse, we can make only tentative generalizations.

We do know that women will not all take the same stands, even on war. Although the first woman elected to Congress, Jeannette Rankin, is the only member ever to vote twice against taking America to war—she voted against our entering both the First and the Second World Wars, and lost her seat in Congress each time as a result—women have always swelled the numbers of wartime patriots. When asked to name her toughest decision, Nancy Kassebaum first inclined to name her vote to give President Bush the authority to take the United States into war in the Persian Gulf. But then she corrected herself: that decision, ultimately, was not hard because she thought it the only one possible, since the country "had to do it." Although Kassebaum speculates that her office got 75 calls opposing the use of force in the Gulf for every one that supported it, she believed the president's policy was the only way to stop Saddam Hussein. "You have to weigh the calls you get with the larger constituency out there that you don't hear from," Kassebaum says, "and then you have to use your own judgment."

Maxine Waters agrees with Kassebaum on the process: neither takes polls or lets them influence her vote. On the issue, however, she disagrees fundamentally with the senator.

A woman who considers war "an obsolete means of resolving conflict," Waters was one of the Persian Gulf War's most unrelenting opponents. Although she was only a neophyte member of Congress and emotions were volatile, no one tried to influence her to mute or modify her stand: "People know I have strongly held positions." When asked whether she thought her vote expressed the will of her district, she replies, "I don't legislate that way. I try to let people know who I am all the time, so they will understand where I'm coming from on issues. I don't pull very many surprises. I think the people voted for me because they kinda liked where I was coming from."

Waters will keep on opposing policies like those that led to the Persian Gulf War—even though they gave President Bush the highest poll ratings of any president in history. In the aftermath of the war, as the Kurds were fleeing toward the Turkish and Iranian borders, she insisted that "we should not only provide humanitarian aid, we should be absolutely honest with the American people about what we're doing there. They need to know that this administration is supporting Saddam Hussein's staying in office."

If women disagree on fundamental issues, there is nonetheless some evidence that they do approach public office differently from the way men do. Mayor Kathryn Whitmire of Houston, Texas has suggested, for starters, that women are usually ready to try new things: since each was once the new kid on the block, innovation does not set them to trembling. Whitmire herself demonstrated a positive relish for breaking precedent when she appointed Lee Brown to be Houston's chief of police—the first white mayor to appoint a black to that office. Long after Brown had left Houston to head New York City's police department, Whitmire remembered one letter to the editor at the time he first came that said, Well, it could have been worse: she could have appointed a woman. And indeed, in 1990, Houston's chief of police was the first in the country to need maternity uniforms for herself.

Although Senator Nancy Kassebaum does not expect women's burgeoning political presence to change policy significantly because she suspects they are not "that different" from men, she agrees with the common perception that women bring "a certain perspective and sensitivity" to bear. Kassebaum herself, for instance, will not play "political hardball"—a game at which "some of my colleagues are masters." She recognizes that refusing to play that game can put her at a disadvantage, but feels that it is simply "against my nature." Convinced that women can be firm in their resolve without resorting to trickery, Kassebaum associates political hardball with "innuendo, vindictiveness . . . threats," and a willingness "to use everything that's out there in order to get your own way."

In Texas, on the other hand, political hardball is a synonym for politics. In his Pulitzer-prizewinning *The Making of the President 1960*, Theodore White described that state's political tradition as among the most "squalid, corrupt, and despicable" in the nation. During the 1988 elections, U.S. Senator Lloyd Bentsen was widely quoted as saying that Texas politics is a contact sport, and hardball politics there is known as paying your dues.

At a political roast in Austin after she defeated Republican Clayton Williams to become governor of Texas, Ann Richards reportedly turned to *Washington Post* reporter David Broder and taunted, "Well, do you think I'm tough enough now?" Many reporters had speculated that Richards wasn't, indeed, tough enough to win, but she had proved herself willing to offend even her most faithful supporters by attacking her Democratic primary opponents in ads that Austin columnists called "wretched" and "misleading." Of former Governor Mark White, she said that he had used taxpayers' money to line his own pockets; of Attorney General Jim Mattox, that he had been indicted. (By omitting the fact that Mattox had been acquitted in his trial for bribery, Richards violated the cardinal principle of American jurisprudence: that a person is innocent until proven guilty.) One after another, three male candidates lost their political composure and self-destructed at the goading of Ann Richards, and their doing so was largely a tribute to the skill with which she played the game of political hardball.

This skill put her in the most powerful position in Texas government to affect the delivery of human services, which Bill Hobby, her close friend and the former lieutenant governor, believes she cares about more than anything else in politics. Richards would not disagree with Mayor Carrie Saxon Perry when she says, "Most women I know are on missions." They are "evangelical" in their commitment to serve others. Nor, probably, would she disagree when Perry says, "It's very selfish: you get a good feeling about what you do. Women really believe that one person can make a difference."

Near the end of her gubernatorial campaign, Richards frequently closed her stump speeches by citing the time Eleanor Roosevelt looked out her train window to see clothes hanging on a line behind an unpainted wood house and wrote in her diary that she "saw Thrift hanging there." Richards celebrated Roosevelt for being able to see the people behind the thing, the human beings behind the statistics. The story clearly stood as an implicit promise about the kind of governor she intended to be.

Being a woman has proved a plus for those who have known how to take their advantages where they find them. For Carrie Saxon Perry, it meant that when she first went to the state legislature, "they started off *not* on guard." People look at a woman who's gotten herself elected to a respectable office and they think: "She must have worked for it!" In the case of a man, Perry points out, "they might think he knew somebody." Nancy Kassebaum has been invited to speak on stellar occasions "because I'm a Republican woman in the Senate" when most of the men who came into the Senate at the same time she did have been overlooked. "I think you have to work rather hard not to flaunt that and take undue advantage," she warns, "because that can lose you support [in whatever your political forum]—and that's ultimately where you want it."

Ann Richards calls it the "two-headed cow" syndrome: After she was elected Travis County commissioner in 1976, she was invited to speak all around the state. "There were not that many elected women to invite to make speeches," she remembers, and she liked doing it because she met so many women "just like I was in the early years—starved to hear" from someone who had done it that there is no mystery involved in running for office and winning. "It was wonderful." Richards says: "Still is! You'd tell 'em 'You're smart. You're good. You just don't have the experience or the techniques to do the things you need to do. And here's how to do it . . . !' "

Like so many of her peers, Richards enjoys giving other women the chance, as Lena Guerrero puts it, "to think beyond the world [they] live in, to find some other tracks." Since 1982, when she was elected state treasurer, Richards has considered it her duty, as Texas's highest elected woman official, to help other women along if they are competent.

"When they're not," she says, "they reflect on all of us."

Nancy Kassebaum tries to campaign for women all around the country, encouraging them to run for school boards, for city and county commissions, and, particularly, for the state legislatures, where she thinks many of the political initiatives of the 1990s will come from. "The excitement's going to be at that level," Kassebaum has concluded, "I've seen the vitality here erode since I've been in the Senate."

Kassebaum will tell any candidate who asks that "it's very important in politics to be yourself. You don't have to be aggressive to be tough. But you do have to know what you care about and keep focused on that." Like Richards, Kassebaum defied her opponent's insistence that she give the public information she thought none of its business and, by taking a stand on principle, risked losing her election. She refused to release tax statements that involved her estranged husband's business, while Richards refused to say whether she had ever taken illegal substances.

Both went down in the polls as a result of those refusals, and both said "I don't care." Neither was willing to be pushed into doing something fundamentally against her principles merely to win, and both had to fight off well-meaning friends who told them they were making a mistake. One editorial called Kassebaum "an injured wren," and newspapers all over Texas echoed Richards's opponents in demanding that she "Answer the question!" At least in part because the public saw them take a tough stand and hold it, they won despite a barrage of criticism.

Carrie Saxon Perry is convinced that "women are more result-oriented" than men. "They're human: they don't mind recognition," she hastens to add, "but they get into it because they're unhappy with the way the school board has been running the schools, or because there should be a black woman sitting up there, or because city government should be more responsive." You can't stay in the business of politics, Perry says, unless you learn not to take things personally "because you get lambasted!" And once in, "it's like a bottomless pit: people have such needs that they want someone to deliver, and you have to find ways to make them be more reasonable."

Politics can be a lonely business and very, very hard. But for all the women we interviewed, the satisfaction of doing the job, and doing it superbly, is proving worth the pain and trouble. Congresswoman Maxine Waters says, "I can't think of anything better to do with my life! I like working on behalf of people who don't have paid lobbyists. It's like fighting City Hall from the inside." And as Governor Ann Richards puts it, "The important thing . . . is not the election itself. It is the follow-through. And we are following through on everything we said we would do. That's the fun part!"

TWO Women of Color and the Campaign Trail

IRENE NATIVIDAD

AT A GATHERING of women state legislators in 1987, a former Congresswoman threw a challenge to this powerful audience with her opening remarks. "I am Shirley Chisholm," she said, "a bearer of a double jeopardy in this nation because I'm simultaneously a woman and a black person. And if I dared to do the things that I've been able to achieve in spite of my gender and my race, then every one of you in this room must dare and I would be most angry if you don't."

Little did Ms. Chisholm know that in 1991, a mere four years after this speech, the capital city of the nation would be headed for the first time by an African American woman, Sharon Pratt Dixon. Nor did she foresee that the number of women of color members of the U.S. House of Representatives would be at an all-time high: four African Americans (Cardiss Collins [D-Illinois]; Barbara-Rose Collins [D-Michigan]; Eleanor Holmes Norton [D-District of Columbia]; and Maxine Waters [D-California]) along with one Asian American (Patsy Mink [D-Hawaii]) and one Hispanic American [Ileana Ros-Lehtinen (R-Florida)]. To top this off, the first Hispanic to be elected to the powerful Los Angeles Board of Supervisors after 116 years was a woman, former L.A. City Council member Gloria Molina.

The emergence of these women in the national political

Shirley Chisolm *Credit: AP/Wide World Photos*

scene underscores the fact that women of color politicians are no longer an anomaly. Instead, many have followed Ms. Chisholm's lead and have sought public offices with the same tenacity and determination for which Ms. Chisholm is known. Unsurprisingly, local politics has provided the most opportunity for women of color. According to Rutgers University's Center for the American Woman and Politics (CAWP), 133 served as state legislators in 1990 or 10.5 percent of the 1,273 women state legislators nationwide.

Among these women, African American officeholders form the overwhelming majority. Based again on CAWP's figures for 1990, 100 women of color are in the state legislatures; 75 in county governing bodies; 651 in municipal council seats; and 70 in mayoral seats. Among the latter, Sharon Pratt Dixon of the District of Columbia and Carrie Saxon Perry of Hartford, Connecticut are the only two women of color mayors of cities with populations over 100,000.

The predominance of African American women in politics when compared to other women of color is an outgrowth of their longer-term experience as community leaders, church leaders, and as "leaders" of families often bereft of men. Having had to enter the workplace far earlier than white women, African American women have also "tended to be more assertive with their men" as Shirley Chisholm accurately points out. They have also been participants in the civil rights struggle in the United States—an ongoing battle that has given many of them considerable political training.

While the pool of approximately 1,000 African American women elected officials may seem small, there is another group of women politicians who add significantly to these numbers. According to the Joint Center for Political Studies, about 50 to 60 percent of Democratic Party state officials are African American women. David Bositis, one the center's senior researchers opines that "this is mainly due to the Democratic Party's aggressive affirmative action programs, which have provided openings for African American women who can literally be counted twice—as women and as persons of color."

Asian American women, in comparison, are relatively new entrants into the political process. While African American women are longstanding and consistent voters (in 1988, 67.4 percent were registered to vote compared to 60.4 percent of African American men, based on figures provided by the Joint Center for Political Studies), their Asian sisters have not yet made a significant presence in the voting booths, let alone in the governing bodies of this country. Outside of U.S. Representative Patsy Mink, there is only one other high-ranking Asian American woman elected official—March Fong Eu, California's long-time secretary of state. Additionally, only 17 Asian American women currently serve as state legislators.

Part of the reason for these paltry numbers is that many are relatively new arrivals, since the largest influx of Asian Americans has taken place only within the last two decades. While focusing their energies primarily on business and the professions, Asian Americans have tended to shun politics until recently because it was an activity that would have called attention upon them as a community. This is understandable given the United States' long history of exclusionary laws that prevented the immigration of Asians to this country. It is hard to remember that it was not until 1950 that Asians not born in the United States were conferred the right to be naturalized citizens.

Hispanic American women, like their Asian American sisters, do not vote in large numbers either, although compared to Hispanic American men, their voting participation is greater. In 1990, the National Association of Latino Elected Officials (NALEO) counted 792 Hispanic American women officeholders, the majority of whom were in Texas or California. NALEO pointed out that this number accounts for about 20 percent of all Hispanic elected officials, which is the same proportion of women public officeholders in the United States as a whole.

Only two Hispanic American women hold statewide offices—New Mexico's Secretary of State Stephanie Gonzalez and Texas Railroad Commissioner Lena Guerrero. While there are 14 women currently serving as state legislators, NALEO reports that the largest number of Hispanic American women elected officials are school board members—358 to be exact. Just as the civil rights movement was the propellant for many African American women to become involved in politics, the schools have been the breeding grounds for Hispanic American women politicians who have had to wage battles for bilingual education, let alone simple access to education for their children in an Anglo world.

For Native American women, political empowerment has been obtained primarily within their tribal structures, as epitomized by the election of Wilma Mankiller in 1987 as the first woman to head the Cherokee nation. Some, however, have managed to enter mainstream politics as signified by the election in 1990 of five Native American women to state legislative seats. This is not a large number when compared to the other groups mentioned above, but as Tomasina Jordan, national chair for the American Indian Cultural Exchange, points out, "The Native American woman's bid for mainstream political power has had to take a back seat to her community's struggle to gain official recognition from the United States."

Within tribes themselves, Ms. Jordan notes that women have always had the right to vote, way before their white sisters. Women, in fact, had a more equal role in leadership, as exemplified by a Woman's Council in the Cherokee nation, whose advice was sought on tribal matters—a prevalent practice before the arrival of the white man.

The diminution of the role of women as tribal leaders was a direct result of European acculturation, according to Wilma Mankiller. She feels that the press attention attendant upon

Wilma Mankiller *Credit: AP/Wide World Photos*

her election had more to do with the white stereotype that a
woman could not be a "chief" of a tribal nation. She points
out that prior to her election, there were other women who
served as chiefs—Ada Deer, for one, who was the chief of the
Menominee Tribe of Wisconsin, and Ramona Bennett who
headed the Puyollop Tribe in Washington state, for another.
Both she and Ms. Jordan acknowledge that the voyage from
tribal politics to mainstream politics will be a difficult one for

Native American women, but not necessarily insurmountable considering their history.

Given demographers' projections that minorities could be the majority of the population in some important states by the next century and taking into account the increased presence of women as a whole in the political arena—both as candidates and voters—it is safe to assume that many more of our nation's leaders will be women of color. The possibilities for advancement of these women as officeholders are indeed limitless with the explosive growth of the minority population. The challenge, however, lies in the rate such progress will take place. Will the barriers attendant upon the double jeopardy of being a woman and a person of color decrease in the future? Or will such barriers fail to dissipate even with an increasingly ethnic population? Equally important, will the different racial and ethnic groups' grab for a political place in the sun result in minorities (women *and* men) being pitted against each other? This is a critical question as political maps are redrawn to reflect the findings of the 1990 census, and as politicians of all colors begin to deal with what a multicultural future means.

To be able to assess the future prospects of women of color candidates, one must take a look at the challenges they currently face in their bids for political leadership. If the American woman still confronts tremendous difficulties in running for public office, imagine then the hurdles encountered by a candidate who is both a woman and a person of color. The barriers are similar in many cases, but the difference is in degree.

As campaigns become more media driven and therefore more expensive, *money*, or the lack of it, is the major barrier faced by women of color candidates. Miriam Melgar, a Hispanic woman who lost her bid for a seat on the Wilmington (Delaware) County Council in 1986, stated the reason succinctly, "We simply do not have the connections that bring money in," she said.

Women of color are less likely to have access to the contacts and networks that traditionally fund candidates. Hence, they're frequently locked out of the "money loop." Even when a candidate has proven herself by winning the primary election, the traditional party's cynical perception of her chances of winning prevent the party from going all out in terms of support. Personal financial resources, on the other hand, are equally scant, whether one's own or one's family's, so funding one's own campaign is often out of the question.

Faye Williams, a 1986 and 1988 congressional candidate from Louisiana, raised almost a million dollars for each campaign, much of it from outside of her state. Each time she "kept hoping that the (Democratic) party would come out and support her outright," especially after she won her primary in 1986, but that was not to be. She feels that her groundbreaking run as the first African American woman congressional candidate from Louisiana was too threatening to the traditional politicians who ran the state. She lost her first race by a mere 5,000 votes—a loss that she thinks could have been averted if she had had the funds to cover last minute media buys. While there were other reasons for her failure to capture this seat, certainly her limited coffers did not help things any. As a result, she still has campaign debts from both her 1986 and 1988 congressional races.

Problems in acquiring sufficient campaign funds are very much related to another hurdle faced by women of color—*credibility*. Because the experience that brings a woman of color to decide to run for office may not always be known to a larger group beyond her immediate community, there is always a perception that she somehow brings less credentials as a candidate. The reality, of course, is that she is often overqualified when compared to her male opponents. She usually brings more community leadership experience, as well as better academic credentials. Faye Williams, for instance, ran against a businessman, Clyde Holloway, who only possessed a high school degree, while Ms. Williams was a law school graduate who also held a master's degree in public administration from the University of Southern California. One can safely say that Ms. Williams' academic *bona fides* didn't hurt her candidacy. The same can be said of former Delaware County Council candidate Miriam Melgar who credits her education and profession as a biochemist for giving her credibility among some voters, specifically white voters, with whom she was the number two vote getter.

Shirley Chisholm recalls that when she decided to run for a congressional seat in 1968, she had already served as a state legislator, was a former district leader, and was also a national Democratic committeewoman. Compared to her male opponents, she brought tremendous credentials to the race, but the political powers that be felt that the seat should go to a man. Despite the fact that she was not her party's choice, she won—partly because her political experience brought her a significant base, partly because of a district that had a ratio of two-to-one female voter registration, and partly because of her own charismatic personality that made her connect with voters more easily.

Mary Scott Boria, a former vice chair of the Cook County Democratic Women in Chicago and a political activist who has worked on numerous campaigns, attributes the problem of credibility to women of color not having much "visible" political experience that brings them name recognition to a constituency other than their own minority community. That is why Texas Railroad Commissioner Lena Guerrero advises women of color interested in running for public office to extend their networks by getting on advisory boards or "mainstream" organizations that will broaden their reach, not to mention refine leadership skills in another setting.

A third problem frequently mentioned by women of color as a major hurdle in their political advancement is what Lena Guerrero calls "the cultural resistance from men of color." When she ran for her state legislative seat for the first time, male Hispanic community leaders exhausted all of the possibilities for a male candidate before settling on her. This is similar to Shirley Chisholm's experience almost a decade earlier. "Men can't believe we're ready, because it wasn't too long ago that they got in," according to Lena Guerrero.

Shirley Chisholm echoes this view when she states, "Black males feel that the political seats are owed to them because of historical circumstances; therefore, opportunities should redound to them first of all." When Ms. Chisholm first sought election to Congress in 1968, there had not been an African American person representing that district in Brooklyn. So, when redistricting created an opportunity for African American representation, there seemed to be a consensus among community leaders that this new seat should go to a man—hence, the opposition and lack of support for her candidacy from among the African American male leaders in the district.

"That we should step aside and be supportive of our male *compañeros*," states former Delaware County Council candidate Miriam Melgar, stems from the misperception that a woman of color candidate is "taking away opportunity from the male peers in the community." The consequence for women of color is that, contrary to expectations, they do not always receive the support of their own community (as expressed through its leaders who are mostly men) in their bid for political power. This lack of support does not always spell defeat, as both Lena Guerrero and Shirley Chisholm have demonstrated, but it does create additional complications for campaigns that are already filled with difficulties, given the combined factors of race and gender.

How successful women of color politicians have dealt with this hurdle is to target all women voters (regardless of race or ethnicity) in their districts, as Shirley Chisholm did in her 1968 race. The other technique is to widen their electoral bases by reaching out to other constituencies. Ms. Chisholm's ability to speak Spanish fluently was not missed by the Hispanic voters in her district. Lily Lee Chen, an Asian American who challenged incumbent California Congressman Matthew Martinez in 1988, made sure that she had a committee of supporters from the Hispanic American, the African American, the women's, and the business communities when she launched her campaign. While she did not win her race, her attempt at outreach beyond the Asian American community is one frequently emulated by women of color candidates, especially those running in multiracial districts.

Another impediment shouldering the door against women of color candidates is the need to break the cultural barrier of expectations—expectations that account, in part, for the resistance posed by men of color to the candidacies of women from their community. For the Hispanic woman, for instance, there is an understood role—to take care of her family. Leaving her family without dinner to run to a political meeting runs counter to that role and is often viewed as unacceptable. Lena Guerrero finds this to be the case more in those areas where minorities form the majority culture, as opposed to those areas where they are combined with peoples of other races or ethnicity.

For Asian Americans, the rigid family structure defines roles for everyone. Margaret Chin, a 1991 city council candidate for a new district being carved in New York City, states her mother's perception of Ms. Chin's political activities, "A daughter doesn't go out and mind other people's business." Not only must an Asian American woman candidate face the stereotype about a woman's role as sole nurturer, but also that of the daughter, who is not perceived traditionally as being as important as the son. Her objections, notwithstanding, Ms. Chin's mother has proven to be her staunchest ally.

To solidify support for herself with her larger family—the Chinese American community—she also had to forge a link between the older, powerful Chinatown families and the new breed of young, aggressive community leaders to whom she belonged. Adroitly balancing both worlds, she has managed to get their support for her groundbreaking run for a seat never held by an Asian American. But it has not been easy. This support comes after two successful races for the Democratic State Committee from New York's 61st Assembly District; so in effect, she already had a winning record to demonstrate her mettle to the community.

Because women of color politicians do not fit the norm as prescribed by the larger white society, the barrier of image, presence, or appearance is also one they must confront. They will always look or sound different from the majority of the electorate, not only because they are of a different race or ethnicity, but because they are also women.

When Miriam Melgar decided to make a run for the Dela-

Margaret Chin

ware County Council, some of her Hispanic friends thought her heavy Panamian accent might be a barrier in communicating with voters. Ms. Melgar's solution was to have someone tutor her on how to make public presentations—speeches, debates, and press question-and-answer sessions. Similarly, Lily Lee Chen, in her preparations for her 1988 congressional run, resorted to lessons at a nearby university to minimize her Chinese accent. What both of these women were reacting to was a perception, whether correct or not,

that an accent underscored "foreignness" and being an outsider. While both of them knew that what they said was more
important than the accent with which it was conveyed, they
could not be blamed for being apprehensive about anything
that would emphasize even more their differences from voters
in their districts. Both women lost their races, but the reasons
had less to do with accents and more with cogent political
factors such as the incumbency of their opponents or lack of
funds.

The implications of being viewed as an outsider were just
as real in Shirley Chisholm's first congressional race in 1968.
She felt that an undercurrent in the opposition against her
had to do with her Caribbean heritage. Ms. Chisholm's family was Barbadian, and she spent much of her childhood in
Barbados. There were some political leaders in her community who felt that the first African American to hold that
congressional seat should be one who was of native U.S.
stock.

For Asian American women, the majority of whom are
not native born, being taken seriously as candidates is frequently hampered, they feel, by their often short, slight, and
youthful appearances. When combined with accents or softspoken demeanors, they seem to embody the stereotype of
Asian Americans as not being "leadership material" in a society that ties leadership to size and an outgoing personality.
Congresswoman Patsy Mink of Hawaii, whose small stature is
typical of Asian Americans, nevertheless counters this stereotype with her booming voice, eloquent delivery and, yes, an
outgoing personality. New York City Council candidate Margaret Chin, on the other hand, does not possess Representative Mink's "larger" personality and has a quieter presence.
This has not stopped her from winning, twice. Her appear-

ance, in fact, belies a "steel mettle" personality forged from a deep well of commitment, hard work, persistence, and belief in her capacity to create change for the Asian American community. That personality has obviously managed to convey itself and convince voters of her sincerity. So the bottom line is that appearance may be a *perceived* detriment to women of color politicians, but it has very little to do with the winability of a candidate who has the appropriate credentials and the ability to convey her message to the voters.

Less a barrier to a woman of color's candidacy than just a difficult balancing act is how to juggle the issues of importance to the voters of one's district versus the issues of concern to one's racial or ethnic community versus the issues paramount among women. New York City Council candidate Margaret Chin poses succinctly the question in the voters' minds, "Are you going to serve everyone or just your community?"

On those issues pertinent to race, the white community makes assumptions that women of color candidates will automatically support such issues. On the other hand, the racial or ethnic community to which they belong may often blame their women candidates for not being supportive enough of their grievances. This may seem to be a no-win situation, but former Colorado state legislator Polly Baca thinks otherwise. In her 10-year tenure, she sponsored more legislation supporting women and peoples of color than most of her colleagues, even though her district was predominantly white and seemingly conservative. This very same district elected her five times with at least 62 percent of the vote. Polly Baca answers, "If you take care of your district's needs, you can also take care of the needs of your racial community and women as a whole. You don't have to choose between being a woman and a minority. You can't and shouldn't."

Wilma Mankiller, the first woman elected chief of the Cherokee nation—the second largest Native American tribe in the United States—agrees, "Women, in general, bring an interconnectedness to things; we have a broader perspective on issues." And women of color who have experienced the dual barriers of race and gender discrimination bring a special understanding to many issues linked to women. Child care, for instance, has now become a mainstream concern for most Americans for whom the two-earner family is the norm rather than the exception. For women of color, who usually have to become wage earners much earlier than white women, child care has always been and continues to be paramount. Hence, this is a problem whose saliency women of color candidates recognize immediately.

There is one issue that throws a monkey wrench into this balancing act—reproductive choice. This issue presents a problem for some Hispanic and Asian American women candidates who may be supportive of women's issues in general, but whose view of "choice" is reduced to a categorical statement, "access to abortion is wrong," based upon long-held religious beliefs. Polly Baca notes that she was always and continues to be pro-choice, but she was not a leader in the movement to preserve that right. Had she been one, she feels that it would have affected her candidacy to her detriment, both because she's Hispanic and because of her district. For Maria Berriozabal, 1991 mayoral candidate in San Antonio, Texas, her anti-choice position has caused some women activists and organizations to not formally endorse her run. Clearly, given the spotlight on this issue after the Supreme Court's *Webster* decision in July 1989, reproductive choice will continue to present some problems for those women of color candidates unsupportive of the issue but who are also interested in targeting the women's vote, a slight majority of which is pro-choice.

Given the difficulties outlined above for women of color candidates, it is a wonder that the numbers of women running and winning elective offices has increased at all. Part of the motivation for many of these candidates is to open doors for others from their own communities through their own candidacies. As Faye Williams, the first African American and the first woman to make a bid for a Louisiana congressional seat, sees it, "Just in running [for office], I broke ground." This perspective was echoed by Delaware County Council candidate Miriam Melgar, who said, "Even when you don't win, the impact of your running is that you open up the horizons of the voters. You educate them as to who we are. If you don't do it, there's no exposure for your people." New York City Council candidate Margaret Chin counts as her greatest achievement "helping to push for a positive image of Asians and Asian Americans. By my being out there [as a politician], people had a better sense of my community."

This sense of one's candidacy as having reverberations within one's own racial or ethnic community as well as one's personal career is a powerful propellant for many women of color to take the risk and run for public office. While many white women candidates have made the transition from politics as a mission to politics as a career, the majority of women of color politicians still see the breakthrough implications of their candidacies. In other words, the "mission" aspect of their bids for public office is very much alive.

There is evidence from surveys and studies conducted by the National Women's Political Caucus (NWPC)—a 20-year-old bipartisan organization whose aim is to increase the number of women public officeholders—to buttress the claims of women of color candidates that "in the running is winning." Voters are much more likely to consider the candidacy of a woman once they have had exposure to a political race where a woman was a contender. For instance, NWPC's 1984 post-election survey indicated that 29 percent of the voters polled would be more likely to support a woman candidate in the future because of Geraldine Ferraro's candidacy for the vice presidency.

By extension, the more voters become accustomed to women of color running for public office, the more open they will be to such candidacies in the future. In addition, the increasing presence of peoples of color and women involved in politics will also help to create an atmosphere of acceptance, especially at a time when diversity will define America's population in the next century.

This is not to say, however, that running for office will be any less difficult. The fact of the matter is that no one ever gave away a seat of power because it's the right thing to do. One must compete for that seat. Furthermore, campaigns will not cost any less in the future nor will the power of incumbency (the major detriment to women and peoples of color gaining access to elective office) be mitigated unless a cap on congressional or state legislative terms is established nationwide. Given this scenario, women of color candidates must be better prepared in the art of running for office, must develop a network of support that is broad, and must learn how to raise significant sums of money. Texas Railroad Commissioner Lena Guerrero feels that women of color interested in getting elected must not only get training in campaign skills but also in reading budgets, conducting meetings, or running organizations in general. In her view, winning public office is one thing, governance is another. It can be argued that many male candidates have run, won, and gotten re-elected without all of this preparation and with lesser credentials. That is true—but the experience of numerous women candidates of all races and ethnicity indicates that for a woman to be qualified to run she must be overqualified.

Numerous women's organizations have created programs in response to the need of women of color candidates for support either in terms of training or a network. In 1984, former U.S. Representative Shirley Chisholm formed the National Black Women's Political Caucus. Its thrust was to get more African American women to run for office and to be more visible politically. Ms. Chisholm points out that part of the impetus for the formation of this organization was her perception that both African American and white men did not include African American women when it came time for candidate selection. Her own experience as a congressional candidate showed the reluctance of African American men to support their women for public office. Similarly, she faults 1984 presidential candidate Walter Mondale for not reaching out to African American women in his vice presidential search. Whatever the reason for its formation, the National Black Women's Political Caucus has obviously hit a nerve among its targeted constituency—500 women from 32 states attended its first convention in Atlanta in 1985. At present, it has 37 chapters with more continually being formed.

In January 1986, the National Women's Political Caucus inaugurated its first "Minority Women Candidates Training Program." The program was intended to provide sophisticated campaign skills to women across racial and ethnic lines—from developing a campaign plan to fundraising to media skills. To provide role models, the instructors chosen were women of color campaign professionals as well as officeholders, including Donna Brazile, former Deputy Field Director for the Dukakis campaign; Leslie Winner, an Asian American who ran former California Assemblywoman (now Congresswoman) Maxine Waters' first state legislative campaign; and Lena Guerrero, then a Texas state representative. The training was specifically intended to focus on running for local offices, since that is where most women of color begin their political careers.

While the skills gained were considered invaluable by the participants, the network that emerged was even more so. One of the attendees was Virginia Nell Webber, who had run unsuccessfully for the Dallas City Council twice prior to this training session. After participating in the program, Ms. Webber said that the enthusiasm and support of her sisters at that training as well as her newly honed skills propelled her to go for a third try at the city council seat. She won—the first African American woman on the Dallas City Council.

NWPC's program has since been replicated in numerous cities across the country. Similarly, other organizations like the YWCA have provided training to promote political participation as a whole. The National Women's Education Fund, an organization formerly dedicated to providing campaign skills to all women, also targeted women of color candidates many years before the NWPC or the YWCA. Most recently, black sororities have also offered political skills training to their members.

Despite these efforts, there could not possibly be sufficient training conducted for all of the women of color who will seek to lead government at varying levels in this country in the next decade. The United States is now in the midst of the second great wave of immigration (the first being at the turn of the century); and a third of its population growth in the

1980s was fueled by new arrivals, primarily from Asia and Latin America. The potential increase in the number of women of color who will be politically active defies calculation.

The challenge for these candidates in the coming years is not just how to gain acceptance from a majority white electorate, whose numbers are shrinking dramatically, but how to win seats in increasingly multiracial districts. New York City Council candidate Margaret Chin finds that it's hard work "to learn to relate to different constituencies." But that's precisely what future women of color candidates will have to do in order to win. This requires an openness to different cultures, an understanding of the commonality of human experience and human needs, and a determined willingness to look beyond stereotypes that various groups may still have of each other.

This is not an easy task, especially when various ethnic and racial groups try to carve out districts that will give them long-awaited access to political power. Sometimes this process works out as in Gloria Molina's case, when the formation of the new Hispanic supervisorial district in Los Angeles, in recognition of the size of the Hispanic community, was largely uncontested. But in other instances, ethnic and racial groups will have to compete in the redefinition of legislative districts. Margaret Chin is currently in the midst of such an effort— depending on how the lines are drawn, either Hispanic Americans or Asian Americans will be the minority group that will define that district. Needless to say, Ms. Chin and her supporters are involved in delicate negotiations with the Hispanic community over this matter. Should her forces win, the city council seat created would be the first one to be held by an Asian American in New York City.

The stakes are high, but they are always that way for women of color who take a stab at political power. Margaret Chin is clear as to why she wants to undergo the travails of another campaign, "I want a seat at the table and open the door for others," she says. That resolute claim has echoed over the years and will reverberate in the future as women of color continue to fulfill their yearning to lead. Former U.S. Representative Shirley Chisholm, who ran for the presidency in 1972, agrees vehemently with this goal, but points out an equally compelling motive for herself and other women politicians, "I ran . . . despite hopeless odds to demonstrate sheer will and refusal to accept the status quo."

THREE **Do Women Officeholders Make a Difference?**

RUTH B. MANDEL AND
DEBRA L. DODSON

Introduction[1]

WOMEN ARE THE "new kids on the block" when it comes to political power in the United States. Shut out of even the right to vote until well into the twentieth century, women generally had no choice during the first two-thirds of our nation's history but to use the tactics and strategies of outsiders if they wanted to influence government action on issues about which they cared. Many of the early women reformers held firm convictions born of religious, political, and social values that championed human rights and decried injustice. To make government reflect their values, these women needed allies among men in authority—men who were accountable on Election Day to other men who most likely opposed women reformers' policy preferences.

Times have changed, but not as much as many would like. On the one hand, more women than ever are on the "inside" influencing policy as officeholders. As of 1991, women hold about 18 percent of elected statewide and state legislative of-

[1]An earlier version of portions of this chapter appears in Ruth B. Mandel, "Outside/Inside: The Continuing Tradition of U.S. Women's Political Leadership," a paper prepared for *Meeting the Challenge: Women as Leaders*, The Radcliffe Conferences, Cambridge, Massachusetts, May 1989.

fices, more than quadruple their representation a mere generation ago (*CAWP Fact Sheet*, 1991). On the other hand, almost three-quarters of a century after winning the right to vote, women still are far from achieving parity among officeholders at any level of government. In the U.S. Congress, men outnumber women 17 to one among the 535 voting members. Even after a generation of incremental progress for women at the state legislative level, male legislators outnumber women by more than four to one.

Why should we care whether women have parity with men in holding public office? One good reason is that the under-representation of women among our public leaders symbolizes the failure of American society to provide equality of opportunity for all its citizens. Another is that the under-representation of women means that half the nation's talent remains largely untapped—a waste in any era, and particularly costly today, when rapid change and complex, almost insurmountable problems face us locally, nationally, and globally.

A third—and very significant—reason that we must be concerned with women's under-representation in elected positions is that the presence of women in public office promises something new in policymaking—new and valuable perspectives and priorities that might otherwise be ignored because they are not typically the perspectives and priorities men have brought to public office. In a 1979 address to a conference on minorities and women in public service, Donna Shalala, then Assistant Secretary of Housing and Urban Development, stated that the importance of minority and female participation in public service "goes beyond the need to utilize our natural human resources. It extends to the need to incorporate varying perspectives into the governmental structure—

perspectives that can be provided only by minorities and women themselves, whether elected or appointed" (Shalala, 1979). Describing the first meeting of the National Women's Political Caucus (NWPC) in 1971, a *New York Times* reporter wrote, "One theme recurred in the speeches regardless of the race, age or political affiliation of the speaker: that an increase in political power held by women would set the nation on a course toward more 'humanitarian' policies" (Shanahan, 1971). An examination of women's political leadership suggests that the idealism expressed at the NWPC conference was not so wide of the mark.

Ever since women began holding public office, more than a few women officials have joined with their activist sisters outside institutional politics to support progressive and egalitarian measures, especially where these concerned equality for women. A government monograph about women in Congress between 1917 and 1976 observes that many of them "stood out for their strong identification with humanist issues: peace, child care, health and welfare, and other social issues. And regardless of their party or political ideology, the vast majority supported some form of women's rights" (Tolchin, 1976). In her book about the impact of the women's movement on public policy in the early 1970s, Jo Freeman wrote: "The fact that almost all of the approximately two dozen bills relevant to women [introduced in the 93rd Congress] originated in the House [where 16 women held seats], with few comparable ones as yet introduced into the Senate [where no women served], illustrates the importance of having sympathetic *women* in Congress, rather than merely sympathizers. . . . While several male legislators have sponsored women's legislation, there is usually a feminist in the background someplace" (Freeman, 1979).

Is public policy different because women hold public office? Would policy change if those women were replaced by men? Not so long ago, those who believed that the answer to both these questions is "yes" had to rely largely on isolated examples and general impressions to support their claim. In recent years, however, scholars at the Center for the American Woman and Politics (CAWP) and elsewhere have been systematically gathering and analyzing information about women in public office. Since 1975, CAWP has conducted four national surveys of elected officials; these—and especially the most recent of them—furnish broad-based evidence that, when it comes to policy and to leadership more generally, the perspectives that women bring to public office tend to differ in important respects from those of men.

Why Should We Suspect That Women Might Make a Difference?

It appears to be virtually impossible to separate nature from nurture, or ascriptive from acquired characteristics. In any case, an American woman enters public office having been raised as a female in a patriarchal culture. Inevitably, she will see the world through lenses tinted by her gender, experiencing life differently from her brother, husband, or male colleague. Even if she has spent her days rejecting the social imperatives of her gender identity and resisting society's pull toward orthodox sex roles, her personal history is that of a female in rebellion, but never that of a male.

On the surface, elected women and men in the last several decades may seem to be much alike. By and large, elected officials of both sexes come from the middle class, are middle-aged, fairly well-educated, Caucasian, and Protestant. The majority are married and have had children.

However, there are also some suggestive gender differences among public officials. For example, elected women are less likely than elected men to be *currently* married or to be the parents of *young* children. Elected women are also more likely than elected men to say that the age of their children influenced their timing in running for office. Considering these differences, as well as the fact that it is women who are the more likely to have had the daily responsibility of caring for children, elderly relatives, or other family members and friends, the implications are clear: elected women are more likely than their male counterparts to have had the hands-on responsibility of family caregiving and to have had to make trade-offs when family responsibilities and public life conflict.

The occupational and employment experiences of female officials also tend to be quite different from those of their male colleagues. For example, a smaller proportion of the women than of the men have law degrees. A smaller proportion of the women than of the men are employed for pay while holding elective office. And the elected women who are employed are much more likely than their male colleagues to work in traditionally female occupations—nursing, social work, teaching, secretarial work.

In part because of such differences in life experience, women and men typically come into elective offices by different routes, bringing with them the influences not only of their different occupational backgrounds and employment histories, but also of their different informal networks, organizational memberships, and campaign constituencies (Carroll and Strimling, 1983). A woman state senator who is a teacher, for example, might belong to her professional association, and to the League of Women Voters, the American

Association of University Women, and the Women's Political Caucus. It would not be surprising if she had perspectives on some issues, or an agenda and set of priorities, that differ considerably from those of a male senatorial colleague whose law firm specializes in real estate and commercial property development, and who belongs to the state bar association, the Rotary Club, and a veterans group.

Understanding that women come to public office with life experiences very different from those of their male colleagues is key to understanding why the priorities and attitudes of women in public office often differ from those of men.

Measuring the Impact of Women in Public Office

The Center for the American Woman and Politics has conducted four surveys of elected officials. In 1975 and 1977, mail surveys of all women serving in federal, state, and local offices were designed primarily to gather, in a systematic way, information about such characteristics of elected women as their personal and political backgrounds, their attitudes toward current issues, and their ambitions. The third study, conducted in 1981, also collected this kind of information, but in addition looked more closely at how women and men had come into elective office. It was the first study to provide nationwide data comparing female and male officeholders, including analyses of their attitudes on a number of public policy issues. The fourth CAWP survey, conducted in 1988, had a more ambitious purpose still: it sought to measure what impact women state legislators may be having on public policy.

While findings from all four of CAWP's surveys inform

this chapter, the 1988 survey of a national sample of women and men lawmakers is the basis for all of the figures and most of the following discussion about legislators.[2] Funded by a grant from the Charles H. Revson Foundation, the study allowed us to assess differences between female and male legislators with respect to both their attitudes on certain policy issues and three aspects of their policy actions: their work on legislation addressing problems specific to females; their legislative priorities; and their effectiveness in getting their policy priorities passed.

To what extent is the expression of gender difference among officeholders affected by variations in age, occupation, party affiliation, ideology, or race? Is it affected by the numbers and proportions of female colleagues, the level of feminist consciousness, or by women officeholders' ties to networks that value and support women's distinctive contributions to public life? To answer these questions, we asked the legislators of both sexes how they identified themselves ideologically (we already knew party affiliations), and whether they considered themselves feminist. We gathered demographic data—age, race, marital and parental status, and educational and occupational history. In addition, we asked the women legislators whether they belonged to various women's organizations outside the legislature and—if their state had a legislative women's caucus—whether they attended caucus meetings.

---

[2]For more information about CAWP surveys, and for details about the 1988 survey, see the appendix to this chapter. For more detailed information and/or copies of CAWP's studies, contact: Center for the American Woman and Politics (CAWP), Eagleton Institute of Politics, Rutgers University, New Brunswick, New Jersey 08901.

Do Women and Men Differ in their Policy Attitudes?

Most research in the 1970s and early 1980s that compared the attitudes of elected women and men on policy issues found that women were more likely than men to support feminist or liberal policies (Merritt, 1980; Stanwick and Kleeman, 1983). In CAWP's three national surveys of elected men and women, women officials were more likely to have feminist and liberal views than their male counterparts within the same political parties, and in the same self-identified position on the spectrum of political ideology (i.e., conservative, moderate, liberal).[3] Independent studies conducted recently under CAWP's sponsorship have confirmed these findings (Havens and Healy, 1991; Welch and Thomas, 1991).

Like CAWP's earlier surveys, the 1988 survey found that women state legislators were more likely than their male colleagues to support feminist policies. In 1988, women lawmakers were more likely than men to favor ratification of the Equal Rights Amendment (ERA), less likely than men to favor banning abortion, and more likely than men to oppose requiring parental consent for a minor's abortion (Figure 1). The women legislators were also more likely than men to express liberal attitudes on issues not usually thought of as "women's issues": the ability of the private sector to solve economic problems with minimal federal regulation, the death penalty, and nuclear power. Indeed, the gender gaps on these three issues were as large as the gap on the issue of

---

[3]"Feminist," as we use the term to characterize policies, attitudes, or positions, means reflecting or consistent with the policy agendas and policy preferences of the major feminist organizations, such as the National Organization for Women (NOW) and the National Women's Political Caucus.

banning abortion. On the other hand, virtually the same proportion of the male as of the female legislators supported government provision of child care and increased taxes for social services. How legislators stand on these two issues seems driven more by party (and party-oriented views about the appropriate role of government and government spending) than by gender, with Democrats generally more supportive of both policies than their Republican colleagues.

Our survey also found that on some issues, the views of black women legislators tended to differ from those of their white counterparts.[4] In considering the possible implications of this finding, it should be noted that since all of the black women serving as state legislators in 1988 were Democrats, all of the black women we interviewed were Democrats. The white women lawmakers in our sample were more evenly divided along party lines—about two in five were Republicans. When we compared the women legislators on the basis of race alone (i.e., ignoring other factors such as party affiliation), we found black women much less likely to support the death penalty than their white female colleagues. Black women unanimously favored government-subsidized child care, while only two out of three white women supported it. Black women were more likely than white women to believe that state and local taxes should be raised to support social services, and that the ERA should be ratified. None of the black women legislators we interviewed thought that abortion should be banned, although about one out of four of the white women did.[5] However, we found virtually no difference

[4]Of the 1,176 women serving in state legislatures in 1988, 95 were black. Our sample included 33 black women. The sample had too few women lawmakers of other racial groups for a more extensive and complete analysis of racial differences.

[5]Among Democratic women, however, black and white women had similar views on most of these issues.

Figure 1 • LEGISLATORS' ATTITUDES ON SELECTED POLICY ISSUES BY SEX

Percent Who Favored Ratifying the Equal Rights Amendment

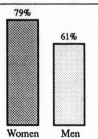

79% 61%

Women   Men

Percent Who Favored the Death Penalty

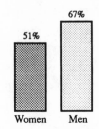

51% 67%

Women   Men

Percent Who Opposed Requiring Parental Consent for a Minor's Abortion

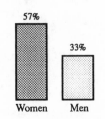

57% 33%

Women   Men

Percent Who Favored Prohibiting Abortion

26% 39%

Women   Men

Percent Who Favored Building More Nuclear Power Plants

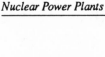

16% 29%

Women   Men

Percent Who Agreed That the Private Sector Can Solve Economic Problems with Minimal Regulation

47% 59%

Women   Men

Percent Who Favored Government-Provided Child Care

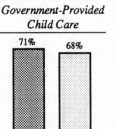

71% 68%

Women   Men

Percent Who Favored Increasing Taxes for Social Services

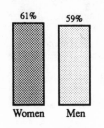

61% 59%

Women   Men

by race with respect to the women officials' confidence in the ability of the private sector to solve economic problems, their position on nuclear power, and their views on laws requiring parental consent for minors' abortions.

While the attitude differences between women and men legislators suggest that the increased presence of women in legislatures might make substantial differences in the outcome of floor votes and in legislative agendas, attitudinal differences are never guarantees of behavioral differences. Do women's different attitudes translate into differences in actions inside male-dominated legislatures?

Do Women Make a Difference in Policy?

There is good reason to believe that women officeholders might make government more sensitive to the special concerns of women if only because they themselves are more sensitive to these issues. For example, while an official of either sex may be concerned about crime and violence, a woman is more likely to understand the gravity of rape. Because a woman is more likely than a man to be a family caregiver, she is more likely to have seen firsthand the economic and health care problems of the aged. She may also identify with the aged more closely than a man does, since such a large proportion of the frail elderly are of her sex. And, while both male and female public officials are likely to be parents, women are more likely to know from their own experience about the need for child care and parental support systems.

Newly elected to Congress in 1986, then-Representative Patricia Saiki, a Republican from Hawaii, drew on personal experience when she explained why she considered child care a top priority for legislative attention:

Without adequate child care options, the 71 percent of working mothers with children under the age of 18 who work full time cannot hope to realize their dreams. Without adequate child care, the millions of families headed by females who live in poverty cannot hope to break the cycle of despair that grips their lives. As the mother of five children, I know what is involved in trying to raise a family and pursue a professional career. It is not easy, even under the best of circumstances. For most families, the best of circumstances is simply out of reach (Rix, 1988).

Most legislators of both sexes believe that the kind of perspective reflected in Saiki's comments is having an effect on policymaking. Eighty-five percent of the female legislators, and 74 percent of the male legislators, in CAWP's 1988 survey thought that the increased presence of women influenced the extent to which legislators consider how legislation will affect women as a group. Eighty-seven percent of the women, and 76 percent of the men, thought that women's increased presence affected the number of bills that were passed dealing specifically with the problems faced by women. Most legislators also thought that women have had an impact on the spending priorities of their particular states—75 percent of the women and 60 percent of the men. (Such perceptions are not confined to state legislators. A study of state cabinet-level officials in Connecticut found that a majority believed women have made a difference in policymaking in their state, particularly with respect to making sure that how policies will affect women is taken into consideration [Havens and Healy, 1991].)

The impressions of the legislators surveyed by CAWP that women in state legislatures have made a difference in policy are supported by the two measures of action from the survey: (1) whether the legislator had worked on at least one *women's rights bill* and (2) whether the legislator's top priority was in an area we call *women's distinctive concerns*.[6] Work on women's rights bills is measured using legislators' responses to the following, essentially "yes or no," question:

Of all the bills that you have worked on during this session, are there any where the bill itself or specific provisions of the bill were intended to help women in particular?

To answer this question affirmatively, lawmakers need not have spent much time on the bill or have considered it an important item on their own legislative agendas—they simply had to have done some work on a bill aimed specifically at helping women.[7] Some of these bills might not fit conventional definitions of "women's rights" legislation, but all reflected a concern that government must give equal attention and resources to the problems of the female half of the population (for example, as with legislation requiring insurance coverage for mammograms).

Our findings on legislators' priorities are based on their responses to this more open-ended question:

Although you may have worked on a number of bills . . . we want you to pick out the *single* bill that you would say has been your own *personal top priority* for the current session. Can you briefly describe the focus of this bill?

Based on the legislator's description of his or her priority bill, we determined whether the bill did, or did not, meet our

[6]"Women's rights" bills dealt specifically with issues of direct concern to women generally (e.g., legislation concerning rape, teen pregnancy, or women's health) or focused on their specific concerns as wage earners (e.g., pay equity), working mothers (e.g., maternity leave, day care) or marital partners (e.g., domestic violence, spousal retirement benefits, or division of property in divorce).

[7]If a legislator reported work on such a bill but could not recall the nature of the bill, or described an anti-feminist bill, or described a bill that did not directly benefit women, the legislator's affirmative response was reclassified as a "no."

criteria for what we call a women's distinctive concern. In this category we included legislation addressing such broad, humanistic concerns/"people issues" as health care, welfare of children and adults, education, environment, and social services, as well as the type of measure that met our definition of a women's rights bill. Measures dealing with such issues as budget, finance, and transportation we classified as "not a women's distinctive concern."

Our findings both about work on women's rights bills and about legislative priorities lead us to believe that the increasing presence of women in public office is changing legislative agendas. We found that women legislators were noticeably more likely than their male colleagues to have worked on a women's rights bill: about three in five female legislators, but only slightly more than one in three of the men, had done so in the most recent session. Black women legislators were the most active in this respect; 85 percent reported work on women's rights bills. And we found that women were also more likely than men to have made a women's distinctive concern their top priority bill. Slightly more than half of the women legislators (both black and white), but only slightly more than one-third of the men, had done so (Figure 2).

These results are consistent with other research conducted by CAWP-sponsored independent scholars. One of these studies found that women cabinet-level appointees in Connecticut were more likely than their male colleagues to consider family issues—such as family leave—important (Havens and Healy, 1991). Another—a study of legislators in 12 states—found that women legislators were more likely than their male counterparts to support—and work toward—policies reflecting women's distinctive concerns (Welch and Thomas, 1991).

Indeed, in various forums over the years, many women

Figure 2 • POLICY ACTIONS OF LEGISLATORS BY SEX

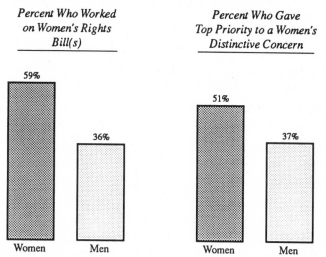

lawmakers have expressed to CAWP a conviction that women in office are making a difference in the public policy agenda. As one legislator put it during a CAWP focus group conducted in November 1987:

They [men] were not tuned in to child care, spousal abuse, rape, and all of that stuff. Here we [women] came along and we said, "You know, these are your children, these are your mothers, your wives. If you are *not* going to take care of them, we *are* going to take care of them." And there were a lot of locker room jokes, [but] now they come around begging for money for another spouse abuse center in their area.

This legislator is by no means alone among women leaders in her conviction that a great many important issues, too long neglected by politicians, command her attention. Women leaders describe their advocacy for women's concerns as a special obligation, a form of social nurturing—"if I don't do it, who will?"

Reviewing her work on issues of domestic violence and child support enforcement at a CAWP-sponsored panel in October 1988, Delegate Anne Perkins of the Maryland legislature told an audience of researchers, "These issues fall on me." And she catches them. At the same forum, Minnesota's Secretary of State, Joan Growe, explained what it means to say that women leaders in political office are making a difference: "It means they are willing to take on the special, extra agenda of women's issues and needs and serve a broader constituency than their particular district." And former Federal Trade Commissioner Patricia Price Bailey noted that women are "connected because they suffer the same experience. Something is there that we share that causes us to have a connectedness to each other." Women like Bailey believe they are affected in their perceptions, sensibilities, and behavior by something we might term a woman's consciousness—an amalgam of nature and nurture, gender-related personal experiences, patterns of culture and history. They do not question whether their presence in leadership will make a meaningful difference, especially to other women. They know it will.

Of course, some women officials shun any notion of gender consciousness and are most proud of the way they "fit in," declining to differentiate themselves from men in any politically relevant sense. Yet even women who deny that gender is of significance in shaping leadership behavior sometimes acknowledge its influence. For example, soon after her historic appointment to the Supreme Court, Justice Sandra Day O'Connor maintained that she brought "to the court differences in background that are more germane than my gender," citing her experience as a state legislator as giving her a "different perspective." But she also noted that she would "bring to the court the perspective of a woman primarily in a sense that I am female, just as I am white, a college graduate, etc." Developing her view a bit, she added, "Yes, I will bring the understanding of a woman to the court, but I doubt that that alone will affect my decisions. . . . I think the important fact about my appointment is not that I will decide cases as a woman, but that I am a woman who will get to decide cases" (Associated Press, 1982).

Factors Affecting Women's Impact

To determine whether women's impact was due primarily to certain subgroups of women legislators, and to see whether institutional characteristics, such as the presence of a women's caucus, affect the likelihood that women will diverge from their male colleagues, CAWP's 1988 study took a close look at how feminist identification, political ideology, and connection to the organized women's community affected policy action. We found that while such factors may explain some of the differences between men and women with respect to attitudes toward and action on policy, they don't explain them all.

The Effects of Feminist Identification

Our analysis of CAWP's 1988 survey found that both gender consciousness and feminist self-identification[8] affected whether legislators worked on women's rights bills. Women

[8]To determine who the feminists were, we asked the following question: I am going to read you a list of labels that some people reject, but others use to describe themselves. For each, we would like to know whether you do or do not identify with the label . . . Feminist? . . .

who were feminists were by far the most likely to have worked on a women's rights bill (about three out of every four had); men who were not feminists were the least likely to have done so (about one out of three). But there was only a small difference in this respect between feminist men and nonfeminist women: about half of each of these groups had worked on a women's rights bill (Figure 3). This pattern is not confined to legislators. A recent CAWP-sponsored independent study of women and men on the bench found that feminist women judges were the most likely to exhibit support for women's rights in hypothetical cases, nonfeminist men the least likely, and nonfeminist women and feminist men about equally likely (Martin, 1991).

The inference from these findings is that those who are especially interested in making policies more attuned to the special problems facing women in society should try to bring more feminists *and* more women into public office. Women make a difference, feminists make a difference, but feminist women make the *most* difference when it comes to work on women's rights bills.

When it comes to legislative priorities, a slightly different pattern emerges (Figure 3). Among the women, the nonfeminists were nearly as likely as the feminists to have made a women's distinctive concern their top priority. This finding suggests that the experience of being female may create, even in women who do not consider themselves feminist, a sensitivity to the human issues reflected in legislation addressing the broad array of women's concerns, if not to the female-specific problems of the type addressed by women's rights bills.

Among the male legislators, the gap between those who were feminist (a small group—just one-fifth of the male legis-

Figure 3 • POLICY ACTIONS OF FEMINIST AND
NONFEMINIST LEGISLATORS BY SEX

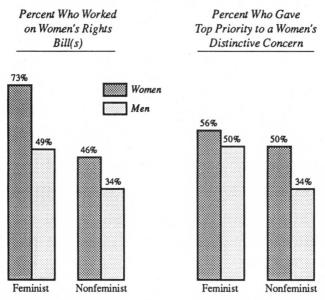

| Percent Who Worked on Women's Rights Bill(s) | Percent Who Gave Top Priority to a Women's Distinctive Concern |

lators we surveyed) and those who were not was about as large
when it came to legislative priorities as it was for work on
women's rights bills. Indeed, the percentage of feminist men
who gave top priority to a women's distinctive concern
equaled that of the nonfeminist women, and was much closer
to the comparable percentage of the feminist women legislators than to that of the nonfeminist men.

Although feminist men were less likely than their feminist
women colleagues to have worked on women's rights bills, it
may be that men who regard themselves as feminists are more
likely than their nonfeminist male colleagues to be politically
liberal—that is, to be generally supportive of government
programs for social services (Klein, 1984). In any case, the
effect on policy is that when it comes to giving priority to

women's distinctive concerns, women make a difference and feminists of both sexes make a difference.

The Effects of Political Ideology

As might be expected, we found that ideology did have some effect on the actions and priorities of legislators of both sexes: legislators who identified themselves as liberals were the most likely of their sex, and conservatives the least likely of their sex, to have worked on women's rights bills and to have given top priority to women's distinctive concerns. However, as Figure 4 shows, among the legislators of each ideological group—conservative, moderate, and liberal—the women were more likely than the men to have worked on women's rights bills and to have as their legislative priority a women's distinctive concern. While the gender gaps vary, and differ somewhat depending on which of the two measures we use, the message is clear: all across the ideological spectrum, women's distinctive concerns are more likely to be on the agenda if an elected official is a woman. Indeed, conservative women are as likely as moderate men to work on a women's rights bill and to have as their top priority a women's distinctive concern.

Consider the implications of these findings in, for example, an election district that is known to reject liberals in favor of "middle-of-the-road" candidates. Knowing that women's distinctive concerns are likely to be significantly more important to the moderate official the voters choose to represent them if she is a woman, advocates in that district who are particularly concerned about such issues might do well to concentrate their efforts on getting a woman moderate on the ballot.

Figure 4 • POLICY ACTIONS OF LEGISLATORS BY POLITICAL IDEOLOGY AND SEX

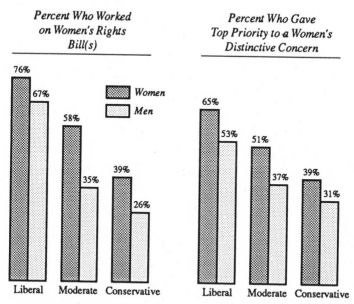

The Effect of Membership in Women's Organizations

CAWP's data show that even elected women who are not particularly active in or connected with women's organizations are likely to give higher priority to women's distinctive concerns than men do. However, our findings suggest that women's organizations play an important role in training and encouraging the women who are most likely to make a difference once in office.[9] The more women's organizations a legislator belonged to, the more likely she was both to work on a women's rights bill and to cite a women's distinctive concern as her top priority. Even among women legislators with

[9]We asked about membership in the National Federation of Business and Professional Women's Clubs, the American Association of University Women, the League of Women Voters, NOW, the NWPC, and any other feminist group.

shared points of view on policy, those who belonged to women's groups were more likely to work on women's rights bills than those who did not belong.

The Effects of Occupation

Because occupational history is yet another factor that might account for the differences we found between female and male lawmakers, we analyzed the legislative priorities of legislators of each sex by type of occupation—i.e., by whether the legislator had worked in a traditionally female or traditionally male occupation (Figure 5). We found that even among legislators of the same or similar types of occupations, the women were still more likely than the men to work on women's rights bills and to give priority to bills dealing with women's distinctive concerns.

Women in traditionally female occupations were, it is true, the most likely to mention a women's distinctive concern as their top priority, with men employed in female-dominated occupations and women in male-dominated occupations almost tied for second place. However, when legislators were asked to list their top *three* priorities, the women in traditionally male occupations were about as likely as their sisters in traditionally female occupations—and more likely than men in either occupational category—to have a women's distinctive concern on the list. This finding suggests that women who have broken sex stereotypes in employment have not turned their backs on the issues about which members of their sex have traditionally been especially concerned, even though they may consider other issues important as well.

Figure 5 • LEGISLATIVE PRIORITIES OF LEGISLATORS BY
TYPE OF OCCUPATION AND SEX

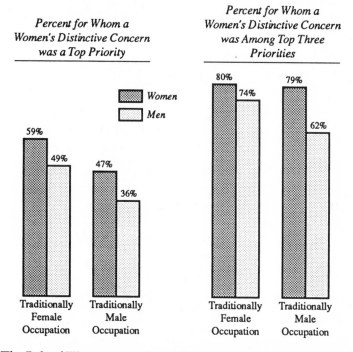

The Role of Women's Legislative Caucuses

Women legislators in the U.S. Congress and in a number of states have organized formal caucuses, or meet on an informal basis, to facilitate collaborative and concentrated efforts to make policy more reflective of women's concerns. The Congressional Caucus for Women's Issues (founded in 1977 as the Congresswomen's Caucus and renamed in 1981 when membership was opened to congressmen) supports federal policy initiatives to improve the status of women and families. In the 100th Congress (1987–1989), for example, the Caucus and its executive committee members (all female) were active in a wide range of work, family, and equity issues: child care; family and medical leave; job training, education, and child care for welfare recipients; sex discrimination in institutions of education supported by federal aid; maternal and child health; the supplemental food program for women, infants, and children (WIC); improving access to government contracts for women-owned businesses; domestic violence; eating disorders; AIDS and young children; homeless families; federally funded screening programs for breast and uterine cancer; family planning programs; pay equity; and the concerns of elderly women (Rix, 1988).

Across the country, similar concerns about issues that particularly affect women and children have emerged in legislative women's caucuses, and in the programs of elected women's associations in states where women officeholders have organized formally or informally.[10] Typical issues on the agendas of women's state legislative caucuses in the late 1980s included: home care for the elderly; domestic violence and child abuse; comprehensive health education; compensation for crime victims; abortion counseling for rape victims; child care; AIDS; family-oriented personnel policies, including family leave; pay equity; adolescent pregnancy and parenting; women and corrections; latchkey children; and adoption consent.

CAWP's findings suggest that women's legislative caucuses are playing a particularly important role in directing

[10]In 1988, women in 11 state legislatures met on a regular basis in a formal caucus, and 12 states had cross-jurisdictional statewide elected women's organizations. As of 1991, women in the following state legislatures meet on a regular basis in a formal caucus: California, Connecticut, Hawaii, Illinois, Iowa, Louisiana, Maryland, Massachusetts, Montana, New York, North Carolina, Rhode Island, and Virginia. Cross-jurisdictional statewide elected women's associations exist in California, Illinois, Maryland, Minnesota, Nevada, New Jersey, New York, Oregon, Pennsylvania, South Carolina, and Washington.

their members' attention to and coordinating their efforts on the gender-specific program and policy needs of females in our society. As Figure 6 shows, elected women who attended formal or informal women's caucuses were considerably more likely to work on a women's rights bill than women who did not attend such caucuses (66 percent vs. 46 percent). Caucuses probably provide an environment that facilitates work on bills intended to help females specifically and brings more women legislators into this process.

In contrast, caucus attendance had little effect on whether women gave top priority to a women's distinctive concern: our survey found that women who did not attend caucuses were almost as likely to give a women's distinctive concern

Figure 6 • POLICY ACTIONS OF FEMALE LEGISLATORS BY ATTENDANCE AT WOMEN'S LEGISLATIVE CAUCUS

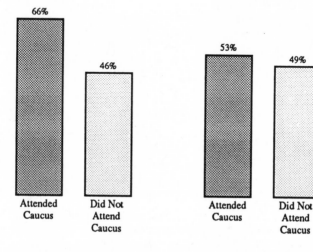

top priority as women who did attend caucuses. Life experience itself may be enough to sensitize women on these broader social and human issues. Yet caucuses may be important in identifying priority issues and coordinating effective action on them, as well as in mobilizing the support of male colleagues. A woman legislator who participated in a CAWP focus group in November 1987 explained how the women's caucus in her legislature works:

Our caucus has a retreat and brings in all of the organizations that women dominate throughout the state to tell us what they have as their priorities for legislation. Out of that day of hearings we choose three, at most five, priorities. This gives all of the women [in the caucus] an opportunity to really feel involved in at least these issues, which are usually unanimously adopted. They are the big issues that we know we will be dealing with. The women's caucus not only supports them by its action of adopting them, but it also develops the means of getting the bills passed, developing the bill and the lobbying strategy and bringing in the support. That means that women [caucus members] can then focus [more of their personal attention] on their own constituents' needs. They can go back home and talk about what they did on women's issues, but . . . [they also have] the opportunity and the freedom to work on transportation, the budget, economic development.

Another woman legislator, participating in the same discussion, explained how the women educate their male colleagues and enlist their support:

The male legislators have discovered that women get a lot of publicity with their kinds of issues. . . . We are always glad to have an advocate. . . . We'll help get the research . . . and baby them along . . . because it goes a lot quicker if a male stands up and advocates something for children . . . and families or health care. We have sensitized them to issues and also made our issues more in the mainstream of public policy.

Outcomes

Evidence from CAWP's (and others') studies showing that women in public office often have perspectives, attitudes, and priorities that differ from those of their male colleagues suggests that women are having a significant effect on the extent to which legislative agendas address both the special concerns of females in our society and broader human and family concerns. Moreover, the evidence from our survey reveals that women in public office are getting action on the issues that concern them. Two-thirds of both the women and men we surveyed in 1988 reported that their top priority bill was passed in a satisfactory form, and whether the bill focused on a women's distinctive concern or not had no impact on the likelihood of success. Furthermore, of the legislators who reported work on a women's rights bill, the great majority—76 percent of the men and 67 percent of the women—reported that the bill they had worked on passed in satisfactory form.

Conclusion

In the past 20 years, every election cycle has brought an increase in the numbers of women winning office, especially in state legislatures. Judging by the results of CAWP's survey, as well as by the findings of independent scholars, these women lawmakers are having an effect on the priorities of legislative bodies and on the attention that policymakers pay to issues both narrowly and broadly defined as "women's concerns." Elected women themselves generally believe that they are making a difference, as do their male colleagues. This is all the more remarkable in light of the still small proportion of women among officeholders. But since the political world is not static, CAWP's findings must be understood as early information about a changing situation. At this point we can go so far as to say that having more women in public office is bringing new perspectives to issues, new issues onto the docket, and different priorities, values, or emphases—perhaps even different styles of leadership—into the public policy arena. We will have to wait until the numbers of women and men in office are more evenly distributed across the board before we can really begin to understand the full consequences of gender-balanced public leadership in the United States.

APPENDIX

The discussion in this chapter of differences between elected women and men draws on findings from the three most recent national surveys of elected officials conducted by the Center for the American Woman and Politics (CAWP) at the Eagleton Institute of Politics, Rutgers University. (We do not refer to the first study, which was undertaken in 1975, because it provided no data comparing women with men.) The 1977 data are reported in Johnson and Carroll, *Profile of Women Holding Office II*, 1978. Results from the 1981 survey, sponsored by a grant from the Charles H. Revson Foundation, are reported in a monograph series entitled *Bringing More Women Into Public Office*, issued by CAWP. Findings about elected officeholders are analyzed in Carroll and Strimling, *Women's Routes to Elective Office*, 1983. Findings from the 1988 study of the impact of women in public office (also sponsored by the Charles H. Revson Foundation) are summarized in several reports issued by CAWP in 1991. It is the 1988 survey that is the basis for all the figures and most of the discussion about legislators throughout this chapter.

During the summer of 1988, CAWP conducted a nation-wide telephone survey of state legislators. Four samples of legislators were drawn: all women state senators (N=228); a systematic sample of one-half of women state representatives (N=474); a systematic sample of male state senators, stratified by state and sampled in proportion to the number of women from each state in our sample of women state senators (N=228); and a systematic sample of male state representatives, stratified by state and sampled in proportion to the number of women in each state in our sample of women state representatives (N=474). The more women serving in the legislature of a state, the more men sampled from the state. This was to ensure that we actually compared female and male colleagues rather than women from one type of state with men from another type of state. We asked for the legislators' subjective evaluations of the effect of women's increased presence on policies and processes within their own legislatures. We also asked questions about their own behaviors and views that allowed us to make more objective assessments of women's impact.

The telephone interviews, lasting approximately one-half hour each resulted in the following response rates: 86 percent for female senators; 60 percent for male senators; 87 percent for female representatives; and 73 percent for male representatives. Respondents and nonrespondents did not differ significantly in their party affiliations, the one variable for which we have data for all legislators. The analysis combines responses of senators and representatives, statistically weighting responses to ensure that the upper and lower house members' proportions within our sample of women and our sample of men reflect women's presence in legislatures.

F O U R **Different Voices, Different Views: The Politics of Gender**

CELINDA C. LAKE
AND VINCENT J. BREGLIO[1]

Introduction

THE EMERGENCE AND PERSISTENCE of the gender gap is one of the dominant features of the politics of the 1980s and early 1990s. Although there has been evidence for 40 years that men and women are likely to differ considerably in their attitudes about war and peace, it was not until 1980 that a sharp divergence between the sexes became manifest with respect to their perceptions of the presidential candidates and their perspectives on a broad range of issues and policy trade-offs that faced the public in that presidential election year. Those dif-

[1]The authors are political consultants with particular expertise in polling and survey analysis. Lake is a partner in Greenberg-Lake Associates, The Analysis Group, which has a largely Democratic clientele. Breglio is president of Research/ Strategy/Management, Inc., which has a largely Republican clientele.

The opinion data discussed and analyzed in this chapter have been gathered by the authors over the years from various published national polls and surveys as well as from private national polls done by Greenberg-Lake, The Analysis Group, and Research/Strategy/Management, and from focus groups conducted by the authors. The source for data on foreign policy was the "Americans Talk Security" series. Sources for data on the economy and economic and social issues included Gallup polls, CBS/*New York Times* polls, *Washington Post*/ABC News polls, and the University of Michigan National Election Study series; sources for data on election outcomes were CBS/*New York Times* exit polls, ABC News exit polls, and the networks' consortium of exit polls for 1990. Readers wishing more information about the data sources should contact the authors in care of WREI.

ferences persisted throughout the Reagan years and came to be reflected not only across specific issues, but in general political orientation, including party identification—perhaps the most important difference because of its potential long-term impact on voting behavior.

Political analysts first described a gender gap in the early 1980s. From the Eisenhower years (when surveys first looked at the opinions of men and women separately) through the Carter administration, men and women had not differed significantly in their assessments of, and approval ratings for, incumbent presidents or presidential candidates. But in 1980, surveys taken during the Reagan-Carter race showed that women were less likely than men to hold positive opinions about Ronald Reagan, and more likely than men to have doubts about what his presidency would be like. By 1984, there was a 14 to 18 percentage point gender gap in overall job approval for Reagan's presidency, as women and men disagreed about the defense and domestic priorities of that administration. In fact, there were several years during President Reagan's second term when the majority of women disagreed with the majority of men in their assessment of Reagan's job performance, with the majority of women disapproving and the majority of men approving of his performance.

Throughout the 1988 presidential campaign, the margin of difference in support between Democratic candidate Michael Dukakis and Republican candidate George Bush fluctuated largely because of the relative preferences of men and women voters. Bush won because of his strong support among men and his ability to reduce a nearly 20 point gender gap before the Republican convention to a six to eight point gap prior to Election Day. Part of his success in narrowing the gender gap was a result of his heightened emphasis on the theme of a "kinder, gentler nation." Exit polls on Election Day 1988 showed five to seven percentage points more support for Dukakis among women than among men.

Why have there been gender gaps at all? What lies behind the persistent differences that surveys and elections show with respect to men's and women's preferences for candidates and political parties? The answers are rooted in issues, particularly economic issues, and, specifically, in the differences between men and women in how they tend to see issues and in what they consider priorities. A vivid example of the differences between men's and women's perspectives comes from a poll done for the United Auto Workers in the late 1980s by Lalley and Lauer, who looked at voters' views of the roles and responsibilities of corporations. Seventy-one percent of the women in the survey, but only 49 percent of the men, felt that the first responsibility of corporations was to provide jobs for people and to help their communities. Conversely, 39 percent of the men thought that corporations' first responsibility was to make a profit, but only 19 percent of the women thought so. In general, women tend to emphasize community, connectedness, and caring, while men stress competition and individual rights. And at every income level, women are much more likely than men to feel vulnerable economically.

Throughout the 1980s, women were consistently more likely than men to be pessimistic about the direction the country was going in, and, as the survey results in the following table show, that pattern has continued into the 1990s. In none of these four polls did a majority of women express optimism about the direction of the country—although a majority of men did in two of them—and the smallest gender gap was nine points (in October 1990, when pessimism was deep among men as well as women). Even after the conclusion of the Persian Gulf War—a time of some general good feeling among Americans and of relative optimism among the majority of men—a plurality of women remained pessimistic about the general direction of the country (February 1991). By April, optimism had faded somewhat among men, but women were still considerably less likely to think the country was headed in the right direction.

	Nov. '89[1]		Oct. '90[2]		Feb. '91[3]		Apr. '91[4]	
	M	F	M	F	M	F	M	F
Percent Who Felt U.S. Was Going in Right Direction	53	41	24	15	55	41	47	37

[1]Research/Strategy/Management (R/S/M) National Study (N=1200).
[2]Washington Post/ABC News Poll (N=1500).
[3]R/S/M National Study (N=1000).
[4]Washington Post/ABC News Poll (N=1500).

Areas of Divergence

The differences between women and men in their perceptions of the general direction of the country are related to differences in perspectives and priorities. While the issue agendas of women and men do not differ dramatically, women and men do see the world, especially their own economic situations, quite differently. Women and men often reach similar conclusions, but, as this chapter will discuss, they often arrive at those conclusions for quite different reasons. Surveys taken during the 1988 presidential election campaign showed that women were somewhat more likely than men to worry about health care, education, helping the poor, homelessness, and protecting American jobs; men were more likely to worry about the deficit, taxes, energy, and defense policy. When asked to cite the national policy issues that concern them most, women are generally more likely than men to mention social problems, and men are more likely than women to mention fiscal and foreign policy concerns. Women typically have somewhat different priorities for government action than men, and want a more active role for the government in domestic and family policies. Women tend to feel much more economically vulnerable than men and, as a result, women take a broader view of what constitutes an economic agenda. Women are more likely than men to regard issues like health care, day care, and balancing work and family as basic economic issues as well as life-style or role issues.

Economic Issues: Work, Wages, and Family

During the 1980s, women's labor force participation increased steadily; by the end of the decade, 58 percent of America's women were in the workforce. Many women are working to help their families' incomes keep ahead of inflation during a period when men's wages have been declining in real terms. And as the number of female-headed families has risen during this period, more and more women are working to provide basic support for themselves and their children. Mothers of young children are in the labor force in record numbers and proportions, and the evidence is that they are working primarily to help their families survive financially. For example, one-third of women workers with preschool children are either their family's only wage earner or have husbands who earn $15,000 or less.

Women's daily struggles with the trade-offs between earning needed dollars and taking care of family responsibilities almost certainly contribute to a more broadly pessimistic outlook among women than among men. Frustration about their paid jobs may also be a factor: it is notable that women are more likely than men to feel that they face low wages and poor jobs, a perception that often reflects real differences in women's and men's jobs, and in their wages. Two-thirds of women believe that women do not get paid the same wages for the same work as men. In addition, women are much more likely than men to work in the lower-paying service-sector and pink-collar jobs, and, overall, women's wages are typically still a lot lower than men's—as of 1989, women working full time earned only 68 cents for every dollar earned by men working full time. (Not surprisingly, women have consistently been more likely than men to favor raising the minimum wage.) Women are more often recent hires than their male counterparts, and are consistently more likely than men to feel that they may lose their jobs.

Finally, women are more sensitive than men to rising prices, a reflection of both women's more limited incomes and their economic roles within the family. Throughout the 1980s, women were less likely than men to think that the Reagan administration had curbed inflation, and research showed that men and women had different items in their mental shopping carts when they assessed what had happened to prices. Women were more likely than men to think about food, health care, and medicine—all items whose costs rose more steeply than the overall inflation rate during the 1980s. Men were more likely to focus on housing and appliances.

Stands on economic issues contributed most heavily to the gender gap after the 1982 recession. In August of 1983, for example, 58 percent of men, but only 38 percent of women, thought that the economy had improved in the previous six months. Similarly, 64 percent of men, but only 27 percent of women, thought the economic situation of women generally had improved. This difference in economic perspective translated into different assessments of Reagan's performance and, in some elections, differences at the ballot box. In June of 1984, only 45 percent of women, but 64 percent of men, approved of Reagan's job performance.

Differences between the economic perspectives of women and men persisted throughout Reagan's second term. In 1987, before the 1988 campaign to elect Reagan's successor got underway, 60 percent of men, but only 47 percent of women, thought the economy was in good shape. More important: as men and women reviewed the Reagan era of "prosperity," women were far more likely than men to be critical of his administration's economic performance, and felt more economically vulnerable than men. In 1988, 55 percent of men, but only 42 percent of women, thought that they were better off than they had been in 1980. And 63 percent of women believed that the country's economic recovery had been bought at the expense of future generations, a perception with which 51 percent of men agreed. By the election in November of 1988, a majority of men—52 percent—thought their family's economic situation would get better and were hopeful for the future of the country's economy. But a majority of women—56 percent—thought either that their economic situation would get worse or that it would stay the same.

These differences have remained in the early 1990s. In early 1991, 59 percent of men, but only 48 percent of women, thought the country's economic situation was good. And, while President Bush enjoys enormous popularity among voters in the post-Gulf War era, women have been about 10 percentage points less approving of his overall job performance than men, and, further, disapprove more often than men of his handling of the economy.

Women are more likely than men to want both the public sector and the private sector to address the problems facing families, and, not surprisingly, view these as basic economic issues. As a result, women are more likely than men to support government helping families even if it means an increase in taxes. A considerable majority of women—62 percent—think that the federal government should spend more money to ensure adequate day care for working parents; only 52 percent of men agree. Seventy percent of women want to see more government money spent on improving health care. While the majority of both sexes support having the federal government require that employers provide health insurance for their employees, women are even more likely than men to do so. (In one 1990 statewide survey in a southwestern state, 84 percent of women, compared with 72 percent of men, agreed that the federal government should insist that employers provide health insurance.)

Similarly, it is working women of the baby-boom generation[2] who are most likely to support increased government spending for long-term health care. Theirs is the first generation to be faced with having not just one, but often two generations of older family members (typically, older women—mothers and grandmothers) to be concerned about. As the primary caregivers in their families, women baby-boomers worry about who will care for the frail elderly if there is no

[2]The large population cohorts born in the post-World War II period. As of 1992, most will be in their early 30s to mid-40s.

program providing long-term health care. Popular news accounts have described the women born in the post-war baby-boom years as a "sandwich generation," currently trying to balance work outside the home with raising their children, and facing the prospect of taking on the responsibility of caring for elderly family members as well.

Reflecting the dramatic changes in women's roles and work lives, women's attitudes about issues where work and family intersect have changed considerably during the last dozen years or so. In 1978, for example, less than half of women who worked outside the home thought that companies should provide day care for their employees' children. Today, over three-fourths of working women think so—a proportion that is almost 30 percentage points higher than among their male counterparts. Backing for government help for working families is most intense among younger, working women, but exists among all groups of women. While women in every demographic group are more likely to support day care programs than men, college-educated, baby-boomer men with young children have been rapidly changing their opinions, and these men are now nearly as likely as their female peers to support more government and corporate action to help working families cope.

Women tend to feel that they are not well served by the economic and social status quo. On the eve of the 1988 presidential election, men split evenly over whether they preferred the status quo—things staying as they were—or change, but almost two-thirds of women opted for change.

War and Peace

At least since 1952 (the first year for which we have relevant opinion data by sex), women have typically been less willing than men to support U.S. involvement in any military conflict, less willing than men to escalate U.S. involvement, and less willing than men to commit troops at any given point of a conflict. This has held true for the conflicts in Korea, Vietnam, Lebanon, Grenada, Central America, Panama, and the Persian Gulf.

The biggest differences in opinion about war have traditionally been between blue collar men, the most "hawkish" voters, and younger, college-educated women, the least hawkish voters. Attitudes toward war, along with attitudes toward women's issues, have also accounted for the largest gender gaps between Republican men and Republican women voters.

Just months after the conclusion of the war in the Persian Gulf, 53 percent of men, but only 39 percent of women, wanted America to take the lead military role in the world. And at most points in time in the months before and during the Persian Gulf War, men and women differed about U.S. involvement in, and escalation of, the conflict. For example, in January 1991, a majority of men (56 percent) wanted the United States to begin military action against Iraq, while a slight majority of women (52 percent) wanted to wait longer. In February 1991, only several weeks after the war began, a majority of women (53 percent) said it was time to start negotiations, while the same percentage of men said it was not yet time.

In any conflict women are more likely than men to worry about the loss of life—both military and civilian, ally and

enemy—and weigh such losses more heavily in choosing between policy options. Attitudes toward the Persian Gulf War
exemplify this difference. Before the war started, 56 percent
of men, but only 35 percent of women, thought it would be
worth it if several thousand American troops lost their lives
in a ground war with Iraq. At the height of the war, 64 percent of men, but only 37 percent of women, thought that
American bombers should attack all military targets, including those in heavily populated areas where civilians might be
killed.

While the differences in women's and men's attitudes toward war long predate the current gender gap, in recent years
they have led to substantial differences in opinion on social
programs, defense spending, and relative budget priorities.
Women have been consistently more likely than men both to
believe that more spending on the military meant that less
money would be available for social programs and to give
higher relative priority to social programs. Even after the success of the Persian Gulf War—which over three-fourths of
both men and women believed was a great victory for the
United States—54 percent of men and 64 percent of women
believed that the money spent on the war would have been
better spent on problems here at home. Women were also
more likely than men to be cynical about what the war will
cost, and while 54 percent of men believed that America's
allies in the Persian Gulf would end up contributing their
share, only 38 percent of women believed that.

At the turn of the last decade, the geopolitical shape of
the world changed dramatically. In this new era of foreign
policy, women are still forming their opinions about the
shape of the new world order and how dangerous the international situation is for the United States. Ironically, women are

more likely than men to be worried about war and less likely to trust the Soviet Union and Gorbachev. For example, in a 1990 survey, a plurality of women characterized the Soviet Union as aggressive (48 percent), while a plurality of men characterized it as peace-loving (41 percent). Fifty-seven percent of men thought the U.S. government should invest in the U.S.S.R., but only 38 percent of women did. Forty-four percent of men, but only 25 percent of women, had a favorable view of Gorbachev.

Energy and Environment

On most issues involving energy and the environment men and women typically have remarkably similar views. One exception stands out starkly—the issue of nuclear power. While a majority of both men and women currently oppose building more nuclear power plants in the United States, the opposition among women is significantly greater and more intense than among men. Even in the early 1980s, when nuclear power was generally more in favor than it is now, the majority of women opposed, and saw as risky, building more nuclear power plants. Today, among men, opponents of nuclear power outnumber proponents by 11 percentage points (54 percent to 43 percent). However, among women, opponents outnumber proponents by a whopping 48 percentage points (71 percent to 23 percent). Throughout the 1980s and in the 1990s to date, the issue of nuclear power has produced one of the biggest gender differences in policy preferences.

In general, women are more likely than men to favor government intervention to deal with problems and thus, not surprisingly, women are more likely than men to approve of tough regulations to deal with environmental problems.

Women, particularly younger women, are also consistently less likely than men to worry about the trade-offs between the environment and the economy. Today, the majority of both women and men favor maintaining current environmental regulations, although women are more intensely supportive than men. And women were ahead of men on this issue: when the debate on environmental regulations first raged in 1980, the majority of men (54 percent) favored relaxing the then-current environmental regulations, but the majority of women (57 percent) wanted to keep those regulations in force.

Overall, while more women than men are concerned about the environment, both sexes worry about the deteriorating environmental quality in this country. Today, approximately the same proportion of women as of men (only one out of five) feel that the environment will be better in three years than it is now; moreover, men are about as likely as women to take a gloomier view: approximately four out of 10 of both sexes feel that it will not be as good.

However, when men and women discuss environmental problems, their different life perspectives become apparent. For example, in focus groups on toxic waste, women and men show equal levels of concern, but women talk about the problems in terms of birth defects, threats to the health of their children, and other health issues. Men, on the other hand, tend to talk more about economic effects and declining property values.

Men are somewhat more likely than women to know about some of the more technical environmental issues. For example, consistently more men than women have been aware of global warming: in late 1989, 85 percent of men, but only 73 percent of women, claimed to be aware of global warming. A year later, 91 percent of men claimed such aware-ness, compared to 81 percent of women.

At the same time, however, men and women did not dif-fer in their belief that the United States should be taking the lead in solving the problem of global warming: nearly equal proportions of men and women (seven out of 10) believed that the United States should be taking the lead rather than waiting for an international agreement to deal with global warming. This shared sense of urgency also extends to many energy conservation measures. For example, men and women agree in favoring the adoption of the 40-mile-per-gallon "cor-porate average fuel economy" (CAFE) standard for automo-biles by the year 2000.

Social Issues: Issues about People

Women tend to worry about social issues more than men do and to seek greater government involvement in solving these problems. They have tended to support an activist role for government to help the poor, the elderly, and the unem-ployed. Feeling more economically vulnerable than men do, women also are more likely than men to worry about the affordability of such services as health care, long-term care for the elderly, and day care. Women are also more likely than men to support government spending to help the poor and minorities even if it means an increase in their taxes.

Throughout the 1980s, as voters have focused on the costs of social programs and rising budget deficits, men have worried more about taxes and deficits, while women have worried more about maintaining social programs. Men and women have tended to take different sides in the debate about the size and role of government that has underlain much of the broader political debate for the last 12 years. Women have consistently been more likely than men to support government spending for health care, urban problems, education, and welfare, and they have been more willing than men to cut defense and space programs to find the money for social programs. In 1983, for example, as this debate began in earnest, 50 percent of men, but only 25 percent of women, wanted to cut government services to reduce spending. Similarly, in 1988, men favored a smaller federal government by 56 percent to 36 percent; women, on the other hand, slightly favored an expanded federal government, 46 percent to 41 percent.[3]

At the end of the 1980s, health care emerged as one of the major concerns on voters' minds and especially on women's minds. While all voters worry about rising health care costs and the availability of health insurance, two-thirds of women, but only half of men, worried about the implications for them personally of the costs of long-term illness and disability, the costs of hospital and physician care, and the cost of nursing home care. For women, these issues are more salient than for men: they see themselves as both the primary caregivers for elderly parents and grandparents, and as the likely recipients of health services in old age. Women are also more likely than men to be concerned about the viability of the Social Security system (76 percent to 60 percent) and about the current costs of health insurance (81 percent to 67 percent). And, as mentioned earlier, women are more likely than men are to support the federal government insisting that employers provide health insurance for their employees. This suggests a greater willingness on the part of women to involve the private sector

---

[3]Percentages do not add to 100 because some survey respondents had no opinion on this question.

in serving people's needs, and to use the government to require that involvement.

Public Safety Issues

Women, particularly older women, are more likely than men to worry about crime. While women and men are about equally likely to support the death penalty (a majority do), women are more likely than men to favor stricter gun control. In one western state, for example, only 30 percent of men, but a majority (52 percent) of women, favored stronger gun control laws; and only 36 percent of men, but 52 percent of women, favored a ban on semi-automatic rifles made in the United States.

In general, where public safety is concerned, women show the same reservations about risk that we have seen in the policy areas of war and peace and nuclear power. Thus women are typically more supportive than men of drunk driving laws, seat-belt laws, and speed limits. Men tend to be more individualistic than women on these issues and to oppose what they more often than women see as government interference in their personal freedom.

Women's Rights and Abortion

Contrary to conventional wisdom, opinions on the issues that are generally thought of as "women's issues" have been less of a factor in the gender gap than differences in perspectives on issues like the economy and priorities for the budget. Still, no discussion of the women's vote in the 1980s and 1990s would be complete without a discussion of abortion, which became more important in voting decisions following the Supreme Court's 1989 ruling in *Webster v. Reproductive Health Services*. Men and women support the right to abortion in nearly equal proportions—in 1991, 58 percent of men and 55 percent of women described themselves as pro-choice, while 34 percent of men and 39 percent of women described themselves as pro-life. Women are, however, more likely than men to consider this issue central to their voting decisions and to be active in either pro-choice or pro-life politics. In 1990, 48 percent of women, versus 39 percent of men, said they would give time and money in support of their position on the abortion issue; 59 percent of women, versus 48 percent of men, would call or write an elected official on the issue.

Age and education are factors in how people, especially women, feel about abortion. Older, non-college-educated women tend to be more strongly pro-life than their male counterparts. Men are more likely than women to support allowing abortion under all circumstances (19 percent versus 13 percent)—that is, men are more likely than women to believe that a woman should be able to get an abortion if she wants one, no matter what her reasons. At the same time, younger, college-educated men and women are equally supportive of abortion rights generally, although the women in this group tend to be much more active on the issue than the men, and—where a clear contrast exists between the positions of the candidates—more likely to cross party lines to support the pro-choice candidate.

Just a few months after the *Webster* decision, younger and suburban women who supported the pro-choice position elected Douglas Wilder governor of Virginia and David Dinkins mayor of New York, and ensured James Florio an early, solid lead in his race for governor of New Jersey. In 1990, defections of pro-choice women across party lines helped account for the gender gaps in a number of statewide races, and affected the outcome in several, in some cases benefiting Democrats (e.g., Ann Richards, the gubernatorial victor in Texas) and in others benefiting Republicans (e.g., Jim Edgar, the gubernatorial victor in Illinois).

With respect to women's rights more generally, there is often not as much difference in the positions of men and women as one might expect. Men and women are equally likely to support equal rights for women, but women are much more likely than men to make their voting decisions on the basis of the candidates' positions on these issues. Women are also much more likely than men to favor government action to ensure women's rights. In 1988, for example, when an Equal Rights Initiative was on the ballot in Vermont, 56 percent of women, but only 45 percent of men, voted for it. Surveys in 1990 and 1991 showed that women are much more likely than men to consider ending discrimination an important government goal—the proportion of women who thought so was 17 percentage points higher than the comparable proportion of men. And women are also much more likely than men to think that women are discriminated against—the proportion of women who felt that was the case was 25 percentage points higher than the comparable proportion of men.

Partisan Preference and Voting Behavior:
Differences at the Ballot Box

The differences in the perspectives and priorities of women and men have produced differences in party identification and at the ballot box. Throughout much of the 1980s, women were significantly more Democratic in their vote and party identification than men. For the last 10 years, when women have been asked which political party they most closely identify with, the proportion who have named the Democratic Party has consistently exceeded, by about seven percentage points, the proportion naming the Republican Party. Conversely, when men have been asked which party they most closely identify with, the proportion who have named the Republican Party has consistently exceeded, by seven or more percentage points, the proportion naming the Democratic Party. (For example, in a February 1991 survey, 46 percent of women, but only 35 percent of men, identified themselves as Democrats; 47 percent of men, but only 39 percent of women, identified themselves as Republicans.) In the 1980, 1984, and 1988 elections, that persistent gap translated into more support among women than among men for the Democratic presidential candidates and for Democratic candidates at all levels.

The reason that the margin of preference for the Democratic Party has been so stable is that the party preferences of men and women—men for the Republican Party and women for the Democratic Party—have offset each other. Over the last two years, men have consistently selected the GOP label 44 to 47 percent of the time. Among women, the percentage identifying themselves as Republicans has been equally consistent, but lower—between 37 and 40 percent.

In 1991, when asked which party is more attuned to the real problems facing the country in the 1990s, a plurality of women—42 percent—named the Democratic party (32 percent named Republicans), while a plurality of men—45 percent—named the Republican party (35 percent name Democrats). It should be noted, however, that despite the consistent Democratic edge in party identification among women, women are only slightly more likely than men to identify themselves as liberals.

As is obvious from the very figures demonstrating that there is an overall gender gap in party preferences, both women and men are far from solid blocs when it comes to party preference. In fact, as much or more variance in preferences exists among people of the same gender as *between* the genders. Through the 1980s, it was younger, college-educated women working outside the home and nonmarried women who accounted for much of the gender gap.

Men's and women's differences have affected the outcome in some statewide and congressional races. In the 1986 senatorial elections, black voters of both sexes and women voters gave the winning margin to nine Democratic candidates and, as a result, control of the U.S. Senate switched from Republican to Democratic hands. Exit polls on Election Day in 1990 showed significant gender gaps in 13 statewide races. In six of those races the majority of women actually voted for different candidates than the majority of men. The margin of men determined the winner in two of these six (the gubernatorial races in Vermont, where Republican Richard Snelling was elected, and in Michigan, where Republican Dick Engler was elected). In the other four races, it was the margin provided by women that decided the outcomes (the senatorial races in Minnesota [Democrat Paul Wellstone won] and New Jersey [Democrat Bill Bradley was reelected], and the gubernatorial races in Oregon [Democrat Barbara Roberts won] and Texas [Democrat Ann Richards won]).

The largest gender gaps frequently occur when there are women candidates in the race. Younger, working women tend to be more supportive of women candidates of both parties than their male counterparts. Compared to older voters, these younger women generally pay less attention to candidates, decide on how they will vote later in the campaign, and are more likely to split their tickets. However, when there is a woman candidate in the race, younger women (under 45 years of age) decide early, and often enthusiastically, for the woman candidate. In 1990, this phenomenon helped produce a whopping 15 point gap for Ann Richards in the Texas gubernatorial general election, and a double digit gap for Dianne Feinstein in the California gubernatorial primary.

On the other hand, women candidates often have trouble holding the support of older women voters, many of whom feel conflicted about women running for major public office. Slippage of support among older women can reduce the overall gender gap in some races. Finally, both men and women voters share many of the gender stereotypes about women candidates. For example, in one 1990 survey in a large northeastern state, men and women both thought the male candidate would be somewhat better at dealing with deficits and large budgets and agreed that the female candidate would more likely be honest and care about people.

Women's Voting Participation

Women's numbers as well as women's preferences have made a difference at the ballot box.

During the four decades following 1920, when women were first granted the vote, women's voting participation—the proportion of eligible women who voted—increased only gradually, and before 1960, the voting participation of men significantly exceeded that of women. During the 1960s, however, there was a rapid increase in voting participation by women, probably in large part as a result of women's increasing education levels and their increasing likelihood to work outside the home. In 1968, two-thirds of eligible women went to the polls, and the voting participation gap between men and women had closed to only a couple of percentage points by 1978.

Nineteen eighty marked the first year that women in every racial group registered and voted in higher numbers than their male counterparts, and that pattern continued throughout the decade. In most of the presidential elections in the last 12 years, there have been six to 10 million more women than men among those registered to vote. That differential has increased the political clout of women and heightened the impact of the gender gap at the polls.

Conclusion

Men and women do not always have dramatically different positions on issues, although they do often have quite different perspectives on them. They may reach similar conclusions for quite different reasons. The gender gap represents an important change in our political system, but has a direct impact on the outcome of an election only when the differences between men's and women's perceptions, priorities, and agendas are so pervasive and significant that they translate into a margin of support for a particular candidate among voters of one sex that more than offsets the margin of support the opposing candidate enjoys among voters of the other sex. The candidates also need to draw a strong contrast between themselves and their opponents on the issues that matter to women. The election of a number of Democratic U.S. senators in 1986, and several senators and governors in 1990, as previously discussed in this chapter, makes this point. The one political contest that has not yet fit this model is the campaign for the presidency.

Despite a persistent gender gap favoring the Democratic nominee for president, Republicans have won handsomely since 1980, even among women. In 1980, Reagan beat Carter by five percentage points among women (47 percent for Reagan vs. 42 percent for Carter), according to ABC News exit polling. In 1984, Reagan increased his margin of victory among women to eight percentage points over Walter Mondale (54 percent for Reagan vs. 46 percent for Mondale). The 1988 contest, Bush versus Dukakis, was the closest among women—a one percentage point victory for George Bush (50 percent for Bush vs. 49 percent for Dukakis).

Why has the apparent negative impact of the gender gap on Republican statewide and lesser races been unable to shift a majority of women to vote against presidential candidates who stand for many of the policies that help produce the attitudinal differences that define the gender gap?

It may have to do with voters' perceptions of job priorities. The job of president has two overriding priorities—to protect the country and to keep the economy healthy. Decisions on whom to vote for between two presidential candidates focus mostly on who can best fulfill these two priorities. As we look toward the 1992 election, these will be particularly important.

It has already been shown in this chapter that women hold somewhat conflicting views on national defense issues. When these are couched in terms of war and peace, women opt for peaceful alternatives more often than men. On the other hand, they are less trusting of the peaceful intentions of the world around them than men. In 1992, for example, women may choose the presidential candidate they perceive to be stronger on defense, despite women's general preference for peaceful solutions and the lower priority they place on defense spending.

Leadership on the economic front is of particular importance to women because, as noted earlier, women tend to perceive themselves as economically vulnerable. In the last three presidential elections, two economic themes were dominant. In 1980, Ronald Reagan offered "time for a change"—relief from double-digit inflation and soaring interest rates. In 1984, and again in 1988, Reagan and George Bush proclaimed "If it ain't broke, don't fix it"—i.e., a continuation of relatively good times. Both arguments were helpful in securing the support of some women otherwise disenchanted with the Republican candidates but concerned about their families' economic situation. George Bush actively targeted women with domestic issues—presenting himself as the "kinder, gentler" president focused on education, children, and the environment. That reduced an early "gender canyon" to a modest gender gap.

Still, we can expect the growing clout of women to influence the political agenda and to determine the outcome of races at every level for some time to come.

American Women Today: A Statistical Portrait

Section 1: Population

The racial[1] and gender composition of the population of the United States depends on many factors, among them birth and death rates and life expectancy.

Notable Trends

- Although whites constituted a majority of the U.S. population, 1989 population estimates and 1990 decennial figures indicate that between 16 and 20 percent of Americans were nonwhite (see Figures 1–1, 1–2, 1–3, and 1–4 and Table 1–1).

- In 1990, there were approximately seven million more women than men in the United States, an imbalance particularly marked at age 65 and older (see Figures 1–2 and 1–5).

- As a group, females outlive males—a girl born in 1988 is expected to outlive a boy born in the same year by almost seven years (see Table 1–3).

- Birth rates have declined steeply since 1960, but began to level off around 1980 as the post-World War II "baby

Note: The statistical tables and figures in the following sections were prepared by Nancy Peplinsky.

[1]Please note that the Census Bureau does not classify Hispanic as a racial category; therefore persons of Hispanic origin may be of any race and cannot be added with whites, blacks, and other races to obtain a total for the population.

boom" generation of women began to have children of their own (see Figure 1–7).

• Although death rates for males and females of all races decreased considerably from 1960 to 1988, the death rate for black men in 1988 was one and a half times the rate for white men, almost twice the rate for black women, and nearly three times the rate for white women (see Figure 1–8).

• Infant mortality rates are at an all-time low, nine per 1,000 live births. However, in 1990 black babies were twice as likely as white babies to die in their first year (see Figure 1–9).

Figures 1-1, 1-2, 1-3, and 1-4 and Table 1-1

Whites constituted the substantial majority (84 percent) of the American population in 1989. Nevertheless, as Figure 1–1 shows, this country is becoming considerably more racially diverse. Between 1970 and 1989 the Census Bureau estimates, the nonwhite proportion of the population increased from 12 percent to 16 percent. The proportion of persons of Hispanic origin also increased, nearly doubling from four percent in 1970 to eight percent in 1989 (see Figure 1–2). Over the 20-year period females consistently outnumbered males in the overall population, 51 percent to 49 percent, and in 1989 there were more women than men in virtually every racial group.

Data on the U.S. population by both race and sex from the 1990 decennial census were unavailable as *The American Woman* went to press. However, population data based on the 1990 census were available by race only and Figure 1–3 shows that in 1990, 20 percent of the U.S. population was nonwhite. (It should be noted that because of different classification procedures used by the Census Bureau, population estimates [upon which the population distribution in Figure 1–1 is based] are not exactly comparable to decennial census numbers [upon which the population distribution in Figure 1–3 is based]. Also recall that according to the Census Bureau, persons of Hispanic origin may be of any race.) In 1990, Hispanics accounted for nine percent of the total U.S. population. As Figure 1–4 indicates, the majority of the Hispanic population was Mexican.

Figure 1-1 • ESTIMATES OF THE POPULATION OF THE UNITED STATES[1] BY SEX AND RACE, 1970 AND 1989 (percent distribution)

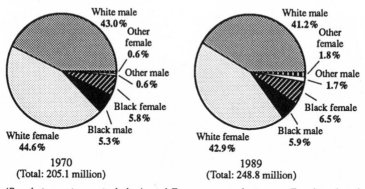

[1]Population estimates include Armed Forces personnel overseas. For the sake of consistency, data for both 1970 and 1980 are based on population estimates because decennial data were not available for 1990 by both race and sex at publication deadline. However, the population distribution derived from the decennial census and the population estimate do not vary significantly.

Source: U.S. Bureau of the Census, *Preliminary Estimates of the Population of the United States by Age, Sex, and Race: 1970 to 1981,* July 1982, Table 4 and *U.S. Population Estimates by Age, Sex, Race, and Hispanic Origin: 1989,* March 1990, Table 1.

Figure 1-2 • ESTIMATES OF THE POPULATION OF THE
UNITED STATES BY SEX AND HISPANIC ORIGIN, 1970 AND
1989 (percent distribution)

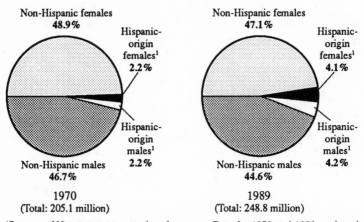

Non-Hispanic females
48.9%

Hispanic-
origin
females[1]
2.2%

Hispanic-
origin
males[1]
2.2%

Non-Hispanic males
46.7%

1970
(Total: 205.1 million)

Non-Hispanic females
47.1%

Hispanic-
origin
females[1]
4.1%

Hispanic-
origin
males[1]
4.2%

Non-Hispanic males
44.6%

1989
(Total: 248.8 million)

[1]Persons of Hispanic origin may be of any race. Data for 1970 and 1989 are based
on Census Bureau population estimates because data from the 1970 decennial census
does not include a breakdown of persons of Hispanic origin by sex, nor are 1990
census data available by both Hispanic origin and sex at publication deadline.

Source: U.S. Bureau of the Census, *General Population Characteristics: United States
Summary,* May 1983, Table 39 and *U.S. Population Estimates by Age, Sex, Race, and
Hispanic Origin: 1989,* March 1990, Table 1.

Figure 1-3 • POPULATION OF THE UNITED STATES BY RACE, 1990[1] (percent distribution)

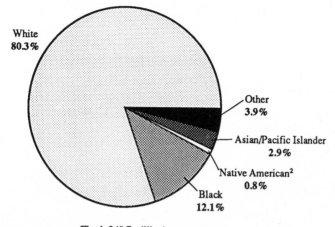

White
80.3%

Other
3.9%

Asian/Pacific Islander
2.9%

Native American[2]
0.8%

Black
12.1%

(Total: 248.7 million)
(Females: 127.5 million Males: 121.2 million)

[1]Based on the 1990 census. Please note that inconsistencies with Figure 1-1 are due to different classification procedures in estimates and decennial census data.

[2]Includes Eskimos and Aleuts.

Source: U.S. Department of Commerce, Press Release CB91-215, June 12, 1991, Table 1.

Figure 1-4 • HISPANIC ORIGIN POPULATION OF THE UNITED STATES BY COUNTRY OF ORIGIN 1990[1] (percent distribution)

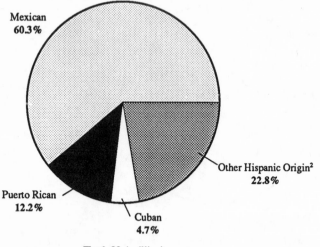

Mexican
60.3%

Other Hispanic Origin[2]
22.8%

Puerto Rican
12.2%

Cuban
4.7%

(Total: 22.4 million)

[1]Based on the 1990 census.

[2]"Other Hispanic origin" includes persons from other Spanish-speaking countries of the Caribbean, Central or South America, or Spain.

Source: U.S. Department of Commerce, Press Release CB91-215, June 12, 1991, Table 1.

Table 1-1 • POPULATION OF THE UNITED STATES
BY RACE, 1990[1]

Race	Number
White	199,686,070
Black	29,986,060
American Indian, Eskimo, or Aleut	1,959,234
American Indian	1,878,285
Eskimo	57,152
Aleut	23,797
Asian or Pacific Islander	7,273,662
Chinese	1,645,472
Filipino	1,406,770
Japanese	847,562
Asian Indian	815,447
Korean	798,849
Vietnamese	614,547
Hawaiian	211,014
Samoan	62,964
Guamanian	49,345
Other Asian or Pacific Islander	821,692
Other races	9,804,847
Total, all races	248,709,873

[1]Based on the 1990 census.

Source: U.S. Department of Commerce, Press Release CB91-215,
June 12, 1991, Table 1.

Figures 1-5 and 1-6

While females outnumbered males in the overall population in 1989, they did not predominate in every age group.
Men constituted the majority of Americans under age 35, as
Figure 1–5 shows. At age 35 and over, however, the data
illustrate that the older the age group, the more females
predominated. For example, women accounted for almost 60
percent of the population over age 65. This can be explained
by the fact that women typically live to an older age than men

(see Table 1–3). More than 14 percent of all women in 1989 were age 65 and over, while men in the same age group constituted only 10 percent of the male population. As the large World War II baby boom generation gets older, projections for the year 2030 show marked shifts in the elderly proportion of the population, with 24 percent of females and 20 percent of males in the age 65 and over category.

Figure 1-5 • POPULATION OF THE UNITED STATES[1] BY SEX
AND AGE, 1989

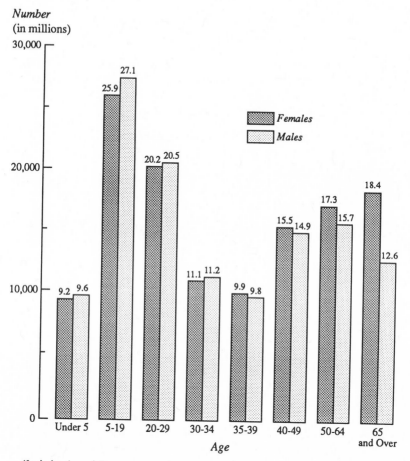

[1]Includes Armed Forces personnel overseas.

Source: U.S. Bureau of the Census, *U.S. Population Estimates by Age, Sex, Race, and Hispanic Origin: 1989*, March 1990, Table 1.

Figure 1-6 • POPULATION OF THE UNITED STATES[1] BY SEX
AND AGE, ESTIMATED 1989 AND PROJECTED 2030
(percent distribution)

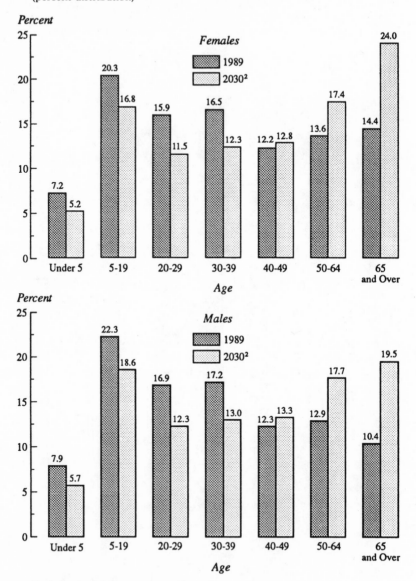

[1]Includes Armed Forces personnel overseas.

[2]Using middle series projections.

Source: U.S. Bureau of the Census, *Projections of the Population of the United States
by Age, Sex, and Race: 1988 to 2080*, January 1989, Table 4 and *U.S. Population
Estimates by Age, Sex, Race, and Hispanic Origin: 1989*, March 1990, Table 1.

Table 1-2 • AGE DISTRIBUTION AND MEDIAN AGE OF
FEMALES BY RACE AND HISPANIC ORIGIN, ESTIMATED 1989
(percent distribution)

Age	All Races	White	Black	Other Races	Hispanic Origin[1]
Under 5	7.2	6.9	8.8	9.1	10.7
5–14	13.5	12.9	16.7	16.6	18.6
15–19	6.9	6.6	8.5	7.7	8.5
20–24	7.3	7.2	8.5	7.6	9.1
25–34	17.2	17.0	18.3	18.4	19.3
35–44	14.5	14.6	13.5	16.0	13.3
45–54	10.0	10.2	9.0	9.7	8.2
55–64	8.9	9.3	7.3	7.2	6.1
65 and over	14.4	15.4	9.5	7.8	6.1
Total percent	100.0	100.0	100.0	100.0	100.0
Total number (in thousands)	127,317	106,774	16,136	4,407	10,190
Median age	33.8	34.7	29.1	30.1	26.5

[1]Persons of Hispanic origin may be of any race.

Source: U.S. Bureau of the Census, *U.S. Population Estimates by Age, Sex, Race, and Hispanic Origin: 1989*, March 1990, Table 1.

Table 1-2

In 1989, women over age 65 comprised 15 percent of the white female population compared to six percent of the Hispanic and 10 percent of the black female population.

Conversely, 38 percent of Hispanic females and 34 percent of black females were under 20 years old in 1989 compared to 26 percent of white females. It follows, then, that the median ages of Hispanic and minority females were younger than for white women.

Table 1-3 • AVERAGE LIFE EXPECTANCY AT BIRTH BY RACE
AND SEX, SELECTED YEARS, ACTUAL 1960–1988 AND
PROJECTED 2000 AND 2010 (in years)

Year	White		Black		All Races	
	Women	Men	Women	Men	Women	Men
1960	74.1	67.4	—	—	73.1	66.6
1970	75.6	68.0	68.3	60.0	74.7	67.1
1980	78.1	70.7	73.6	65.3	77.4	70.0
1988	78.9	72.3	73.4	64.9	78.3	71.5
2000[1]	80.9	74.0	77.1	69.9	80.4	73.5
2010[1]	81.7	74.9	78.5	71.4	81.3	74.4

[1]Using middle series projections.

Source: U.S. Bureau of the Census, *Projections of the Population of the United States,
by Age, Sex, and Race: 1988 to 2080,* January 1989, Table B-5 and National Center
for Health Statistics, "Advance Report of Final Mortality Statistics," *Monthly Vital
Statistics Report,* November 28, 1990.

Table 1-3

Projections on the growing elderly segment of the U.S.
population, in particular the increase of older women, reflect
not only increasing longevity among people of both sexes, but
also the fact that women will continue to outlive men by a
number of years.

While life expectancy at birth increased for Americans
overall by approximately five years (slightly more for females,
slightly less for males) between 1960 and 1988, the life expectancy of a girl was almost seven years longer than for a boy
born in 1988. Life expectancy was shorter for black females
and males than for their white counterparts (although longer
for black women than for white men) and the gap between
females and males was wider among blacks than among
whites.

The average American girl born in the year 2000 is projected to live past her eightieth birthday—still nearly seven years longer than the average boy born in that year.

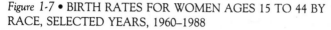

Figure 1-7 • BIRTH RATES FOR WOMEN AGES 15 TO 44 BY RACE, SELECTED YEARS, 1960–1988

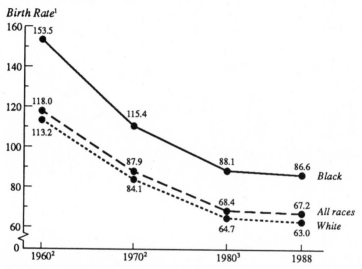

[1]Live births per 1,000 women.

[2]Based on a 50-percent sample of births.

[3]Based on 100 percent of births in selected states and on a 50-percent sample in all other states.

Source: National Center for Health Statistics, "Advance Report of Final Natality Statistics, 1988," *Monthly Vital Statistics Report*, August 15, 1990, Table 1.

Figure 1-7

Birth rates in recent years have been far lower than they were a generation or so ago. However, the steep decline after 1960 leveled off around 1980, as the large post-World War II "baby boom" generation of women began to have children of their own. The difference between the birth rates for white and black women also narrowed between 1960 and 1988.

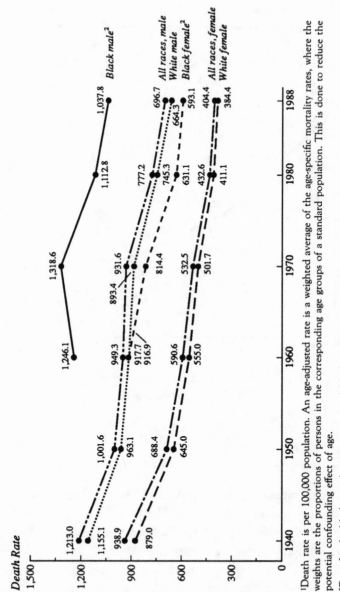

Figure 1-8 • AGE-ADJUSTED DEATH RATES[1] IN THE UNITED STATES BY SEX AND RACE, SELECTED YEARS, 1940–1988

Death Rate

Black male[2]

All races, male
White male
Black female[2]

All races, female
White female

[1]Death rate is per 100,000 population. An age-adjusted rate is a weighted average of the age-specific mortality rates, where the weights are the proportions of persons in the corresponding age groups of a standard population. This is done to reduce the potential confounding effect of age.

[2]Data for the black population were unavailable for years prior to 1960.

Source: National Center for Health Statistics, "Advance Report of Final Mortality Statistics, 1988," *Monthly Vital Statistics Report,* November 28, 1990, Table 1.

Figure 1-8

Death rates for males and females of all races have declined considerably since 1960, although the rates for women of all races remain well below those of their male counterparts. The death rate for black males, while recently declining, has been consistently the highest—one and a half times the rate of white males, almost twice the rate of black women, and nearly three times the rate of white women in 1988.

Figure 1-9 • INFANT MORTALITY RATES IN THE UNITED STATES BY RACE, SELECTED YEARS, 1960–1990

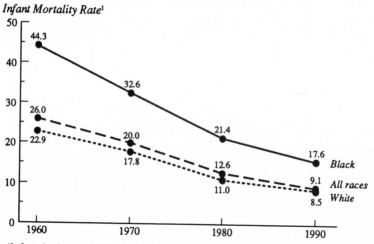

Infant Mortality Rate[1]

[1]Infant deaths per 1,000 live births.

Source: National Center for Health Statistics, "Advance Report of Final Mortality Statistics, 1988," *Monthly Vital Statistics Report*, November 28, 1990, Table 13.

Figure 1-9

Infant mortality rates dropped significantly between 1960 and 1990 for all races. Even after 30 years, however, black babies were still twice as likely as white babies to die in their first year.

Section 2: Health

This section presents a snapshot of women and their health. Topics range from birth and death to diseases such as AIDS and cancer to preventive practices such as the use of mammograms and contraceptives.

Notable Trends

- In 1988, a woman was twice as likely as her mother to have her first child after the age of 25, a trend largely reflecting birth rates among white women (see Figure 2–1 and Table 2–1).

- While birth rates (live births per 1,000 women) for unmarried women of all races increased steadily from 1970 to 1988, there was a slight decrease in the out-of-wedlock birth rate among black women. However, births to unmarried women as a percent of all live births rose dramatically during this time period for women of all races (see Table 2–2 and Figure 2–2).

Encouraging Trends

- Birth rates of teenage girls ages 18 and 19 have decreased 29 percent since 1970 (see Table 2–3).

- Thirty-three percent of all women age 40 and older performed breast self-examinations (BSEs) at least once a month in 1987. Black women in this age group were significantly more likely than white women to perform BSEs on a weekly basis (see Table 2–6).

- The proportion of single women using condoms doubled between 1982 and 1988 (see Table 2–10)

Discouraging Trends

- Although women with AIDS still constituted a minority of all AIDS cases, between 1986 and 1990 the number of new cases increased twice as fast among females as among males (see Figure 2–4).

- Between 1973 and 1988, the incidence of breast cancer among women increased 25 percent. Black women were less likely than white women to be diagnosed with breast cancer, but more likely to die from the disease (see Table 2–5).

Figure 2-1 • AGE OF MOTHER AT BIRTH OF FIRST CHILD, 1960, 1980, AND 1988 (percent distribution)

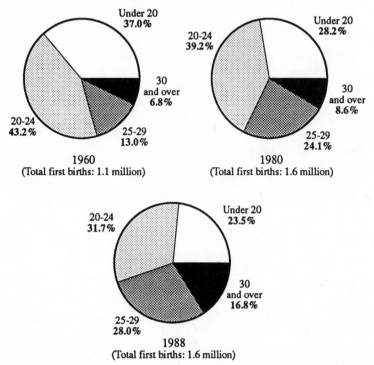

1960
(Total first births: 1.1 million)

1980
(Total first births: 1.6 million)

1988
(Total first births: 1.6 million)

Source: U.S. Bureau of the Census, "Maternity Leave Arrangements: 1961–85," *Work and Family Patterns of American Women*, March 1990, Table A and National Center for Health Statistics, *Monthly Vital Statistics Report*, August 15, 1990, Table 2.

Figure 2-1

Overall, a woman who had her first baby in 1988 was much more likely than her mother to have postponed having children. In 1960, only 20 percent of first births were to mothers age 25 or older, and just seven percent were to mothers over age 29. In 1988, the figures were 45 percent and 17 percent, respectively.

Table 2-1 • AGE OF MOTHER AT BIRTH OF FIRST CHILD BY RACE, 1988 (percent distribution)

Age of Mother	Race		
	All Races	White	Black
Under 20	23.5	20.2	41.7
20–24	31.7	31.9	32.5
25–29	28.0	30.0	17.0
30–39	16.4	17.5	8.6
40 and over	0.4	0.4	0.3
Total percent	100.0	100.0	100.0
Total number (in thousands)	1,596	1,259	258

Source: National Center for Health Statistics, *Monthly Vital Statistics Report*, August 15, 1990, Table 2.

Table 2-1

The pie charts in Figure 2–1 are for American women of all races, and because whites so heavily predominate in the population overall, the graphics largely reflect the pattern among white women. As Table 2–1 shows, delayed childbearing was much less common among black mothers who gave birth to their first children in 1988 than among their white counterparts. Only nine percent of first births to black females were to mothers 30 or older; the comparable percentage for white females was 18.

Table 2-2 • BIRTH RATES[1] OF UNMARRIED WOMEN BY AGE AND RACE, 1970, 1980, AND 1988

Age of Mother	1970[2]			1980[2]			1988[3]		
	All Races	White	Black	All Races	White	Black	All Races	White	Black
15–19	22.4	10.9	96.9	27.6	16.2	89.2	36.8	24.8	98.3
20–24	38.4	22.5	131.5	40.9	24.4	115.1	56.7	38.3	138.2
25–29	37.0	21.1	100.9	34.0	20.7	83.9	48.1	33.8	99.2
30–34	27.1	14.2	71.8	21.1	13.6	48.2	31.7	22.9	58.7
35–39	13.6	7.6	32.9	9.7	6.8	19.6	14.9	11.5	25.3
40–44	3.5	2.0	10.4	2.6	1.8	5.6	3.2	2.6	5.3
All ages, 15–44	26.4	13.9	95.5	29.4	17.6	82.9	38.6	26.6	88.9

[1]Rate is the number of live births per 1,000 unmarried women.

[2]Birth rates for 1970 and 1980 are estimated based on 100 percent of births in selected states and on a 50 percent sample of births in all other states.

[3]Data for states in which marital status was not reported have been inferred and included with data from remaining states.

Source: National Center for Health Statistics, *Monthly Vital Statistics Report*, August 15, 1990, Table 19.

Table 2-2

In 1988, the birth rate among unmarried black women of childbearing years (ages 15 to 44) was less than in 1970, although interestingly enough it was even lower in 1980. By contrast, the birth rate among unmarried white females steadily increased over the time period, and by 1988 the rate had nearly doubled. The birth rate increased among white women under age 25 from 1970 to 1988 and fell slightly in 1980 for ages 25 and above. Among unmarried black women under age 25, birth rates were somewhat higher in 1988 than in 1970, but the net increases were relatively small, and among black females over age 30 there were noticeable net declines in birth rates. Even so, the birth rate among unmarried black women remained much higher than among white women, although the ratio narrowed considerably—from about seven to one in 1970 to about three to one in 1988.

Figure 2-2 • BIRTHS TO UNMARRIED MOTHERS AS A
PERCENTAGE OF ALL LIVE BIRTHS BY RACE AND
HISPANIC ORIGIN, 1970, 1980, AND 1988

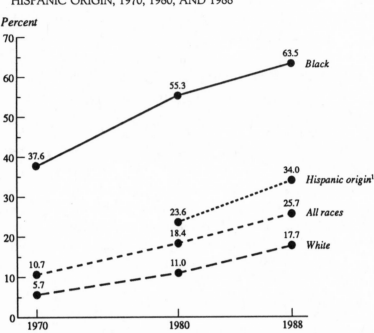

Percent

[1]Persons of Hispanic origin may be of any race. Data on births to Hispanic women
are not available for 1970.

Source: United States House of Representatives, Select Committee on Children,
Youth, and Families, H. Rept. No. 101-356, November 1989, p. 15 and National
Center for Health Statistics, *Advance Report of Final Natality Statistics,* August 15,
1990, Tables 1, 16, and 27.

Figure 2-2

An increasing proportion of all white, black, and Hispanic births have been to unmarried mothers. Since 1980
(the first year for which there were Hispanic data available),
out-of-wedlock births as a percentage of all births rose most
steeply for females of Hispanic origin; black females continued to have the highest and white females the lowest percentages of out-of-wedlock births in 1988.

Table 2-3 • BIRTH RATES[1] OF TEENAGE GIRLS BY AGE OF MOTHER AND RACE OF CHILD, 1970, 1980, AND 1988

Age of Mother	1970			1980			1988		
	All Races	White	Black	All Races	White	Black	All Races	White	Black
10–14	1.2	0.5	5.2	1.1	0.6	4.3	1.3	0.6	4.8
15–17	38.8	29.2	101.4	32.5	25.2	73.6	33.8	25.5	76.6
18–19	114.7	101.5	204.9	82.1	72.1	138.8	81.7	69.2	150.5

[1]Rate is the number of live births per 1,000 girls by age.

Source: National Center for Health Statistics, Monthly Vital Statistics Report, August 15, 1990, Table 4.

Table 2-3

Birth rates for teenage girls (10 to 19 years old) have varied by age and race during the last 20 years. For example, between 1970 and 1980, the birth rate for white and black girls in their upper teens (ages 18 and 19) decreased substantially, by 29 and 32 percent, respectively. Between 1980 and 1988, however, while the birth rate continued to drop for white girls (by four percent) it rose for black girls (by eight percent) in this age group.

Table 2-4 • DEATH RATES FOR THE 10 LEADING CAUSES OF DEATH OF BLACKS AND WHITES BY SEX, 1988

White Male	Death Rate[1]	White Female	Death Rate[1]
Heart disease	336.8	Heart disease	318.0
Cancer	221.4	Cancer	189.3
Accidents	53.7	Stroke and related diseases	74.9
Stroke and related diseases	50.0	Pneumonia and influenza	35.2
Lung disease	44.2	Lung disease	30.0
Pneumonia and influenza	31.8	Accidents	25.2
Suicide	21.7	Diabetes mellitus	17.6
Liver disease/ cirrhosis	14.2	Atherosclerosis	12.0
Diabetes mellitus	13.8	Septicemia/blood poisoning	9.1
HIV/AIDS	10.3	Nephritis/kidney disease	8.6

Black Male	Death Rate[1]	Black Female	Death Rate[1]
Heart disease	276.3	Heart disease	251.2
Cancer	211.7	Cancer	148.9
Accidents	67.1	Stroke and related diseases	65.4
Homicide/legal intervention	58.0	Diabetes mellitus	27.3

Table 2-4 continued

Black Male	Death Rate[1]	Black Female	Death Rate[1]
Stroke and related diseases	56.5	Accidents	24.4
HIV/AIDS	29.3	Pneumonia and influenza	19.8
Pneumonia and influenza	28.3	Conditions originating in the perinatal period	18.4
Conditions originating in the perinatal period	25.8	Nephritis/kidney disease	14.2
Lung disease	25.4	Homicide/legal intervention	13.2
Diabetes mellitus	18.4	Septicemia/blood poisoning	12.7

[1]Rate is per 100,000 population in a specified group.

Source: National Center for Health Statistics, *Monthly Vital Statistics Report,* November 18, 1990, Table 6.

Table 2-4

Heart disease and cancer ranked one and two, respectively, as the leading causes of death for both females and males in 1988. However, the rankings diverge beginning with the third leading cause of death — accidents for men and stroke and related diseases for women. Acquired Immunodeficiency Syndrome (AIDS) was a top-10 killer of men of both races, while homicide/legal intervention ranked fourth for black males and ninth for black females.

Figures 2-3, 2-4, 2-5, and 2-6

More whites contracted AIDS than the other racial groups combined from 1986 through 1990. Still, as Figure 2–3 shows, AIDS cases increased at a much faster rate among Hispanics (309 percent) and blacks (289 percent) than among whites (184 percent).

As Figure 2–4 illustrates, although males accounted for 89 percent of all new AIDS cases reported from 1986 through 1990, AIDS increased nearly twice as fast among women as among men. White women comprised over one-fourth of all female AIDS cases reported through February 1991 while black women made up over half (see Figure 2–5). Women between the ages of 20 and 39 accounted for more than two-thirds (68 percent) of the female AIDS cases, as shown in Figure 2–6. Children under five years old comprised almost seven percent.

Figure 2-3 • REPORTED NEW AIDS CASES[1] BY RACE,
1986–1990

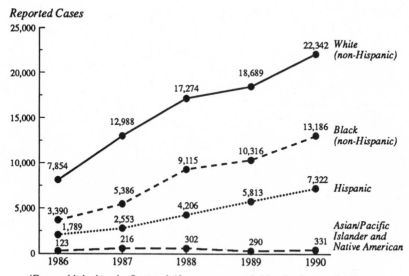

¹Data published in the *Statistical Abstract* are provided by the Centers for Disease
Control (CDC). In determining annual new AIDS cases, CDC advises that the
number of cases reported for any given year may be readjusted at a later date due
to double-counting or miscalculations at the time the data are collected. The numbers provided reflect the most recent adjusted figures available.

Source: U.S. Bureau of the Census, *Statistical Abstract of the United States 1990,*
January 1990, Table 187 and Centers for Disease Control, *HIV/AIDS Surveillance,*
January 1990, Table 3 and January 1991, Table 3.

Figure 2-4 • REPORTED NEW AIDS CASES BY SEX, 1986–1990

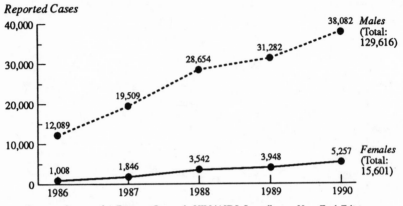

Source: Centers for Disease Control, *HIV/AIDS Surveillance,* Year-End Editions, January 1987, January 1988, January 1989, January 1990, and January 1991, Table 3 in each.

Figure 2-5 • TOTAL REPORTED AIDS CASES[1] BY SEX AND
RACE, FEBRUARY 1991 (percent distribution)

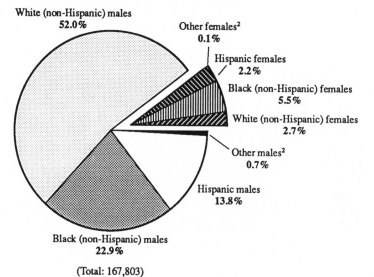

White (non-Hispanic) males
52.0%

Other females[2]
0.1%

Hispanic females
2.2%

Black (non-Hispanic) females
5.5%

White (non-Hispanic) females
2.7%

Other males[2]
0.7%

Hispanic males
13.8%

Black (non-Hispanic) males
22.9%

(Total: 167,803)

[1]Includes all cases reported since 1981, when formal AIDS reporting efforts were undertaken, and approximately 71 cases occurring before 1981 that were later classified as AIDS.

[2]Includes all races not recognized as white, black, or Hispanic.

Source: Centers for Disease Control, *HIV/AIDS Surveillance,* March 1991, Table 7.

Figure 2-6 • TOTAL REPORTED FEMALE AIDS CASES[1] BY
AGE AT TIME OF DIAGNOSIS, FEBRUARY 1991 (percent
distribution)

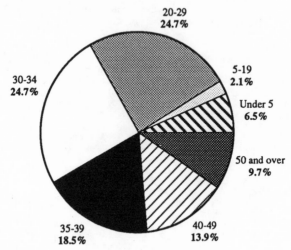

(Total: 17,675)

[1]Includes all cases reported since 1981, when formal AIDS reporting efforts were
undertaken, and female AIDS cases occurring before 1981 that were later classified
as AIDS.

Source: Centers for Disease Control, *HIV/AIDS Surveillance,* March 1991, Table 7.

Figure 2-7 • ESTIMATED FEMALE CANCER INCIDENCE AND
MORTALITY BY CANCER SITE, 1988 (percent distribution)

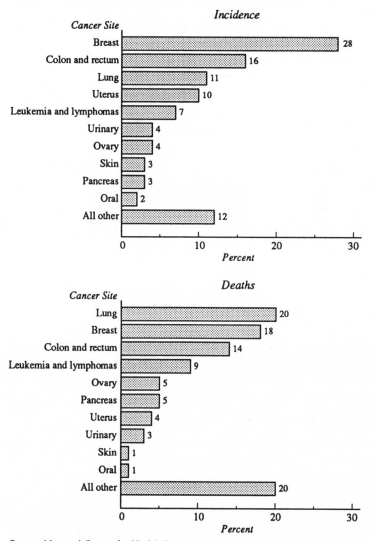

Source: National Center for Health Statistics, *Breast Cancer Risk Factors and Screening: Vital Health Statistics Bulletin, United States, 1987,* January 1990, Figures 1 and 2.

Figure 2-7

Breast cancer was by far the single most common type of cancer occurring among American females in 1988, and ranked second among specific cancer types as a cause of death. However, a woman's chances of surviving breast cancer were clearly a lot better than her chances of surviving lung cancer, which accounted for just over one in 10 cancer cases among women in 1988, but for one in five of all female cancer deaths.

Table 2-5 • AGE-ADJUSTED[1] FEMALE BREAST CANCER INCIDENCE AND MORTALITY RATES BY RACE, 1973-74 AND 1987-88

Race/Rate	Average Rate		Percent Change
	1973–74	*1987–88*	
All races			
Incidence[2]	88.2	111.0	+ 25.8
Mortality[3]	26.8	27.3	+ 1.8
White			
Incidence[2]	89.7	114.7	+ 27.9
Mortality[3]	26.9	27.3	+ 0.2
Black			
Incidence[2]	73.0	93.3	+ 27.9
Mortality[3]	26.3	30.0	+ 14.2

[1]An age-adjusted rate is a weighted average of the age-specific cancer incidence or mortality rates, where the weights are the proportions of persons in the corresponding age groups of a standard population. This is done to reduce the potential confounding effect of age.

[2]Incidence rate is the number of new cancers per 100,000 women in a given year.

[3]Mortality rate is the number of deaths per 100,000 women in a given year.

Source: National Cancer Institute, *Cancer Statistics Review 1973–1988*, July 1991.

Table 2-5

The incidence of breast cancer increased by 26 percent among American women overall between 1973 and 1988, and by close to 28 percent among both white and black females. In 1987–88, black women were less likely than white women to be diagnosed with breast cancer but more likely than white females to die from the disease.

Tables 2-6 and 2-7

The earlier breast cancer is discovered, the better the chance that it can be cured, yet many females age 40 and older — the age group at greatest risk of breast cancer — neglect or omit the practices that make early discovery more likely, including regular breast self-examination (BSE), regular breast examination by a physician (BPE), and periodic mammography. The older the woman, the more likely she is to neglect or omit these procedures.

As Table 2–6 shows, in 1987 women under age 55 were the most likely and women age 75 or older the least likely to perform BSEs. Over half of women under 55 compared to only a third of women over 75 performed BSEs at least once a month. In general, a black woman was much more likely than a white woman to perform a BSE once a week or more.

Similar trends by age and race were evident with respect to BPEs and mammograms, although women 40 and over were more likely to have had a BPE at some point in their lives than they were to have had a mammogram (see Table 2–7). Regardless of race, the older the woman, the less likely she was to have had a BPE or a mammogram. And a black woman was less likely to have had these procedures than a white woman.

Table 2-6 • WOMEN AGE 40 AND OVER WHO PERFORM BREAST SELF-EXAMINATIONS (BSEs) BY RACE AND AGE, 1987 (in percentages)

		Perform BSE				
Race	Age	Less Than Once Per Month	Once Per Month But Less Than Once Per Week	Once Per Week Or More	Other	Unknown Frequency
All races	40–54	24.5	37.4	13.4	5.4	3.1
	55–64	18.6	35.0	14.8	6.4	3.4
	65–74	17.2	30.4	15.7	7.1	3.5
	75 and over	13.1	18.8	15.3	8.0	6.1
	Total, 40 and over[1]	20.0	32.8	14.5	6.4	3.7
White	40–54	26.1	38.2	11.9	5.1	3.0
	55–64	19.0	36.0	13.7	6.8	3.4
	65–74	17.8	31.3	15.1	7.4	3.4
	75 and over	13.8	19.2	14.9	8.3	6.2
	Total, 40 and over[1]	20.9	33.4	13.5	6.4	3.6
Black	40–54	16.3	35.1	20.5	5.8	4.9
	55–64	16.5	32.3	23.5	4.0	4.0
	65–74	12.1	21.4	23.7	4.0	4.4
	75 and over	4.4	14.5	22.1	4.6	5.2
	Total, 40 and over[1]	13.7	28.4	22.2	5.0	4.6

[1]Percentages are age-adjusted.

Source: National Center for Health Statistics, Vital and Health Statistics Bulletin, *Breast Cancer Risk Factors and Screening: United States, 1987*, January 1990, Table O.

Table 2-7 • WOMEN AGE 40 AND OVER WHO HAVE HAD A MAMMOGRAM OR A BREAST PHYSICAL EXAMINATION (BPE) BY AGE AND RACE, 1987 (in percentages)

Examination Status and Race	Age				
	40–54	55–64	65–74	75 and Over	All, 40 and Over
Ever had a BPE					
All races	86.7	83.1	76.8	68.2	81.3
White	88.6	84.8	78.3	70.2	82.8
Black	79.6	78.0	65.7	47.6	71.6
Ever had a mammogram					
All races	42.2	41.1	35.2	24.8	38.1
White	43.9	42.2	36.5	25.5	39.2
Black	33.7	36.4	24.7	17.1	30.1

Source: National Center for Health Statistics, Vital and Health Statistics Bulletin, *Breast Cancer Risk Factors and Screening: United States, 1987,* January 1990, Tables Q and AA.

Table 2-8 • REPORTED LEGAL ABORTIONS IN THE UNITED STATES BY MARITAL STATUS AND AGE, SELECTED YEARS, 1972–1987 (percent distribution)

Marital Status	1972	1978	1984	1987
Married	29.7	26.4	20.5	27.2
Unmarried	70.3	73.6	79.5	72.8
Total percent	100.0	100.0	100.0	100.0
Age				
19 or under	32.6	30.0	26.4	25.8
20–24	32.5	35.0	35.3	33.4
25 and over	34.9	34.9	38.3	40.8
Total percent	100.0	100.0	100.0	100.0
Total number (in thousands)	588	1,158	1,334	1,354

Source: Centers for Disease Control, CDC *Surveillance Summaries,* June 1990, *MMWR* 1990; 39, (No. SS-2), Table 1.

Table 2-8

Between 1972 and 1987, women age 25 and older accounted for a growing proportion, and teenagers for a shrinking proportion, of women having abortions in this country. Two in every five women who got abortions in 1987 were at least 25 years old while only one in four was under age 20. Twenty-seven percent of abortions in 1987 were obtained by married women, a smaller proportion than in 1972.

Table 2-9 • REPORTED LEGAL ABORTIONS IN THE UNITED STATES[1] BY AGE AND RACE, 1987 (percent distribution)

Age	White	Black and Other	All Races
Under 15	0.8	1.6	1.0
15–19	25.7	22.4	24.6
20–24	33.5	33.7	33.6
25–29	20.9	22.7	21.5
30–34	11.7	12.5	12.0
35–39	5.8	5.7	5.8
40 and over	1.6	1.4	1.5
Total percent	100.0	100.0	100.0
Total number[1]	391,228	195,987	587,215

[1]As reported by 31 states.

Source: Centers for Disease Control, *CDC Surveillance Summaries,* June 1990, *MMWR* 1990; 39, (No. SS-2), Table 18.

Table 2-9

The pattern of age distribution differed slightly by race among women who had abortions in 1987. A larger proportion of white girls (27 percent) than of black girls (24 percent) were in their teens when they had abortions. Conversely, a larger proportion of the black women than of the white women were age 25 or older (42 percent versus 40 percent).

Women between the ages of 20 and 24 accounted for one-third of all abortions. Two-thirds of the women who had abortions in 1987 were white.

Figure 2-8 • PERCENT DISTRIBUTION OF ALL WOMEN AGES 15 TO 44, AND WOMEN HAVING LEGAL ABORTIONS, BY FAMILY INCOME, 1987

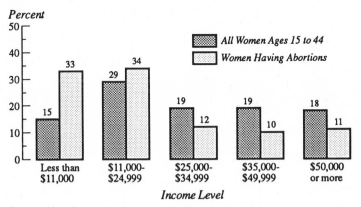

Source: Alan Guttmacher Institute, *Abortion and Women's Health*, 1990, Figure 7.

Figure 2-8

A study by the Alan Guttmacher Institute found that women at the lower end of the income scale had a disproportionate number of all abortions in 1987. For example, females with annual family incomes of under $11,000 accounted for only 15 percent of U.S. women overall, but for 33 percent of the women who had abortions. By contrast, women with household incomes of $50,000 or more accounted for 18 percent of all females, but for only 11 percent of the women who had abortions.

Table 2-10 • CONTRACEPTIVE METHODS USED BY WOMEN AGES 15 TO 44 BY MARITAL STATUS, 1982 AND 1988 (percent distribution)

Contraceptive Method	Never Married		Currently Married		Widowed, Divorced, or Separated	
	1982	1988	1982	1988	1982	1988
Sterile[1]	3.2	5.2	40.9	44.0	38.0	42.6
Birth control pill	18.7	24.7	13.4	15.1	15.8	14.5
Intrauterine device	1.9	0.6	4.8	1.5	6.4	2.1
Diaphragm	4.7	2.1	4.5	4.6	3.7	3.0
Condom	4.1	8.2	9.8	10.6	0.8	3.4
Foam	0.4	0.2	2.0	1.0	1.1	0.5
Periodic abstinence and natural family planning	0.9	0.6	3.2	2.1	1.4	1.1
Withdrawal, douche, and other methods	2.6	2.1	2.3	3.2	2.7	1.7
Pregnant, postpartum, or seeking pregnancy	3.7	3.7	13.9	13.1	4.7	4.5
Never had intercourse	38.4	31.5	—	—	—	—
Nonuser[2]	21.3	21.0	5.0	4.8	25.6	26.6
Total percent	100.0	100.0	100.0	100.0	100.0	100.0
Total number (in thousands)	19,164	21,058	28,231	29,147	6,704	7,695

[1]Includes women and their partners who are surgically and nonsurgically sterile.

[2]Includes women who have had and have not had intercourse in the last three months.

Source: National Center for Health Statistics, Contraceptive Use in the United States, 1973–1988, Advance Data, March 20, 1990, Table 3.

Table 2-10

Between 1982 and 1988 the methods women used to avoid pregnancy varied enormously, particularly by marital status. For example, among currently married women, sterilization (of either wife or husband) was the most common form of contraception, and the percentage of married couples who used this method to prevent pregnancy increased between 1982 and 1988 (in both years, the husband was the sterile partner in over one-third of these couples).

Comparing the distribution of contraceptive methods among currently married women with those of never-married women is complicated by the fact that a significant proportion of never-married women had never had sexual intercourse (32 percent in 1988 — a noticeably smaller proportion than in 1982). Nevertheless, the birth control pill was the contraceptive method most commonly used by never-married women and in 1988 condoms were second. It is encouraging to note that, between 1982 and 1988 condom use increased among women of all marital statuses, doubling for never-married women during this time period.

Section 3: Family and Household Structure

The social and economic events of the past 20 years have affected the structure and composition of many American households.

Notable Trends

- In 1988, the median age of first-time brides reached 24 years old—a figure not matched since 1940 (see Figure 3–2).

- In 1990, the divorce ratio (the number of currently divorced persons per 1,000 currently married persons) was at an all-time high of 166 for women and 118 for men (see Table 3–3 and Figure 3–3).

- In 1990, one out of every four children lived with one parent—usually the mother. This living arrangement was the norm for black children; more than half lived with one parent (see Table 3–6).

- In 1990, young adults ages 18 to 24 were more likely to live with their parents than were their counterparts two decades earlier (see Figure 3–4).

- Most men age 65 and older lived with a spouse in 1990; most women of that age group did not (see Table 3–8).

Table 3-1 • MARITAL STATUS OF PERSONS AGE 18 AND OVER BY SEX, RACE, AND HISPANIC ORIGIN, MARCH 1990 (percent distribution)

Marital Status	All Races		White		Black		Hispanic Origin[1]	
	Women	*Men*	*Women*	*Men*	*Women*	*Men*	*Women*	*Men*
Married, spouse present	56.0	61.3	59.0	63.7	33.6	42.3	54.8	53.5
Married, spouse absent	3.7	3.0	2.9	2.5	9.4	6.9	7.6	7.4
Widowed	12.1	2.7	12.2	2.6	12.4	3.7	6.5	1.5
Divorced	9.3	7.2	9.0	7.2	12.0	8.8	8.5	5.5
Single (never married)	18.9	25.8	16.9	24.1	32.5	38.4	22.5	32.1
Total percent	100.0	100.0	100.0	100.0	100.0	100.0	100.0	100.0
Total number (in thousands)	94,977	88,872	80,624	74,830	11,183	9,137	6,819	6,741

[1]Persons of Hispanic origin may be of any race.

Source: U.S. Bureau of the Census, *Marital Status and Living Arrangements: March 1990*, May 1991, Table 1.

Figure 3-1 • MARITAL STATUS OF WOMEN AGE 18 AND
OVER BY RACE AND HISPANIC ORIGIN, MARCH 1990
(percent distribution)

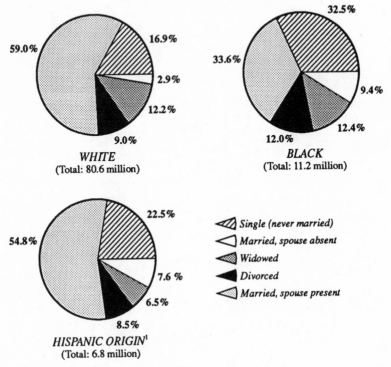

[1]Persons of Hispanic origin may be of any race.

Source: U.S. Bureau of the Census, *Marital Status and Living Arrangements: March
1990*, May 1991, Table 1.

Table 3-1 and Figure 3-1

Approximately three-quarters of American women and men have been married at least once in their lives. In 1990, the majority of adults (age 18 and over) of both sexes were currently married, with spouse present, although a larger proportion of men were married (61 percent) than women (56 percent). Conversely, the never married accounted for a larger proportion of men (26 percent) than of women (19 percent). A much higher proportion of women than of men were widowed (12 percent versus three percent), which was largely a reflection of the fact that a greater proportion of women than of men were age 65 and over (see Figure 1–5).

When marital status is examined by race and Hispanic origin, several differences are apparent. For example, black women were almost as likely to be single (never married) as to be married in 1990. Further, only one-third of black women were currently married compared to 59 percent of white women and 55 percent of Hispanic women.

Figure 3-2 • MEDIAN AGE OF WOMEN AT FIRST MARRIAGE
BY RACE, SELECTED YEARS, 1970–1988

Median Age

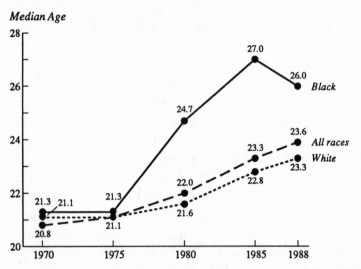

Source: U.S. Bureau of the Census, *Studies in Marriage and the Family,* June 1989,
Table C.

Table 3-2 • NUMBER OF UNMARRIED[1] MEN PER 100 UNMARRIED WOMEN BY AGE, SELECTED RACES, AND HISPANIC ORIGIN, MARCH 1990

								65 and	*Total, 15*

				Ages					
Race	*15–24*	*25–29*	*30–34*	*35–39*	*40–44*	*45–64*	*65 and Over*	*Total, 15 and Over*
White	113	137	134	110	87	61	27	85
Black	98	86	93	64	70	58	37	76
Hispanic origin[2]	124	158	104	118	91	51	29	103

[1]Unmarried includes never married, widowed, and divorced.

[2]Persons of Hispanic origin may be of any race.

Source: U.S. Bureau of the Census, *Marital Status and Living Arrangements: March 1990,* May 1991, Table 1.

Figure 3-2 and Table 3-2

The typical first-time bride in 1988 married at age 24, which was nearly three years older than her counterpart in 1970. In fact, the median age of first marriage had never before been so high for American women. (In 1988, the median age of first marriage for men was 26 years old.)

The trend to marry later was most dramatic for black women. In 1970 the median age was 21 for both black and white women. In 1988, the typical black first-time bride was nearly three years older than her white counterpart. One likely reason, as Table 3–2 shows, was that in every age group the pool of unmarried black men was smaller than the pool of unmarried black women. In comparison, among whites and Hispanics unmarried men outnumbered unmarried women until the age of 40.

Table 3-3 • DIVORCE RATIO[1] BY SEX, RACE, AND HISPANIC ORIGIN, SELECTED YEARS, 1960–MARCH 1990

Race	1960		1970		1980		1990	
	Women	*Men*	*Women*	*Men*	*Women*	*Men*	*Women*	*Men*
White	38	27	56	32	110	74	153	112
Black	78	45	104	62	258	149	358	208
Hispanic origin[2]	—	—	81	40	132	64	155	103
All races	42	28	60	35	120	79	166	118

[1]Divorce ratio is the number of currently divorced persons per 1,000 currently married persons with spouse present. This ratio differs from the divorce rate, which is the number of divorces per 1,000 population.

[2]Persons of Hispanic origin may be of any race.

Source: U.S. Bureau of the Census, *Marital Status and Living Arrangements: March 1990*, May 1991, Table C.

Figure 3-3 • DIVORCE RATIO[1] OF WOMEN BY RACE AND HISPANIC ORIGIN, SELECTED YEARS, 1960, 1970, 1980, AND MARCH 1990

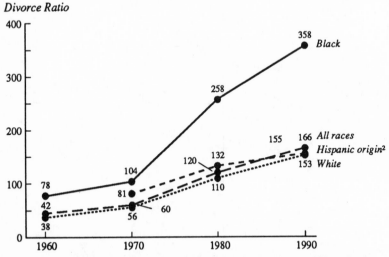

[1]Divorce ratio is the number of currently divorced women per 1,000 currently married women with spouse present. This ratio differs from the divorce rate, which is the number of divorces per 1,000 population.

[2]Data not available for 1960. Persons of Hispanic origin may be of any race.

Source: U.S. Bureau of the Census, *Marital Status and Living Arrangements: March 1990*, May 1991, Table C.

Table 3-3 and Figure 3-3

Already climbing in the 1960s, the divorce ratio (the number of currently divorced persons per 1,000 currently married persons) increased markedly between 1970 and 1990 for whites, blacks, and Hispanics of both sexes. The steepest increase was for black women and men: divorce ratios for both more than tripled in the 1970s and 1980s.

Table 3-4 • PERCENT DISTRIBUTION OF FAMILIES BY FAMILY TYPE, RACE, AND HISPANIC ORIGIN, 1970, 1980, AND 1989

Family Type	1970	1980	1989
ALL RACES			
Married-couple families	86.7	81.7	79.2
Wife in paid labor force	—	(41.0)	(45.7)
Wife not in paid labor force	—	(40.7)	(33.5)
Male householder, no spouse present	2.4	3.2	4.4
Female householder, no spouse present	10.9	15.1	16.5
Total percent	100.0	100.0	100.0
Total number of families (in thousands)	51,237	60,309	66,090
WHITE			
Married-couple families	88.6	85.1	83.0
Wife in paid labor force	—	(42.0)	(47.4)
Wife not in paid labor force	—	(43.1)	(35.6)
Male householder, no spouse present	2.2	3.0	4.1
Female householder, no spouse present	9.1	11.9	12.9
Total percent	100.0	100.0	100.0
Total number of families (in thousands)	46,022	52,710	56,590
BLACK			
Married-couple families	68.0	53.7	50.2
Wife in paid labor force	—	(32.0)	(32.1)
Wife not in paid labor force	—	(21.7)	(18.1)
Male householder, no spouse present	3.7	4.6	6.0
Female householder, no spouse present	28.2	41.7	43.8
Total percent	100.0	100.0	100.0
Total number of families (in thousands)	4,774	6,317	7,470
HISPANIC ORIGIN[1]			
Married-couple families	—	73.1	70.1
Wife in paid labor force	—	(33.8)	(36.4)
Wife not in paid labor force	—	(39.4)	(33.7)
Male householder, no spouse present	—	5.1	6.8
Female householder, no spouse present	—	21.8	23.1
Total percent	—	100.0	100.0
Total number of families (in thousands)	—	3,235	4,840

[1]Persons of Hispanic origin may be of any race.

Source: U.S. Bureau of the Census, *Household and Family Characteristics: 1970*, March 1971, Table 6; *Money Income and Poverty Status of Families in the United States: 1980*, August 1981, Table 1; and *Money Income and Poverty Status in the United States: 1989*, September 1990, Table 7.

Table 3-4

In America, married-couple families still heavily predominate, although their predominance has decreased by more than seven percentage points over the past two decades, as other family types have become more common. Black and Hispanic families are less likely than white families to be married couples; in fact, married couples accounted for only the barest majority of black families in 1989, a drop of nearly 18 percentage points since 1970. In the 20-year period, the percentage of all families that were maintained by single women and men grew, although the proportion of these families maintained by men was quite small compared to those maintained by women, four percent versus 17 percent.

Table 3-5 • FAMILIES BY FAMILY TYPE, PRESENCE OF CHILDREN, RACE, AND HISPANIC ORIGIN, MARCH 1990

Race/ Family Type	Number of Families (in thousands)	Percent With Children Under Age 18
ALL RACES		
Married-couple families	52,317	46.9
Female householder	10,890	60.6
Male householder	2,884	40.0
WHITE		
Married-couple families	46,981	45.9
Female householder	7,306	57.5
Male householder	2,303	40.8
BLACK		
Married-couple families	3,750	52.6
Female householder	3,275	68.2
Male householder	446	38.8
HISPANIC ORIGIN[1]		
Married-couple families	3,395	64.5
Female householder	1,116	66.8
Male householder	329	35.9

[1]Persons of Hispanic origin may be of any race.

Source: U.S. Bureau of the Census, *Household and Family Characteristics: March 1990 and 1989*, December 1990, Table 1.

Table 3-5

In 1990, at least four out of 10 families contained children, although children were more common in families maintained by women than in those maintained by men or married couples. Married couples and females who were black or Hispanic were more likely than their white counterparts to have children. Among families maintained by men, whites were more likely than black or Hispanic men to have children.

Table 3-6

Over the last two decades, living with just one parent—
usually the mother—has become significantly more common
for American children. In 1990, a quarter of all children re-
sided with one parent. While that environment was still the
exception for white and Hispanic children, it has become the
norm for black children, 55 percent of whom lived with only
one parent. Of that 55 percent, an overwhelming majority
lived with their mothers.

Table 3-6 • CHILDREN UNDER AGE 18 LIVING WITH A SINGLE
PARENT BY RACE AND HISPANIC ORIGIN, 1970, 1989, AND
1990

Children Living with a Single Parent	1970	1980	1990
ALL RACES			
As a percentage of all children	11.9	19.7	24.7
Living with mother only	10.8	18.0	21.6
Living with father only	1.1	1.7	3.1
Total number (in thousands)	8,199	12,466	15,867
WHITE			
As a percentage of all children	8.7	15.1	19.2
Living with mother only	7.8	13.5	16.2
Living with father only	0.9	1.6	3.0
Total number (in thousands)	5,109	7,901	9,870
BLACK			
As a percentage of all children	31.8	45.8	54.8
Living with mother only	29.5	43.9	51.2
Living with father only	2.3	1.9	3.5
Total number (in thousands)	2,996	4,297	5,485
HISPANIC ORIGIN[1]			
As a percentage of all children	—	21.1	30.0
Living with mother only	—	19.6	27.1
Living with father only	—	1.5	2.9
Total number (in thousands)	—	1,152	2,154

[1]Persons of Hispanic origin may be of any race.

Source: U.S. Bureau of the Census, *Marital Status and Living Arrangements: March
1990,* May 1991, Table E.

Figure 3-4 • LIVING ARRANGEMENTS OF YOUNG ADULTS
AGES 18 TO 24 BY SEX, 1970, 1980, AND MARCH 1990
(percent distribution)

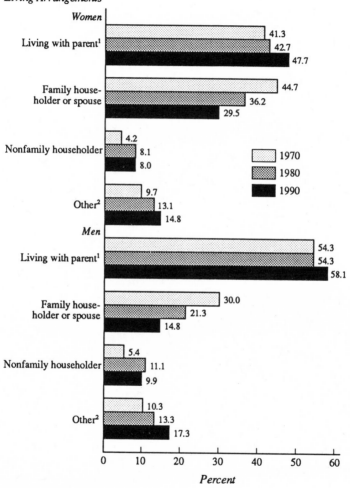

¹Includes unmarried college students living in dormitories.

²Living in the homes of others.

Source: U.S. Bureau of the Census, *Marital Status and Living Arrangements: March 1990*, May 1991, Table J.

Figure 3-4

Young adults (ages 18 to 24) of both sexes were somewhat more likely in 1990 to live with their parents than their counterparts two decades ago, and—not surprisingly, considering that they were typically marrying later—were a good deal less likely to live in their own family households. The proportion of both sexes, however, who did set up their own nonfamily households has nearly doubled from 1970 to 1990.

Table 3-7 • PERSONS AGES 18 TO 24[1] AND 25 TO 34 LIVING WITH THEIR PARENTS BY SEX, MARITAL STATUS, AND PRESENCE OF THEIR OWN CHILDREN, MARCH 1990 (percent distribution)

Living in Parents' Households	Ages 18–24[1]		Ages 25–34	
	Women	Men	Women	Men
Never married/single	96.0	98.1	72.2	84.7
Married, spouse present	1.2	1.0	6.9	3.5
Married, spouse absent	1.8	0.6	8.8	4.5
Widowed	—	—	0.5	0.1
Divorced	1.0	0.4	11.6	7.2
Total percent	100.0	100.0	100.0	100.0
Total number (in thousands)	6,135	7,232	1,774	3,213
Percent with own children	7.8	0.8	29.3	3.9

[1]Includes unmarried college students living in dormitories.

Source: U.S. Bureau of the Census, *Marital Status and Living Arrangements: March 1990*, May 1991, Table 7.

Table 3-7

Overall, nearly eight million women and more than 10 million men between the ages of 18 and 34 lived in their parents' households in 1990. The overwhelming majority of those in the younger age group (18 to 24) have never been married. In the older group, however, over a quarter of the women and 15 percent of the men were either formerly married (divorced or widowed) or currently married. The husbands of about seven percent of the women in the older group were also living with their in-laws; this was double the comparable percentage of wives living with their in-laws. Women ages 18 to 34 who lived with their parents were five times as likely as men to have children of their own living in these (at least) three-generation households.

Table 3-8 • LIVING ARRANGEMENTS OF THE NONINSTITUTIONAL POPULATION AGE 65 AND OVER, 1980 AND MARCH 1990 (percent distribution)

	1980		1990	
Living Arrangement	*Women*	*Men*	*Women*	*Men*
Living alone	39.4	14.6	42.0	15.7
Living with spouse	37.4	75.2	39.7	74.3
Living with other relatives	21.4	8.4	16.1	7.7
Living with nonrelatives only	1.7	1.7	2.2[1]	2.3[1]
Total percent	100.0	100.0	100.0	100.0
Total number (in thousands)	14,268	9,889	17,232	12,334

[1]1990 data include a small number of persons in unrelated subfamilies.

Source: U.S. Bureau of the Census, *Marital Status and Living Arrangements: March 1990*, May 1991, Table L.

Table 3-8

Most men age 65 and older live with a spouse; most of their female counterparts do not. One reason for this disparity is that women typically outlive men, so there are many more older women than older men, especially in the upper age groups (see Figure 1–5). In 1990, an elderly woman had a slightly greater chance to be living alone than to be living with a husband. In contrast, a majority of older men lived with their wives. Elderly women were also more than twice as likely as elderly men to live with other relatives (16 percent) but they were less likely to do so in 1990 than they were in 1980 (21 percent).

Figure 3-5 • FEMALE HOUSEHOLDERS BY TENURE, HOUSEHOLD TYPE, AND PRESENCE OF CHILDREN, MARCH 1990 (percent distribution)

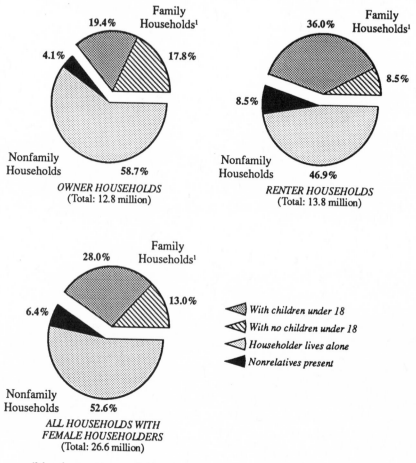

Family Households[1]

19.4%

4.1%

17.8%

Nonfamily Households   58.7%

OWNER HOUSEHOLDS
(Total: 12.8 million)

Family Households[1]

36.0%

8.5%

8.5%

Nonfamily Households   46.9%

RENTER HOUSEHOLDS
(Total: 13.8 million)

Family Households[1]

28.0%

6.4%

13.0%

Nonfamily Households   52.6%

ALL HOUSEHOLDS WITH
FEMALE HOUSEHOLDERS
(Total: 26.6 million)

◨ With children under 18
◨ With no children under 18
◨ Householder lives alone
◨ Nonrelatives present

[1]May also contain nonrelatives.

Source: U.S. Bureau of the Census, *Household and Family Characteristics: March 1990 and 1989*, December 1990, Table 16.

Figure 3-5

Of the nearly 27 million households headed by women in March 1990, over half consisted of women living alone, and less than 30 percent were family households containing children under age 18. Further, nearly three in five women who owned their own homes lived by themselves. (It should be noted that, according to the Census Bureau, widows accounted for more than half of all female owner householders, and for 62 percent of those in nonfamily households.) Only one-fifth of women owners headed families with children under 18. Among women renters, on the other hand, the proportion heading families with children was more than one in three. A female-maintained renter family was considerable more likely than its owner counterpart to have children.

Section 4: Child Care and Support

With increasing numbers of mothers in the labor force, arranging and paying for child support has become an integral part of American women's lives.

Notable Trends

- Over 60 percent of children under age 18 had working mothers in 1988 (see Figure 4–1).

- Nearly two-thirds of all working mothers with children under five years old had their children cared for in a home, either their own or, more commonly, someone else's (see Table 4–1).

- Child care expenses take an enormous bite out of the low-income family budget. In 1987, the average family with an annual income of $15,000 or less spent 20 percent of its money on child care. More prosperous families, those who earned $45,000 or more a year, spent a considerably smaller proportion of their annual incomes on child care—only five percent (see Table 4–3).

- Almost three-fifths of eligible mothers were awarded some form of child support in 1987, although white women were much more likely than either black or Hispanic women to be granted such awards (see Table 4–4).

- Child support is an important buffer against poverty for women with children. In 1987, 25 percent of women awarded child support lived below the poverty line, compared to 46 percent of mothers who were *not* awarded child support (see Table 4–6).

Figure 4-1 • CHILDREN WITH MOTHERS IN THE LABOR FORCE BY FAMILY TYPE AND AGE OF CHILD, SELECTED YEARS, 1970–1988 (in percentages)

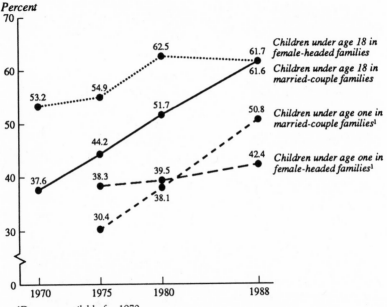

[1]Data not available for 1970.

Source: U.S. Bureau of the Census, *Handbook of Labor Statistics,* August 1989, Table 59.

Figure 4-1

More children than ever before have mothers in the labor force, regardless of whether they live in female-headed or married-couple families. However, in 1988 infants (under the age of one) in female-headed households were less likely than those with both parents present to have their mothers in the labor force.

Table 4-1 • PRIMARY CHILD CARE ARRANGEMENTS OF WORKING MOTHERS FOR CHILDREN UNDER AGE 5 BY RACE AND HISPANIC ORIGIN, 1987 (percent distribution)

Type of Primary Care	All Races	White	Black	Hispanic Origin[1]
Care in child's home	29.9	28.7	32.7	35.0
Care by father	15.3	16.7	6.8	12.8
Care by grandparent	5.1	3.6	10.2	5.1
Care by other relative	3.3	2.2	9.1	5.4
Care by nonrelative	6.2	6.2	6.6	11.7
Care in another home	35.6	35.5	37.1	39.2
Care by grandparent	8.7	8.4	11.2	13.4
Care by other relative	4.6	4.2	7.2	6.7
Care by nonrelative	22.3	22.9	18.7	19.1
Day/group care center	16.1	16.7	13.9	13.4
Nursery/pre-school	8.3	8.0	10.9	7.2
Kindergarten/grade school	1.0	0.6	2.7	—
Child cares for self	0.3	0.2	0.7	—
Mother cares for child[2]	8.9	10.2	2.0	5.2
Total percent	100.0	100.0	100.0	100.0
Total number of children (in thousands)	9,124	7,543	1,311	874

[1]Persons of Hispanic origin may be of any race.

[2]Includes women working for wages either at home or away from home.

Source: U.S. Bureau of the Census, *Who's Minding the Kids?* July 1990, Table 2.

Table 4-1

In 1987, nearly two-thirds of all working mothers with children under age five had their children cared for in a home, either their own or, more commonly, someone else's. Hispanic mothers were the most likely to depend primarily on home care, and the least likely to use organized facilities such as group day care centers or nursery schools. While more than one-third (37 percent) of working mothers overall relied on relatives to watch their children while they worked, the percentages were much higher for black and Hispanic mothers (45 percent and 43 percent, respectively) than for white mothers (35 percent). Grandparents were the relatives black mothers depended upon most for child care—more than one in five in 1987.

Table 4-2

Mothers working full time were considerably less likely than those with part-time jobs to have their children cared for in their own homes in 1987. Both full-time working married mothers and part-time working single mothers were significantly more likely than married mothers with part-time jobs to use organized child care facilities.

Table 4-2 • PRIMARY CHILD CARE ARRANGEMENTS OF WORKING MOTHERS FOR CHILDREN UNDER AGE 5 BY MARITAL STATUS AND FULL- AND PART-TIME EMPLOYMENT, 1987 (percent distribution)

Marital Status of Mother and Child Care Type	Employment Status of Mother	
	Part-Time	Full-Time
Married, husband present		
Care in child's home	38.9	24.2
Care in another home	30.6	38.6
Organized child care facility	16.5	28.1
Kindergarten/grade school	0.3	1.3
Mother cares for child[1]	13.7	7.8
Child cares for self	—	0.1
Total percent	100.0	100.0
Total number of children (in thousands)	8,717	13,666
All other marital statuses[2]		
Care in child's home	41.2	24.3
Care in another home	27.7	40.1
Organized child care facility	24.8	29.7
Kindergarten/grade school	0.6	1.7
Mother cares for child[1]	5.8	2.5
Child cares for self	—	1.6
Total percent	100.0	100.0
Total number of children (in thousands)	1,505	4,954

[1]Includes women working for wages either at home or away from home.

[2]All other marital statuses include married/spouse absent, widowed, divorced, and never-married women.

Source: U.S. Bureau of the Census, *Child Care Arrangements of Working Mothers*, June 1982, Table A and *Who's Minding the Kids?* July 1990, Table 1.

Table 4-3 • CHILD CARE EXPENDITURES OF WORKING WOMEN BY INCOME LEVEL AND POVERTY STATUS, 1987

	Number of Women Paying for Child Care (in thousands)	Mean Monthly Child Care Expenses[1] (in dollars)	Mean Monthly Family Income (in dollars)	Percent of Income Spent on Child Care
Monthly family income				
Less than $1,250	739	170	821	20.7
$1,250–$2,499	1,918	173	1,894	9.2
$2,500–$3,749	1,777	204	3,078	6.6
$3,750 and over	1,735	274	5,655	4.9
Below poverty level	346	153	610	25.0
Near poverty level[2]	228	167	1,025	16.3
Not poor[3]	5,595	215	3,409	6.3

[1]Calculated by multiplying mean weekly child care expenditures by 52 and then dividing by 12.

[2]From 100 percent to 125 percent of poverty level.

[3]125 percent and over poverty level.

Source: U.S. Bureau of the Census, *Who's Minding the Kids?* July 1990, Table 7, Part B.

Table 4-3

Many working mothers rely on unpaid caregivers to look after their children. However, 6.2 million working mothers paid for child care in 1987. Of these, nearly three-quarters of a million had family incomes of less than $1,250 a month ($15,000 a year). Child care expenses took an enormous bite out of the budgets of these low-income families—more than 20 percent. For those below the poverty line, 25 percent of family income was spent on child care. Compared to their low-income counterparts, the most prosperous families ($3,750 or more a month, or $45,000 or more a year) spent, on average, many more dollars on child care; however, as a proportion of total family income, these expenditures were relatively negligible—five percent.

Table 4-4 • CHILD SUPPORT AWARDS BY RACE AND HISPANIC ORIGIN, 1987

	All Races	White	Black	Hispanic Origin[1]
Percent awarded child support	59.0	68.8	35.6	42.4
Total number of women eligible[2] for child support (in thousands)	9,415	6,467	2,686	937

[1]Persons of Hispanic origin may be of any race.

[2]Women eligible for child support had children under the age of 21 whose fathers were not present in the home as of spring 1988.

Source: U.S. Bureau of the Census, *Child Support and Alimony: 1987*, June 1990, Table 1.

Table 4-4

Almost three-fifths of women who were eligible (mothers with children under the age of 21 with no father present) were awarded some form of child support in 1987. White women, however, were much more likely to be awarded child support than either black or Hispanic women, a reflection, perhaps, of the disparate access women have to the resources required to successfully pursue child support awards.

Table 4-5 • RECEIPT OF CHILD SUPPORT AWARDS BY TYPE OF PAYMENT, 1978 AND 1987 (percent distribution)

Payment Status	1978	1987
Received full award amount	48.9	51.3
Received partial amount	22.8	24.9
Did not receive payments	28.3	23.9
Total percent	100.0	100.0
Total number who should have received payments (in thousands)	3,424	4,829

Source: U.S. Bureau of the Census, *Child Support and Alimony: 1987*, June 1990, Table B.

Table 4-5

A chronic problem for many mothers is not receiving the full child support they were awarded. There was some improvement between 1978 and 1987, although it was by no means dramatic. In 1987, of all women who were supposed to receive payments, the proportion getting no payments at all was down by four percentage points from 1978, and the proportion getting full and partial payments was up slightly. It should be noted that while the number of mothers awarded child support increased by approximately 1.4 million (41 percent) over the period, and nonrecipients accounted for a smaller proportion of the total in 1987, there were actually about 185,000 more women who did not receive money in that year than in 1978.

Table 4-6 • POVERTY STATUS OF WOMEN ELIGIBLE FOR
CHILD SUPPORT[1] BY RACE AND HISPANIC ORIGIN, 1987

	All Races	White	Black	Hispanic Origin[2]
Number of women awarded child support (in thousands)	5,554	4,448	956	397
Percent living in poverty	25.4	19.8	51.3	45.3
Number of women *not* awarded child support (in thousands)	3,861	2,020	1,730	540
Percent living in poverty	46.1	38.6	54.4	54.3

[1]Women eligible for child support had children under the age of 21 whose fathers were not present in the home as of spring 1988.

[2]Persons of Hispanic origin may be of any race.

Source: U.S. Bureau of the Census, *Child Support and Alimony: 1987*, June 1990, Table 1.

Table 4-6

While too many female-headed families who are awarded child support live in poverty, it is an important safeguard for women with children. Of the 5.6 million women awarded child support in 1987, 25 percent lived below the poverty level, compared to 46 percent of mothers who were not awarded child support.

Section 5: Education

Historically, women have not attained the same levels of education as men, particularly at the postsecondary level. During the past 20 years, however, women's educational achievements have been converging with, and in some cases surpassing, those of men.

Encouraging Trends

- As of 1989, more than three-quarters of all adults had completed high school, an all-time record (see Table 5–1).

- The undergraduate college student population has become increasingly diverse as more women and ethnic minorities have enrolled in higher education. In 1988, nearly one out of every five students was a person of color; over half of all students were female (see Figures 5–3 and 5–4 and Table 5–4).[1]

- In 1989, the majority of degrees at all levels except doctorates were earned by women (see Figure 5–7).

- The proportion of undergraduate science and engineering degrees earned by women has increased dramatically since 1960. For example, in 1989, one-half of all biological science degrees were earned by females—nearly double the percentage in 1970 (see Table 5–6).

[1]Unlike the Census Bureau, the Department of Education considers Hispanic a racial category which can be added with whites, blacks, and other races in order to calculate the total population.

- At least one out of every five female college graduates in 1988 majored in business/management. Although women tended to concentrate in traditional majors (e.g., the social sciences, the arts, and education), there were interesting variations by race. For instance, Asian/Pacific Islander women were the most likely to major in engineering and the biological sciences and black women to major in protective services (see Table 5–7).

- The number of females graduating from the U.S. military academies increased during the 1980s. For example, in 1991, approximately 14 percent of the graduating class of the U.S. Air Force Academy were women, a 37 percent increase since 1980 (see Table 5–8).

- In 1989, more than one-quarter of all dentistry degrees, one-third of all medical degrees, one-half of all veterinary degrees, and two-fifths of all law degrees were awarded to women. Hispanic and Asian/Pacific Islander females, in particular, made notable gains in dentistry (see Figure 5–8 and Table 5–5).

- In just 12 years (from 1975 to 1987), the number of colleges and universities headed by women increased 100 percent. The proportion of institutions with women presidents nearly doubled during this time period, from five percent to nine percent (see Table 5–14).

Discouraging Trends

- While the percentage of female high school graduates who completed four years of college increased from 16 percent to 25 percent between 1966 and 1987, the percentage of black female high school graduates completing college rose to 18 percent in 1976 but then fell to 14 percent by 1987 (see Table 5–3).

- Although women have made substantial progress in obtaining degrees in traditionally male strongholds, they still constitute a minority in terms of degrees earned in many of these fields. For example, in 1989 women earned only 15 percent of all bachelor's degrees awarded in engineering (see Table 5–6).

- Of all first professional degrees (dental, medical, and law) awarded to females, the proportion earned by black women declined from 1976 and 1989 in all three areas (see Table 5–5).

- In 1910, 20 percent of college faculty were female. In 1985, women constituted 28 percent of college faculty—an increase of only eight percentage points over a period of 75 years (see Table 5–9).

- In 1985, women of color accounted for just three percent of all college faculty (see Table 5–10).

- Sixty percent of female faculty in 1985, compared to 36 percent of male faculty, clustered in the academic ranks of assistant professor, instructor, and lecturer, positions with little job security and low pay (see Table 5–9).

- Women continue to be underrepresented in upper management in higher education. In 1989, only one out of every 10 chief executive officers of a college or university was female. Women of color made up less than two percent of these high-level administrators (see Table 5–13).

Table 5-1 • YEARS OF SCHOOL COMPLETED BY PERSONS AGE 25 AND OVER BY SEX, RACE, AND HISPANIC ORIGIN, 1989 (percent distribution)

Years of School	All Races		White		Black		Hispanic Origin[1]	
	Women	Men	Women	Men	Women	Men	Women	Men
Elementary 0–8 years	11.5	11.8	10.6	10.9	16.3	18.6	34.4	34.4
High school 1–3 years	11.9	11.0	11.2	10.4	18.7	17.2	14.9	14.6
High school 4 years	41.3	35.4	42.3	35.7	36.7	36.3	29.6	26.1
College 1–3 years	17.2	17.4	17.4	17.6	16.5	16.2	12.4	13.9
College 4 years or more	18.1	24.5	18.5	25.4	11.9	11.7	8.8	11.0
Total percent	100.0	100.0	100.0	100.0	100.0	100.0	100.0	100.0
Total number (in thousands)	80,930	73,225	69,325	63,578	9,080	7,315	5,310	5,128

[1]Persons of Hispanic origin may be of any race.

Source: U.S. Bureau of the Census, unpublished data, 1989.

Table 5-2 • YEARS OF SCHOOL COMPLETED BY WHITE, BLACK, AND HISPANIC-ORIGIN WOMEN, 1970, 1980, AND 1989 (percent distribution)

Years of School	1970			1980			1989		
	White	Black	Hispanic Origin[1]	White	Black	Hispanic Origin[1]	White	Black	Hispanic Origin[1]
Elementary 0–8 years	25.5	41.1	50.7	16.5	25.6	41.3	10.6	16.3	34.3
High school 1–3 years	19.4	26.4	18.3	15.5	22.9	16.1	11.2	18.7	14.9
High school 4 years	35.5	22.2	22.3	39.1	30.0	26.0	42.3	36.7	29.6
College 1–3 years	11.1	5.8	5.4	15.6	13.2	10.6	17.4	16.4	12.4
College 4 years or more	8.4	4.6	3.2	13.3	8.3	6.0	18.5	11.9	8.8
Total percent	100.0	100.0	100.0	100.0	100.0	100.0	100.0	100.0	100.0
Total number (in thousands)	51,718	5,661	2,050	60,349	7,300	3,493	69,325	9,080	5,310

[1]Persons of Hispanic origin may be of any race.

Source: U.S. Bureau of the Census, unpublished data, 1989 and *Statistical Abstract of the United States 1990*, January 1990, Table 216.

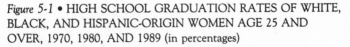

Figure 5-1 • HIGH SCHOOL GRADUATION RATES OF WHITE, BLACK, AND HISPANIC-ORIGIN WOMEN AGE 25 AND OVER, 1970, 1980, AND 1989 (in percentages)

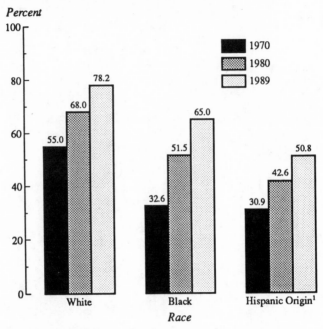

[1]Persons of Hispanic origin may be of any race.

Source: U.S. Bureau of the Census, unpublished data, 1989 and *Statistical Abstract of the United States 1990*, January 1990, Table 216.

Tables 5-1 and 5-2 and Figure 5-1

Obtaining at least a high school diploma has become the norm for most Americans. By 1989, more than three out of four adults age 25 and older had completed four years of high school. (These figures included individuals who finished but did not go beyond high school, those who completed some college course work, and those with bachelor's degrees or higher). Since 1970, increasing proportions of women of all races have completed high school, although white women were more likely than either black or Hispanic women to have done so as of 1989.

Table 5.3 • HIGH SCHOOL GRADUATES COMPLETING AT LEAST 4 YEARS OF COLLEGE BY SEX, RACE, AND HISPANIC ORIGIN, 1966, 1976, AND 1987 (in percentages)

Race	1966		1976		1987	
	Women	*Men*	*Women*	*Men*	*Women*	*Men*
All races	15.9	23.7	24.1	32.0	25.2	26.1
White	15.8	24.4	24.3	32.9	26.2	27.2
Black	13.6	11.0	18.4	16.5	13.6	13.7
Hispanic origin[1]	—	—	8.2	17.9	13.7	15.7

[1]Persons of Hispanic origin may be of any race.

Source: National Center for Education Statistics, *The Condition of Education 1990, Volume 2, Postsecondary Education,* Indicator 2:7.

Table 5-3

As of 1987, more than one-quarter of all high school grad-uates had completed four years of college. The proportion of female high school graduates who obtained college degrees increased steadily, from 16 percent in 1966 to 25 percent in 1987. Among males, however, this proportion peaked in 1976 at 32 percent and then dropped to 26 percent in 1987. These data indicate a disturbing trend—after rising to a re-cord high in 1976, the proportion of black high school gradu-ates of both sexes continuing on to college declined.

Figure 5-2 • RECIPIENTS OF CERTAIN FEDERAL FINANCIAL AID AS A PERCENTAGE OF ALL FIRST-YEAR COLLEGE STUDENTS, SELECTED YEARS, 1979–1989

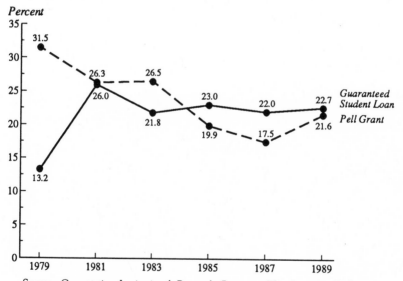

Source: Cooperative Institutional Research Program, *The American Freshman: Twenty Year Trends,* January 1987; *The American Freshman 1987,* December 1987; and *The American Freshman 1989,* December 1989.

Figure 5-2

In 1989, compared to 10 years earlier, higher proportions of students graduated with debts, the result of undertaking loans to help finance their educations. In 1979, students were more than twice as likely to have grants, which do not require repayment, instead of loans to help offset college costs, 32 percent versus 13 percent. By 1989, the proportion with grants had decreased to 22 percent and the proportion with loans increased to 23 percent. This trend of decreased availability of grants (offset by increased borrowing by college students) may partially explain the declining proportions of black high school graduates pursuing college (highlighted in Table 5–3). Since (as shown in Sections 7 and 8) black families tend to have fewer resources than whites families, black college students may be unwilling to incur large debts to attend college.

Figure 5-3 • TOTAL COLLEGE ENROLLMENT BY SEX OF
STUDENT, SELECTED YEARS, 1959/60 to 1988

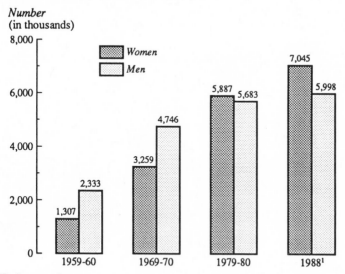

¹Preliminary data.

Source: National Center for Education Statistics, *Digest of Education Statistics 1990,*
February 1991, Tables 156 and 157.

Figure 5-3

Since 1959, the number of females enrolled in colleges
and universities has increased dramatically, and in 1988,
more women were enrolled in college than men.

Figure 5-4 • TOTAL UNDERGRADUATE COLLEGE
ENROLLMENT BY SEX AND RACE OF STUDENT, 1976 AND
1988 (percent distribution)

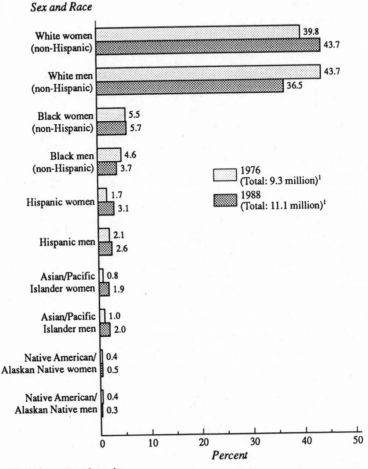

Sex and Race

White women (non-Hispanic): 39.8 (1976), 43.7 (1988)
White men (non-Hispanic): 43.7 (1976), 36.5 (1988)
Black women (non-Hispanic): 5.5 (1976), 5.7 (1988)
Black men (non-Hispanic): 4.6 (1976), 3.7 (1988)
Hispanic women: 1.7 (1976), 3.1 (1988)
Hispanic men: 2.1 (1976), 2.6 (1988)
Asian/Pacific Islander women: 0.8 (1976), 1.9 (1988)
Asian/Pacific Islander men: 1.0 (1976), 2.0 (1988)
Native American/Alaskan Native women: 0.4 (1976), 0.5 (1988)
Native American/Alaskan Native men: 0.4 (1976), 0.3 (1988)

1976 (Total: 9.3 million)[1]
1988 (Total: 11.1 million)[1]

Percent

[1]Excludes nonresident aliens.

Source: National Center for Education Statistics, *Digest of Education Statistics 1990,*
February 1991, Table 191.

Table 5-4 • FEMALE/MALE UNDERGRADUATE COLLEGE ENROLLMENT BY RACE OF STUDENT, 1976 AND 1988 (percent distribution)

| | Female | | Male | |
Race	1976	1988[1]	1976	1988[1]
White (non-Hispanic)	82.4	79.7	84.4	80.9
Black (non-Hispanic)	11.5	10.4	9.0	8.2
Hispanic	3.6	5.7	4.0	5.7
Asian/Pacific Islander	1.8	3.5	1.9	4.5
Native American/Alaskan Native	0.8	0.8	0.7	0.7
Total percent	100.0	100.0	100.0	100.0
Total number (in thousands)[2]	4,475	6,089	4,801	5,010

[1]Preliminary data.

[2]Excludes nonresident aliens.

Source: National Center for Education Statistics, *Digest of Education Statistics 1990*, February 1991, Table 191.

Figure 5-4 and Table 5-4

The undergraduate college student population increased in diversity from 1976 to 1988 as more women and ethnic minorities enrolled in colleges and universities. In 1988, one out of every five students was of minority background and over half of all students were female. The total number of women of all races enrolling in college rose during this time period, with Asian/Pacific Islander and Hispanic women experiencing the greatest increases.

Figure 5-5 • FEMALE COLLEGE ENROLLMENT BY AGE OF
STUDENT, 1970 AND 1990 (percent distribution)

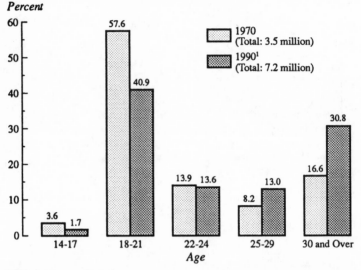

[1]1990 data are projections.

Source: National Center for Education Statistics, *Digest of Education Statistics 1989*,
December 1989, Table 150 and *Digest of Education Statistics 1990*, February 1991,
Table 159.

Figure 5-5

During the past 20 years, the female student population
(graduate as well as undergraduate) has gotten older. In 1990,
women enrolling in college were less likely than their counterparts in 1970 to be under the age of 22 and more likely to be
over 30. Part of this increase can be attributed to increasing
numbers of women over 30 enrolling in graduate and professional schools.

Figure 5-6 • PART-TIME STUDENTS AS A PERCENT OF
ENROLLED COLLEGE UNDERGRADUATES BY SEX, 1970,
1980, AND 1988

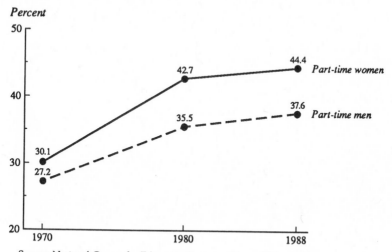

Percent

Source: National Center for Education Statistics, *Digest of Education Statistics 1990,*
February 1991, Table 171.

Figure 5-6

Since 1970, the percentage of undergraduates enrolled in
college part time has increased, particularly among females. In
1988, 44 percent of all women and 38 percent of all men
enrolled in college were there on a part-time basis. To offset
the rising costs of college and the decreasing likelihood of
receiving grants to cover these costs (see Figure 5–2), more
students may have jobs than was the case in the 1970's.

Figure 5-7 • POSTSECONDARY DEGREE ATTAINMENT BY
SEX OF STUDENT, SELECTED YEARS, 1959/60 to 1988/89

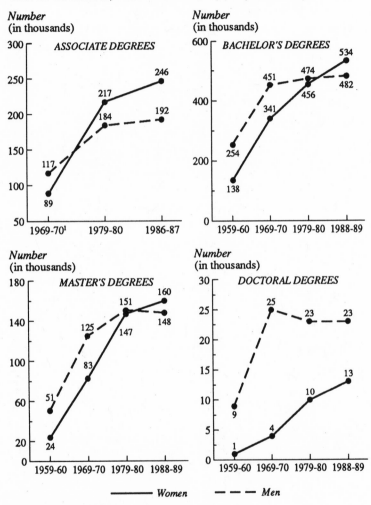

─────── *Women*   ─ ─ ─ *Men*

[1]Earliest data available.

Source: National Center for Education Statistics, unpublished data, 1989 and *Digest of Education Statistics 1990,* February 1991, Table 156.

Figure 5-7

At all levels except doctoral, women surpassed men in postsecondary degree attainment. In 1989, females earned 57 percent of all associate degrees, 53 percent of all bachelor's degrees, and 52 percent of all master's degrees. They lagged behind males only at the highest degree level—earning 36 percent of all doctorates awarded in 1989.

Figure 5-8 • FIRST PROFESSIONAL DEGREE ATTAINMENT BY MAJOR FIELD AND SEX OF STUDENT, 1989[1]

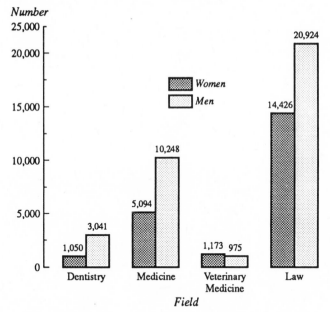

[1]Excludes nonresident aliens.

Source: National Center for Education Statistics, unpublished data, 1989.

Table 5-5 • FIRST PROFESSIONAL DEGREE ATTAINMENT OF WOMEN STUDENTS BY RACE, 1976/77 AND 1988/89

Race	Dentistry		Medicine		Law	
	1976–77	1988–89	1976–77	1988–89	1976–77	1988–89
White (non-Hispanic)	82.8	72.9	86.7	79.8	90.5	87.8
Black (non-Hispanic)	12.0	7.4	9.5	7.8	5.8	5.7
Hispanic	1.6	6.4	1.7	3.8	1.6	3.5
Asian/Pacific Islander	3.0	12.8	1.9	8.0	1.7	2.5
Native American/Alaskan Native	0.5	0.6	0.2	0.6	0.4	0.5
Total percent	100.0	100.0	100.0	100.0	100.0	100.0
Total number of degrees awarded to women	367	1,050	2,543	5,094	7,630	14,426
Percent of all degrees awarded to women	7.3	25.7	19.1	33.2	22.5	40.8

Source: U.S. Department of Health, Education and Welfare, Office for Civil Rights, *Data on Earned Degrees Conferred by Institutions of Higher Education by Race, Ethnicity and Sex, Academic Year 1976–1977* and National Center for Education Statistics, unpublished data, 1989.

Figure 5-8 and Table 5-5

The number of females earning professional degrees is at an all-time high. In 1989, women earned 26 percent of all dentistry degrees, 33 percent of all medical degrees, 55 percent of all veterinary degrees, and 41 percent of all law degrees. While the proportion of dental, medical, and law degrees earned by women increased substantially from 1976 to 1989, this varied by race. Hispanic and Asian/Pacific Islander women made substantial gains, particularly in dentistry; the proportion of dental degrees awarded to these women quadrupled.

Table 5-6 • UNDERGRADUATE DEGREE ATTAINMENT IN VARIOUS FIELDS BY SEX OF STUDENT, SELECTED YEARS, 1959/60 TO 1988/89 (in percentages)

Field	1959–60		1969–70		1979–80		1988–89	
	Women	Men	Women	Men	Women	Men	Women	Men
Business/management	7.4	92.6	8.7	91.3	33.7	66.3	46.7	53.3
Computer sciences[1]	—	—	13.6	86.4	30.2	69.8	30.7	69.3
Education	71.1	28.9	75.0	25.0	73.8	26.2	77.7	22.3
English/literature[2]	62.3	33.7	66.9	33.1	66.1	33.9	66.8	33.2
Engineering	0.4	99.6	0.8	99.2	9.3	90.7	15.2	84.8
Health professions[1]	—	—	77.1	22.9	82.2	17.8	84.9	15.1
Biological sciences	25.2	74.8	27.8	72.2	42.1	57.9	50.2	49.8
Mathematics	27.2	72.8	37.4	62.6	42.3	57.7	46.0	54.0
Physical sciences	12.5	87.5	13.6	86.4	23.7	76.3	29.7	70.3
Psychology	40.8	59.2	43.3	56.7	63.3	36.7	70.8	29.2
Social sciences[1]	—	—	36.8	63.2	43.6	56.4	44.4	55.6
Visual/performing arts[1]	—	—	59.7	40.3	63.2	36.8	61.5	38.5

[1]Data are for 1970–71 rather than 1969–70.

[2]Data are for 1986–87 rather than 1988–89.

Source: National Center for Education Statistics, unpublished data, 1989 and *Digest of Education Statistics 1990*, February 1991, Tables 243, 245, 246, 247, 249, 252, 253, 255, 256, 258, 260, and 262.

Table 5-6

Since 1959 females have made significant inroads into traditionally male-dominated fields, earning bachelor's degrees in majors ranging from business to the sciences to engineering. In 1989, of the nontraditional fields shown in Table 5–6, the biological sciences had the highest proportion of degrees earned by women (50 percent) and engineering the lowest (15 percent). While 15 percent is hardly parity, it is a marked improvement over 1959 when women earned less than one percent of all engineering degrees. Women also made substantial gains in business and mathematics, earning 47 and 46 percent, respectively, of all degrees awarded in these majors in 1989.

Table 5-7 • UNDERGRADUATE DEGREE ATTAINMENT OF WOMEN STUDENTS BY SELECTED FIELDS AND RACE, 1988/89 (percent distribution)

Field	White Non-Hispanic	Black Non-Hispanic	Hispanic	Asian/ Pacific Islander	Native American/ Alaskan Native
Arts/humanities	14.8	9.7	16.9	12.7	14.4
Biological sciences	3.2	3.5	3.8	7.9	3.4
Business/management	21.0	25.3	22.1	23.4	20.4
Education	15.3	8.7	10.8	4.6	16.1
Engineering	1.6	1.9	2.1	6.2	1.6
Physical sciences	2.2	2.1	1.4	4.3	1.4
Professional[1]	13.1	12.6	9.6	10.7	11.2
Protective services	0.9	3.0	1.8	0.3	1.7
Social sciences	19.2	22.6	23.9	20.7	22.7
Other[2]	8.6	10.7	7.6	9.3	7.1
Total percent	100.0	100.0	100.0	100.0	100.0
Total number	451,530	35,651	15,880	18,682	2,278

[1]Includes architecture, health care, home economics, and library sciences.

[2]Includes agriculture, communications, computer sciences, military sciences, and parks and recreation.

Source: National Center for Education Statistics, unpublished data, 1990.

Table 5-7

In 1989, 20 percent of female college students earned bachelor's degrees in business, while virtually another 20 percent obtained degrees in the social sciences. While women undergraduates tend to concentrate in the traditional female subjects (the arts and humanities, education, and the social sciences), there were some interesting variations by race in nontraditional fields. For example, Asian/Pacific Islander women were the most likely to major in engineering and the biological and physical sciences, and black women the most likely to major in protective services.

Table 5-8 • WOMEN GRADUATES OF THE U.S. SERVICE ACADEMIES, 1980 AND 1991

Service Academy	1980		1991[1]	
	Number of Women Graduates	Percentage of Women Graduates	Number of Women Graduates	Percentage of Women Graduates
Air Force	97	10.8	133	13.6
Coast Guard	14	9.2	21	10.2
Military (West Point)	62	6.4	94	9.7
Naval	55	5.8	82	8.6

[1]Estimates are based on projected graduates as of May 16, 1991.

Source: Unpublished data provided by each service academy, November 1990.

Table 5-8

During the 1980s, increasing numbers of women graduated from the U.S. service academies. West Point had the largest increase (52 percent), although females still constituted just 10 percent of the 1991 graduating class. The Air Force Academy had the highest percentage of women graduates (14 percent) in 1991, and the Naval Academy the lowest (nine percent).

Tables 5-9, 5-10, and 5-11

Although the majority of all college students are female and 20 percent are nonwhite, Tables 5–9 and 5–10 show that most faculty members were white males. In 1985, women constituted only 28 percent, and women of color only three percent, of college faculty (Table 5–10). Since 1910 the female proportion of college faculty has increased by only eight percentage points. In addition, women academics in 1985 tended to be relegated to the lower and less secure rungs of the faculty ladder. Only 32 percent of female versus 59 percent of male faculty enjoyed the job security and higher pay associated with full and associate professorial ranks (see Table 5–9). Women academics were twice as likely as men to be instructors and lecturers (29 percent versus 14 percent), positions that tend to be secured by contracts and renewed on a yearly basis, instead of tenured.

This pattern of male faculty at the higher ranks is more pronounced at four-year institutions, which tend to have greater resources than two-year institutions.

Table 5-9 • COLLEGE FACULTY BY SEX AND ACADEMIC
RANK, FALL 1985 (percent distribution)

Academic Rank	Women	Men	Percent Women Within Rank
Full professor	11.7	34.0	11.6
Associate professor	20.3	25.3	23.3
Assistant professor	31.1	21.3	35.8
Instructor	25.1	12.9	42.7
Lecturer	3.6	1.5	47.8
Other faculty	8.2	5.0	38.4
Total percent	100.0	100.0	
Total number	128,063	336,009	

Source: National Center for Education Statistics, *Digest of Education Statistics 1990*,
February 1991, Table 207.

Table 5-10 • FEMALE COLLEGE FACULTY BY RACE AND ACADEMIC RANK, FALL 1985 (percent distribution)

Academic Rank	White (Non-Hispanic)	Black (Non-Hispanic)	Hispanic	Asian/Pacific Islander	Native American/ Alaskan Native	All Faculty (Both Sexes)
Full professor	12.0	9.1	10.6	11.2	10.3	27.8
Associate professor	20.5	18.3	19.1	19.3	16.7	23.9
Assistant professor	30.9	33.9	27.8	34.9	22.9	23.9
Instructor	24.9	28.1	28.0	19.9	38.1	16.2
Lecturer	3.6	3.7	5.7	4.2	5.3	2.1
Other faculty	8.2	6.8	8.8	10.6	6.7	5.8
Total percent	100.0	100.0	100.0	100.0	100.0	100.0
Total number	113,083	8,771	2,344	3,524	341	464,072

Source: National Center for Education Statistics, *Digest of Education Statistics 1990*, February 1991, Table 207.

Table 5-11 • COLLEGE FACULTY BY SEX, ACADEMIC RANK, AND INSTITUTIONAL TYPE, 1984 (percent distribution)

Academic Rank	Two-Year Institutions		Four-Year Institutions	
	Women	Men	Women	Men
Full professor	14.0	25.8	16.2	45.3
Associate professor	19.1	19.3	23.9	27.3
Assistant professor	15.1	8.2	35.8	19.7
Instructor	31.4	27.6	16.0	4.8
Lecturer	1.5	0.6	5.2	2.1
Other faculty	18.9	18.5	2.9	0.8
Total percent	100.0	100.0	100.0	100.0

Source: American Council on Education, *1989–90 Fact Book on Higher Education,* 1989, Table 109.

Table 5-12 • FEMALE COLLEGE FACULTY BY SELECTED
FIELD, 1990 (in percentages)

Field	Percent Female
Physics	3.2
Agriculture and forestry	4.2
Natural science	6.4
Engineering	6.6
Political science	18.0
Law	19.0
Theology	22.8
Economics	22.8
Earth, environment, and marine science	23.5
Trade and industrial	23.7
History	24.3
Computer science	25.0
Medical science	25.3
Chemistry	25.5
Mathematical science	30.5
Business, commerce, and marketing	35.5
Psychology	35.7
Biological science	37.0
Sociology	37.6
Art, drama, and music	37.8
Education	45.7
English	52.8
Foreign language	59.6
Health specialties	70.4
Social work	73.1
Home economics	99.9

Source: U.S. Bureau of Labor Statistics, unpublished data, 1990.

Table 5-12

Women faculty, like female college students, were generally underrepresented in nontraditional fields. In 1990, women constituted less than 10 percent of the faculty teaching in each of the following disciplines: physics, agriculture and forestry, natural science, and engineering. Further, female academics made up at least 70 percent of the faculty in the traditionally female fields of health professions, social work, and home economics.

Figure 5-9 • AVERAGE COLLEGE FACULTY SALARY BY SEX AND ACADEMIC RANK, 1990/91

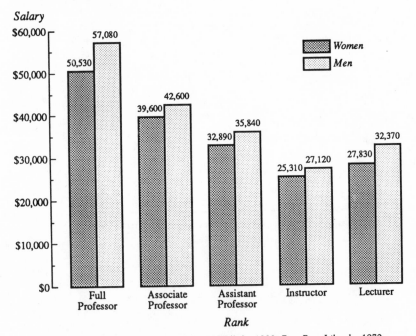

Source: "The Future of Academic Salaries: Will the 1990s Be a Bust Like the 1970s or a Boom Like the 1980s?" *Academe*, March-April 1991, Vol. 77, No. 2.

Figure 5-9

As in other occupations, female academics earn less than their male counterparts, regardless of rank. In 1991, at the highest academic rank—that of full professor—females earned 89 percent of the salaries of their male counterparts. This gap closed, albeit slightly, at the lower academic ranks. At associate professor and instructor positions, women earned 93 percent of men's salaries, and at the assistant professor level, women earned 92 percent. At the lowest rank, that of lecturer, women's salaries dropped to 86 percent of men's salaries.

Table 5-13 • WOMEN COLLEGE ADMINISTRATORS, 1989 (in percentages)

Position	All Women	Women of Color
Chief executive officer	10	1.4
Chief academic officer	17	1.4
Chief business officer	10	0.6
Chief development officer	20	1.2
Chief student affairs officer	25	3.6

Source: American Council on Education, *Fact Book on Women in Higher Education 1990*, 1991, Tables 76 and 78.

Table 5-14 • WOMEN COLLEGE PRESIDENTS BY TYPE AND CONTROL[1] OF INSTITUTION, 1975, 1981, AND 1987

	All Institutions		Public Institutions		Private Institutions		Women's Colleges	
	Number	Percent[2]	Number	Percent[2]	Number	Percent[2]	Number	Percent[2]
1975 total	148	4.8	16	1.1	132	8.2	—	—
Four-year	103	5.4	5	0.9	98	7.2	—	—
Two-year	45	3.9	11	1.2	34	14.2	—	—
1981 total	231	7.0	72	4.8	159	8.9	80	—
Four-year	160	8.0	25	4.4	135	9.4	61	—
Two-year	71	5.5	47	5.0	24	7.0	19	—
1987 total	296	8.6	112	7.2	184	9.8	84	79.2
Four-year	195	9.3	39	6.6	156	10.4	71	82.6
Two-year	101	7.5	73	7.6	28	7.4	13	65.0

[1]Control refers to whether an institution is private or public.

[2]Institutions headed by women as a percentage of all institutions of the type indicated.

Source: American Council on Education, 1989–90 *Fact Book on Higher Education*, 1989, Table 117.

Tables 5-13 and 5-14

   In just 12 years (from 1975 to 1987), the number of colleges and universities headed by women increased 100 percent. Like women academics, however, female administrators
tend to be clustered at the lower levels of college management. As of 1989, women constituted only 10 percent of all
academic chief executive officers (CEOs) compared to 20 percent of all development officers, and 25 percent of all student
affairs officers. Women of color fared even worse—constitut-
ing less than two percent of all CEOs and chief development
officers, and less than four percent of all chief student affairs
officers.

   This pattern held across different institutional types (that
is, two- and four-year colleges as well as public and private
institutions) with women's colleges the notable exception. In
1987, nearly 80 percent of all women's colleges had female
presidents compared to seven percent of public and 10 percent of private institutions.

Section 6: Employment

During the past 25 years, the unprecedented numbers of women entering the paid labor force have significantly altered the profile of the U.S. workforce.

Notable Trends

- More females than ever before are working or looking for work—in 1990, 58 percent of all American women were in the labor force (see Table 6–1).

- Females are projected to comprise almost two-thirds of the net change in the size and composition of the U.S. workforce between 1988 and 2000 (see Figure 6–1).

- Married women are almost as likely as single women to be employed (see Figure 6–3).

- More than half of all married mothers with young children (under age six) were in the labor force in 1990 (see Figure 6–4).

- Of all mothers, divorced women are the most likely to work full time (see Table 6–8).

- In 1990, more than two-thirds of all employed females worked in just two service-sector industries—services and retail trade (see Figure 6–8).

Encouraging Trends

- In 1989, women accounted for 11 percent of military personnel on active duty—the Air Force had the highest percentage of women (14 percent) (see Table 6–15).

- The number of businesses owned by females soared between 1977 and 1987—30 percent of U.S. companies were owned by women in 1987 (see Table 6–16 and Figure 6–11).

Discouraging Trends

- Black and Hispanic females were much more likely than white females to be unemployed in 1990 (see Figure 6–5).

- In 1990, close to half (46 percent) of all women workers were employed in relatively low-paying service and administrative support occupations such as secretaries, waitresses, and health aides, and black females were more likely than white females to work in these occupations (see Figures 6–9 and 6–10 and Table 6–12).

- In spite of the inroads women have made into traditionally male occupations, most jobs tend to be gender segregated (see Table 6–13).

- Corporate boards of Fortune 500 companies continue to be the preserve of white males. A 1989 survey of 264 companies found that only one in eight of their board members was female (see Figure 6–12).

Table 6-1 • CIVILIAN LABOR FORCE PARTICIPATION RATES FOR PERSONS AGE 16 AND OVER BY SEX, RACE, AND HISPANIC ORIGIN, SELECTED YEARS, ACTUAL 1950–1990 AND PROJECTED 2000 (in percentages)

Year	Women				Men			
	All Races	White	Black	Hispanic Origin[1]	All Races	White	Black	Hispanic Origin[1]
1950	33.9	—	—	—	86.4	—	—	—
1960	37.7	36.5	—	—	83.3	83.4	—	—
1970	43.3	42.6	—	—	79.7	80.0	—	—
1980	51.5	51.2	53.1	47.4	77.4	78.2	70.3	81.4
1990	57.5	57.5	57.8	53.0	76.1	76.9	70.1	81.2
2000[2]	62.6	62.9	62.5	59.4	75.9	76.6	71.4	80.3

[1]Persons of Hispanic origin may be of any race.

[2]Using moderate growth projections.

Source: U.S. Bureau of Labor Statistics, *Handbook of Labor Statistics*, August 1989, Tables 4 and 5; "New Labor Force Projections, Spanning 1988 to 2000," *Monthly Labor Review*, November 1989, Table 4; and *Employment and Earnings*, January 1991, Tables 3 and 39.

Table 6-1

More women than ever before are working or looking for work. In 1990, the labor force participation rate for females was 57.5 percent, and since 1980 the labor force participation rate of white women has converged with that of black women. Labor force projections indicate that by the year 2000, female labor force participation will be 62.6 percent, almost double that of 1950 (33.9 percent). Interestingly, men's labor force participation rate declined from 86.4 percent to 76.1 percent from 1950 to 1990.

Table 6-2 • LABOR FORCE STATUS OF PERSONS OF HISPANIC ORIGIN AGE 16 AND OVER BY SEX AND COUNTRY OF ORIGIN, 1990 (percent distribution)

Employment Status	Total Hispanic Origin		Mexican		Puerto Rican		Cuban	
	Women	Men	Women	Men	Women	Men	Women	Men
Not in labor force	47.0	18.8	47.2	17.1	57.2	28.1	44.1	25.1
In labor force	53.0	81.2	52.8	82.9	42.7	71.9	55.9	74.9
Employed	48.6	74.8	48.2	76.3	38.9	65.1	51.7	69.6[1]
Unemployed	4.4	6.4	4.6	6.6	3.8	6.8	4.2	5.1[1]
Total percent	100.0	100.0	100.0	100.0	100.0	100.0	100.0	100.0
Total civilian population (in thousands)	7,210	7,087	4,248	4,494	866	680	433	414

[1]Percentages for "employed" and "unemployed" do not add up to total "in labor force" due to rounding error.

Source: U.S. Bureau of Labor Statistics, *Employment and Earnings,* January 1991, Table 40.

Table 6-2

In 1990, over half of Hispanic women in the United States were in the labor force, although their participation rate varied by country of origin. Of all Hispanic women, Cubans were the most likely (51.7 percent) and Puerto Ricans the least likely (38.9 percent) to be employed. The employment rate of Mexican women fell in between with 48.2 percent of these women working or looking for work.

Table 6-3 • FULL-TIME WORKERS AGE 16 AND OVER BY SEX AND RACE, 1990 (in percentages)

Workers	*Women*			*Men*		
	All Races	*White*	*Black*	*All Races*	*White*	*Black*
Full-time workers as a percentage of all workers	74.8	73.7	82.1	90.0	90.2	88.9
Total number employed (in thousands)	53,479	45,655	6,051	64,434	56,432	5,915

Source: U.S. Bureau of the Census, *Employment and Earnings*, January 1991, Table 7.

Table 6-3

Most U.S. workers of both sexes worked full time, although women (74.8 percent) were less likely to do so than men (90 percent) in 1990. Black women were more likely than white women to work full time, 82.1 percent versus 73.7 percent.

Figure 6-1 • PROJECTED NET CHANGE IN THE LABOR FORCE BY SEX AND RACE, 1988–2000[1] (percent distribution)

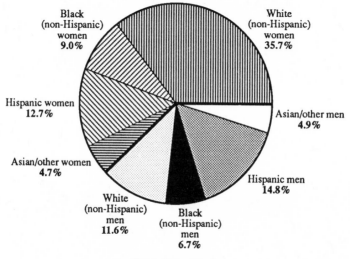

Black
(non-Hispanic)
women
9.0%

White
(non-Hispanic)
women
35.7%

Hispanic women
12.7%

Asian/other men
4.9%

Asian/other women
4.7%

Hispanic men
14.8%

White
(non-Hispanic)
men
11.6%

Black
(non-Hispanic)
men
6.7%

(Total: 18.1 million)

[1]Using moderate growth projections.

Source: U.S. Bureau of Labor Statistics, "New Labor Force Projections, Spanning 1988 to 2000," *Monthly Labor Review,* November 1989, Table 7.

Figure 6-1

Women are projected to account for almost two-thirds of the net change in the size and composition of the labor force between 1988 and the year 2000 (calculated by analyzing labor force entrants and leavers). Of these women, whites are projected to be the largest group, followed by Hispanics and then blacks.

Figure 6-2 • WORKERS AGE 16 AND OVER HOLDING MULTIPLE JOBS BY SEX, SELECTED YEARS, 1970–1989

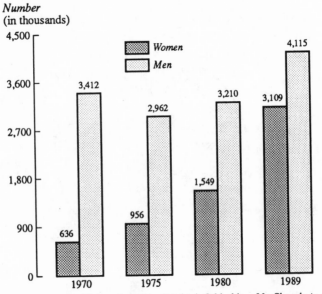

Source: U.S. Bureau of Labor Statistics, "Multiple Jobholding Up Sharply in the 1980's," *Monthly Labor Review,* July 1990, Table 1.

Table 6-4 • WORKERS AGE 16 AND OVER HOLDING MULTIPLE JOBS BY SEX, RACE, HISPANIC ORIGIN, AND REASON, 1989 (percent distribution)

Reason for Multiple Jobholding	Women				Men			
	All Races	White	Black	Hispanic Origin[1]	All Races	White	Black	Hispanic Origin[1]
To meet regular household expenses	40.5	39.3	58.0	50.6	31.7	30.9	41.2	42.7
To pay off debts	9.2	9.4	8.6	6.6	8.7	8.5	12.4	18.2
To save for the future	14.0	14.3	11.6	11.7	17.9	18.1	16.1	15.8
To get experience or build a business	13.1	13.6	5.9	15.9	15.9	16.2	8.1	5.4
Other reasons	23.1	23.5	15.9	15.2	25.8	26.3	22.1	17.8
Total percent	100.0	100.0	100.0	100.0	100.0	100.0	100.0	100.0
Total number (in thousands)	3,109	2,817	236	120	4,115	3,756	278	149

[1]Persons of Hispanic origin may be of any race.

Source: U.S. Bureau of Labor Statistics, "Multiple Jobholding Up Sharply in the 1980's," *Monthly Labor Review*, July 1990, Table 3.

Figure 6-2 and Table 6-4

Between 1970 and 1989, the number of women holding multiple jobs increased by almost 400 percent. In 1970, females accounted for only about one in six of all workers who held more than one paid job at a time. By 1989, the comparable ratio was more than two in five.

Women who worked more than one job in 1989 were more likely than men to do so because they needed the additional earnings to meet regular household expenses. However, there were noticeable variations by race. Among females, for example, whites were the least likely (39.3 percent) and blacks the most likely (58 percent) to hold more than one job in order to meet household expenses.

Table 6-5 • PERSONS AGES 16 TO 64 WITH WORK DISABILITIES BY SEX, SELECTED YEARS, 1982–1988 (in percentages)

	1982		1984		1986		1988	
	Women	Men	Women	Men	Women	Men	Women	Men
Percent with a work disability[1]	8.5	9.3	8.1	9.2	8.2	9.4	8.4	8.7
Percent of the work disabled in the labor force	23.7	41.5	24.4	40.3	25.2	38.0	27.5	35.7
Work-disabled unemployment rate	18.3	16.9	15.4	15.6	17.9	14.5	14.2	14.2

[1]Individuals are classified as work disabled if they have health problems or disabilities that prevent them from working or that limit the kind or amount of work they can do.

Source: U.S. Bureau of the Census, *Labor Force Characteristics of Persons with a Work Disability: 1981 to 1988*, July 1989, Tables B and C.

Table 6-6 • PERSONS AGES 16 TO 64 WITH WORK DISABILITIES
BY SEX, RACE, HISPANIC ORIGIN, AND DEGREE OF
DISABILITY, 1988 (in percentages)

Race and Sex	Total Population (in thousands)	Percent Work Disabled[1]	Percent Severely Work Disabled[2]
All races			
Women	79,826	8.4	4.6
Men	76,716	8.7	4.9
White			
Women	67,202	7.7	3.9
Men	65,790	8.2	4.3
Black			
Women	9,928	13.8	9.5
Men	8,372	13.7	10.3
Hispanic origin[3]			
Women	6,152	7.9	5.2
Men	6,210	8.4	5.9

[1]Individuals are classified as work disabled if they have health problems or disabilities that prevent them from working or that limit the kind or amount of work they can do.

[2]Severely work disabled persons are classified as such based on a number of criteria, such as the presence of a disability that prevents the performance of any type of work or being under age 65 and covered by Medicare or Supplemental Security Income.

[3]Persons of Hispanic origin may be of any race.

Source: U.S. Bureau of the Census, *Labor Force Characteristics of Persons with a Work Disability: 1981 to 1988,* July 1989, Table 1.

Tables 6-5 and 6-6

In 1988, eight percent of women and nine percent of men had work disabilities. Blacks of both sexes were more likely to be work disabled and severely work disabled than either whites or Hispanics. Interestingly, between 1982 and 1988, the labor force participation of work-disabled women increased while that of work-disabled men decreased.

Table 6-7 • CIVILIAN LABOR FORCE PARTICIPATION RATES OF WOMEN BY AGE, SELECTED YEARS, ACTUAL 1950–1990 AND PROJECTED 2000 (in percentages)

Age	1950	1960	1970	1980	1990	2000[1]
16–19	41.0	39.3	44.0	52.9	51.8	59.6
20–24	46.0	46.1	57.7	68.9	71.6	77.9
25–34	34.0	36.0	45.0	65.5	73.6	82.4
35–44	39.1	43.4	51.1	65.5	76.5	84.9
45–54	37.9	49.9	54.4	59.9	71.2	76.5
55–64	27.0	37.2	43.0	41.3	45.3	49.0
65 and over	9.7	10.8	9.7	8.1	8.7	7.6

[1]Using moderate growth projections.

Source: U.S. Bureau of Labor Statistics, *Handbook of Labor Statistics*, August 1989, Table 5; "New Labor Force Projections, Spanning 1988 to 2000," *Monthly Labor Review*, November 1989, Table 4; and *Employment and Earnings*, January 1991, Table 3.

Table 6-7

With the exception of women age 65 and older, the proportion of females of all age groups in the labor force has increased dramatically since 1950. The increase was particularly marked among women ages 25 to 44—in the last 40 years, labor force participation rates increased almost 40 percentage points among women 25 to 34 years old, and 37 percentage points among women 35 to 44 years old. Women's labor force participation is expected to increase into the next century for all age groups except, again, among women age 65 and older.

Figure 6-3 • CIVILIAN LABOR FORCE PARTICIPATION RATES OF WOMEN AGE 16 AND OVER BY MARITAL STATUS, SELECTED YEARS, 1960–1988

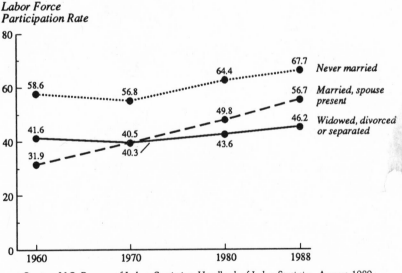

Source: U.S. Bureau of Labor Statistics, Handbook of Labor Statistics, August 1989, Table 6.

Figure 6-3

The labor force participation rate of married women has become more like that of never-married women over the last 30 years. In 1960, the percentage of never-married females who were working or looking for work was about 27 percentage points higher than for married females. By 1988, the difference had narrowed to just 11 percentage points. The labor force participation rate for widowed, divorced, or separated women remained relatively stable, increasing just five percentage points between 1960 and 1988.

Figure 6-4 • LABOR FORCE PARTICIPATION RATES OF MOTHERS WITH CHILDREN UNDER AGE 6, SELECTED YEARS, 1975–1990 (in percentages)

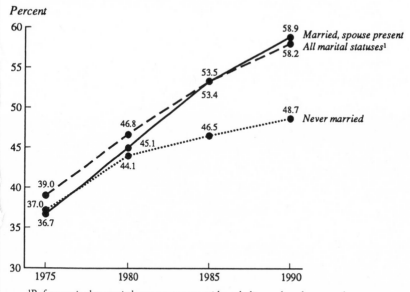

[1]Refers to single; married, spouse present; widowed; divorced; and separated women.

Source: U.S. Bureau of Labor Statistics, *Handbook of Labor Statistics*, August 1989, Tables 56 and 57 and unpublished BLS data, 1990.

Figure 6-4

The increased labor force participation of married women with young children (under age six) is one of the most notable trends of recent decades. In 1975, 36.7 percent of married mothers with children under six were in the workforce; by 1980, the comparable proportion was 45 percent, and by 1990, it was 58.9 percent. The rate for their never-married counterparts also increased between 1975 and 1990, but not nearly as steeply (by only 12 percentage points).

Table 6-8 • MOTHERS[1] EMPLOYED FULL TIME BY MARITAL STATUS AND AGE OF CHILDREN AS A PERCENTAGE OF ALL MOTHERS, 1990 (in percentages)

Marital Status	With Children Ages 14 to 17 (None Younger)	With Children Under Age 14	With Children Under Age 6
Married, spouse present	54.2	42.6	37.8
Married, spouse absent	55.6	46.4	39.3
Never married	55.3	34.5	28.9
Widowed	40.4	37.5	34.8
Divorced	76.7	62.7	53.8

[1]Mothers age 16 and over.

Source: U.S. Bureau of Labor Statistics, unpublished data, 1990.

Table 6-8

The older a mother's children, the more likely she was to be a full-time worker in 1990. This held true regardless of her marital status. Indeed, with the exception of widows, the majority of women whose youngest children were of high school age (between 14 and 18) worked full time. However, divorced mothers were the most likely to work full time regardless of the age of their children.

Table 6-9 • FULL- AND PART-TIME EMPLOYMENT OF MARRIED AND NEVER-MARRIED MOTHERS WITH YOUNG CHILDREN BY AGE OF CHILD, 1980 AND 1990 (in percentages)

Employment Status	All Marital Statuses		Married, Spouse Present		Never Married	
	1980	1990	1980	1990	1980	1990
Total number with children under age 3 (in thousands)	8,508	9,737	7,274	7,530	472	1,269
Percent employed full time	24.4	34.0	23.9	35.5	22.0	22.4
Percent employed part time	12.8	15.5	13.7	17.3	6.1	9.5
Total number with children under age 6 (in thousands)	13,970	16,139	11,590	12,314	703	1,906
Percent employed full time	28.6	37.7	26.8	37.8	25.5	28.9
Percent employed part time	13.5	16.4	14.5	18.3	5.7	9.7

Source: U.S. Bureau of Labor Statistics, *Handbook of Labor Statistics*, August 1989, Tables 56 and 57 and unpublished data, 1990.

Table 6-9

In 1990, employment—especially in full-time jobs—was much more common among married mothers with small children than had been the case a decade earlier. In 1980, less than one-fourth of married mothers who had toddlers (children under three) were full-time workers; in 1990, the percentage exceeded one-third. Among never-married mothers with toddlers, however, the proportion working full time did not grow significantly, although the proportion working part time increased slightly.

Figure 6-5 • UNEMPLOYMENT RATES FOR CIVILIAN WORKERS AGE 16 AND OVER BY SEX, RACE, AND HISPANIC ORIGIN, SELECTED YEARS, 1975–1990 (in percentages)

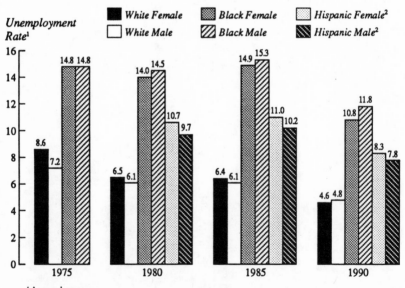

[1]Annual averages.

[2]Persons of Hispanic origin may be of any race. Data unavailable for 1975.

Source: U.S. Bureau of Labor Statistics, *Handbook of Labor Statistics*, August 1989, Table 28 and *Employment and Earnings*, January 1991, Table 39.

Figure 6-5

Overall, civilian unemployment rates were considerably lower in 1990 than they were in 1975. However, the rates for blacks and Hispanics of both sexes were consistently much higher than those of their white counterparts from 1980 to 1990. In most of the years shown, the unemployment rate for black males was higher than that for black females, while the rate for Hispanic women was higher than that for Hispanic men. In 1990, the unemployment rate for white females was slightly lower than for white males.

Figure 6-6 • UNEMPLOYED PERSONS AGE 20 AND OVER BY
SEX AND REASON FOR UNEMPLOYMENT, 1980 AND 1990
(percent distribution)

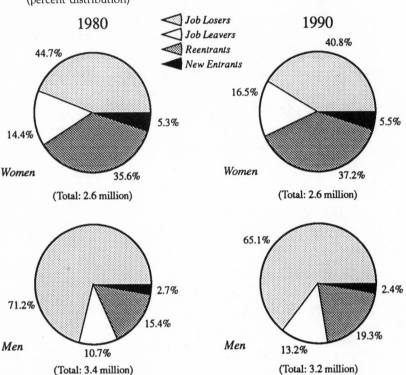

Source: U.S. Bureau of Labor Statistics, *Labor Force Statistics Derived from the Current
Population Survey*, BLS Bulletin 237, August 1988, Table B-22 and *Employment and
Earnings*, January 1991, Table 12.

Figure 6-6

In both 1980 and 1990, adult men (age 20 and over) were much more likely than adult women to be unemployed because they lost their jobs. In both years, larger proportions of unemployed females than of unemployed males were either looking for work after a period out of the labor force (reentrants) or had left their jobs voluntarily.

Table 6-10 • PERSONS NOT IN THE LABOR FORCE WHO WANT A JOB BY SEX, RACE, HISPANIC ORIGIN, AND REASON FOR NOT LOOKING, 1990 (percent distribution)

Reason for Not Looking	Women				Men			
	All Races	White	Black	Hispanic Origin[1]	All Races	White	Black	Hispanic Origin[1]
School attendance	20.5	19.0	24.8	17.8	35.1	33.4	37.3	32.6
Ill health/disability	13.0	13.3	12.3	9.5	23.1	24.3	21.7	25.1
Home responsibility	34.4	34.8	34.5	40.1	—	—	—	—
Think cannot get a job	13.9	13.6	14.3	18.8	18.7	17.5	21.0	21.4
Other reasons	18.1	19.4	14.2	13.8	23.1[2]	24.8[2]	20.0[2]	20.9[2]
Total percent	100.0	100.0	100.0	100.0	100.0	100.0	100.0	100.0
Total number (in thousands)	3,505	2,527	855	421	1,968	1,406	461	187

[1] Persons of Hispanic origin may be of any race.

[2] Includes a small number of men not looking for work because of "home responsibilities."

Source: U.S. Bureau of Labor Statistics, Employment and Earnings, January 1991, Table 36.

Table 6-10

In 1990, nearly twice as many women as men who wanted jobs were not working or looking for work. Females were most likely to cite home responsibilities while males most commonly gave school attendance as reasons for not looking for jobs. Interestingly, women were less likely than men to be out of the labor force because they thought they could not get a job. Men were more likely than women to be unemployed and not looking for work due to illness.

Figure 6-7 • WORKERS ON GOODS-PRODUCING AND SERVICE-PRODUCING NONFARM PAYROLLS BY SEX, SELECTED YEARS, 1960–1988

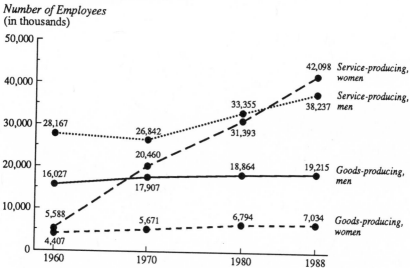

Source: U.S. Bureau of Labor Statistics, *Handbook of Labor Statistics,* August 1989, Tables 68 and 73.

Figure 6-7

Employment in the service-producing sector of the economy more than doubled between 1960 and 1988 (up 138 percent) and women workers accounted for more than three-quarters of that increase. More than nine in every 10 of the 39 million women employees added to American payrolls in the last three decades worked in the service sector. In 1960, less than 20 percent of employees on service-sector payrolls were female; by 1990, the female proportion was more than one in two.

Figure 6-8 • WORKERS IN GOODS-PRODUCING AND
SERVICE-PRODUCING NONFARM INDUSTRIES BY SEX, 1990
(percent distribution)

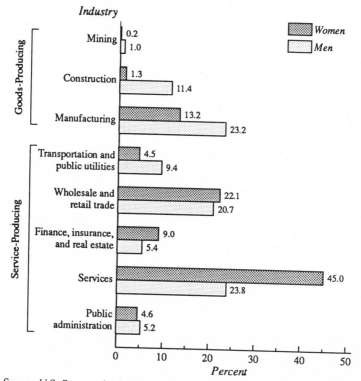

Source: U.S. Bureau of Labor Statistics, *Employment and Earnings*, January 1991,
Table 27.

Figure 6-8

In 1990, more than two-thirds of all employed women
worked in just two service-sector industries—services (com-
prising private household, protective service, and occupations such as teachers, waitresses, and nurses) and wholesale
and retail trade. The service industry alone accounted for 45
percent of all women workers. Men, by contrast, were more
evenly distributed across all industries.

Table 6-11 • PROJECTED EMPLOYMENT BY MAJOR OCCUPATIONAL GROUP, 1988–2000[1] (percent distribution)

Occupation	1988		2000		Projected Percent Change 1988–2000
	Number of Workers (in thousands)	Percent	Number of Workers (in thousands)	Percent	
Executive, administrative, and managerial	12,104	10.2	14,762	10.8	+22.0
Professional specialty	14,628	12.4	18,137	13.3	+24.0
Technicians and related support	3,867	3.3	5,089	3.7	+31.6
Marketing and sales	13,316	11.3	15,924	11.7	+19.6
Administrative support (including clerical)	21,066	17.8	23,553	17.3	+11.8
Service	18,479	15.6	22,651	16.6	+22.6
Agricultural, forestry, fishing, and related fields	3,503	3.0	3,334	2.4	−4.8
Precision production, craft, and repair	14,159	12.0	15,563	11.4	+9.9
Operators, fabricators, and laborers	16,983	14.4	17,198	12.6	+1.3

[1]Using moderate growth projections.

Source: U.S. Bureau of Labor Statistics, "Projections of Occupational Employment, 1988–2000," *Monthly Labor Review*, November 1989, Table 1.

Table 6-11

The four major occupational categories that are projected to show the fastest growth in employment during the 1990s are "technicians and related support" occupations (specific occupations in this category include licensed practical nurses, electrical technicians, computer programmers, and legal assistants), "professional specialty" occupations (e.g., physicians, registered nurses, teachers, and lawyers), "service" occupations (a category that includes child care workers, kitchen workers, police officers, and hairdressers), and "executive, administrative, and managerial" occupations (e.g., accountants, financial managers, education administrators, and inspectors). Currently, women account for nearly half (49 percent) of technicians and related support workers, for 51 percent of professional specialty workers, for 60 percent of service workers, and for 40 percent of executive, administrative, and managerial workers.

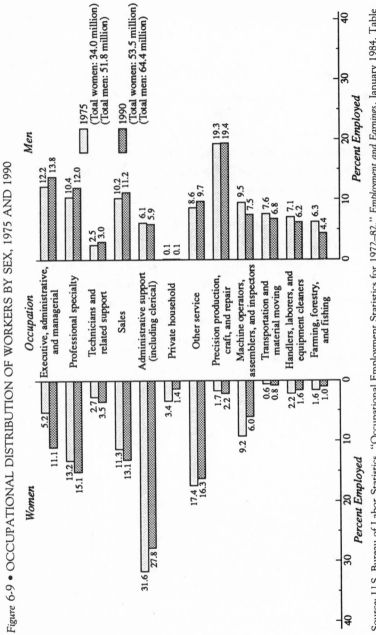

Figure 6-9 • OCCUPATIONAL DISTRIBUTION OF WORKERS BY SEX, 1975 AND 1990

Source: U.S. Bureau of Labor Statistics, "Occupational Employment Statistics for 1972–82," *Employment and Earnings,* January 1984, Table 1 and *Employment and Earnings,* January 1991, Table 21.

Figure 6-9

Between 1975 and 1990, 20 million women were added to the U.S. workforce. Most entered traditionally female occupations. Nevertheless, some traditionally male occupations employed considerably higher percentages of the female workforce in 1990 than in 1970. For example, a larger proportion of all females worked in professional specialty occupations in 1990 and the proportion in executive, administrative, and managerial occupations more than doubled (from five to 11 percent). The proportion in the traditionally female administrative support occupations declined. Nevertheless, because the size of the female workforce increased so much, the number of women in administrative support occupations was higher in 1990 than it had been in 1975.

Table 6-12 • EMPLOYMENT OF WOMEN IN SERVICE AND ADMINISTRATIVE SUPPORT OCCUPATIONS BY DETAILED OCCUPATION, 1990 (percent distribution)

Occupation	Percent Distribution by Detailed Occupation
Administrative support	
Secretaries, stenographers, and typists	30.8
Financial records processors	14.9
Computer equipment operators	3.6
Supervisors	3.0
Mail and message distributors	2.3
Other administrative support, including clerical	45.4
Total percent	100.0
Total number of women (in thousands)	14,870
Service	
Food services	33.7
Personal services	20.9
Health services	19.9
Cleaning and building services	14.5
Private household services	8.0
Protective services	3.1
Total percent	100.0
Total number of women (in thousands)	9,470

Source: U.S. Bureau of Labor Statistics, *Employment and Earnings*, January 1991, Table 22.

Table 6-12

In 1990, over three-quarters of the nearly 15 million women in administrative support occupations were employed as either secretaries, stenographers, or typists, or in "other administrative support jobs." The latter category, which included clerical workers, by itself accounted for 45 percent of all females in administrative support occupations.

Of the more than nine million women in service occupations, one-third had food service jobs (e.g., waitress, cook). Two in five were either health services workers (e.g., health aide, dental assistant) or personal services employees (e.g., hairdresser, child care worker).

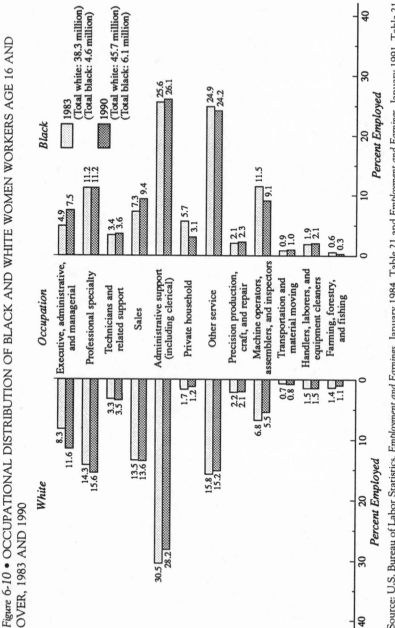

Figure 6-10 • OCCUPATIONAL DISTRIBUTION OF BLACK AND WHITE WOMEN WORKERS AGE 16 AND OVER, 1983 AND 1990

Source: U.S. Bureau of Labor Statistics, *Employment and Earnings*, January 1984, Table 21 and *Employment and Earnings*, January 1991, Table 21.

Figure 6-10

Overall, the occupational profiles of working women in 1990 were not dramatically different from what they were in 1983. There were, however, some interesting differences in the types of occupations of black and white females. For example, in both years, the proportion of all black women workers who were in service occupations was considerably higher than the proportion of white women (27 percent versus 16 percent in 1990), and the proportion of all white women workers who were in managerial occupations was higher than the proportion of black women. However, managers accounted for a larger proportion of both black and white women workers in 1990 than had been the case in 1983.

Table 6-13 • WOMEN AS A PERCENTAGE OF ALL CIVILIAN EMPLOYEES IN SELECTED OCCUPATIONS BY RACE AND HISPANIC ORIGIN, 1990

Occupation	Percent Female All Races	Percent White Female	Percent Black Female	Percent Hispanic Origin[1] Female
Secretaries	99.0	89.5	7.5	5.1
Textile sewing machine operators	89.2	66.5	14.6	18.0
Health aides, except nursing	84.8	65.6	17.0	4.7
Waitresses	80.8	74.2	3.3	4.3
Production inspectors, checkers, and examiners	52.2	42.4	7.9	4.5
Bus drivers	51.5	42.4	8.6	2.3
Financial managers	44.3	41.3	1.8	1.0
Assemblers	43.5	34.1	7.3	5.6
Computer programmers	36.0	30.6	2.4	1.0
Precision food[2]	32.7	25.3	6.7	3.1
Insurance sales	32.6	29.3	2.6	1.3
Stock handlers and baggers	25.0	21.9	2.2	2.3
Farm workers	21.0	19.0	1.3	4.2
Physicians	19.3	16.2	0.5	0.5
Laborers, except construction	18.7	14.4	3.7	1.9
Police and detectives	13.9	9.8	3.9	0.8
Electrical and electronic equipment repairers	8.7	6.5	1.8	0.3
Engineers	8.0	7.0	0.1	0.3
Construction trades	1.9	1.7	0.1	0.1
Total, all occupations	45.4	38.7	5.0	3.0

[1]Persons of Hispanic origin may be of any race.
[2]Includes butchers, bakers, and food batchmakers.
Source: U.S. Bureau of Labor Statistics, unpublished data, 1990.

Table 6-13

In spite of the inroads females have made into some traditionally male occupations, most jobs tend to be gender segregated. For example, in 1990, 99 percent of all secretaries were women, but only two percent of workers in the construction trades were women. Black and Hispanic women were overrepresented in some—usually lower-skilled and lower-paid—occupations such as health aides (85 percent female, 17 percent black female, and five percent Hispanic female) and were underrepresented among the workers in some of the higher-skill, better-paid occupations such as engineers (eight percent women, one-tenth of one percent black women and three-tenths of one percent Hispanic women).

Table 6-14 • WOMEN AS A PERCENTAGE OF ALL FEDERAL CIVILIAN EMPLOYEES BY GRADE[1] AND RACE, 1982 AND 1988

Race	Grades 1-6 ($9,811–21,909)[2]		Grades 7-10 ($18,726–32,795)[2]		Grades 11-12 ($27,716–43,181)[2]		Grades 13-15 ($39,501–71,377)[2]	
	1982	1988	1982	1988	1982	1988	1982	1988
White (non-Hispanic)	51.3	46.6	36.0	37.5	17.1	23.7	7.8	12.7
Black (non-Hispanic)	16.8	19.8	9.3	11.1	4.0	5.6	1.4	2.2
Hispanic	3.2	4.1	1.7	2.4	0.6	1.2	0.2	0.4
Asian/Pacific Islander	1.4	2.0	1.1	1.5	0.5	1.1	0.3	0.5
American Indian/ Alaskan Native	1.7	1.8	0.7	0.8	0.3	0.4	0.1	0.1
Total percent women	74.3	74.4	48.7	53.3	22.4	31.9	9.7	15.9
Total number of employees	599,704	584,059	357,799	391,578	340,987	415,570	209,786	247,626

[1]Includes general schedule positions as well as equivalent positions such as Department of Veterans Affairs doctors and foreign service personnel.

[2]Salaries are based on 1988 levels.

Source: U.S. Office of Personnel Management, *Affirmative Employment Statistics, 1982*, Table 2 and *Affirmative Employment Statistics, 1988*, Table 2.

Table 6-14

Most federal employees at the lowest grade levels (GS-1 through 6) are women and most at the higher grade levels (GS-13 through 15) are men, but women have made noticeable gains. Between 1982 and 1988, the proportion of females among employees in grades 11 and 12 increased by 10 percentage points, and in 1988 women constituted nearly one-third of all employees at these grades. The proportion of women among employees at the highest level also increased, although not as dramatically. While there were some small gains for minority females, their representation among federal employees in the top grades remained very low.

Table 6-15 • ACTIVE-DUTY FEMALE ENLISTED PERSONNEL AND OFFICERS[1] BY MILITARY SERVICE BRANCH AND RACE, FISCAL YEAR 1989[2] (percent distribution)

Percent Distribution

Service and Rank	White	Black	Spanish	Other	Total Percent	Total Number (Both Sexes)	Percent Women
Army							
Enlisted personnel	45.3	47.2	3.0	4.4	100.0	658,119	11.2
Officers	75.3	19.1	1.8	3.9	100.0	107,168	11.4
Navy							
Enlisted personnel	64.3	25.9	6.6	3.2	100.0	514,145	9.7
Officers	87.5	7.1	2.2	3.2	100.0	72,255	10.4
Marine Corps							
Enlisted personnel	61.0	28.4	6.8	3.7	100.0	176,770	5.1
Officers	87.4	8.4	2.0	2.2	100.0	20,047	3.5
Air Force							
Enlisted personnel	69.9	23.5	3.3	3.3	100.0	462,831	13.7
Officers	82.3	11.3	2.3	4.1	100.0	103,699	12.9
Coast Guard							
Enlisted personnel	76.4	16.4	4.0	3.2	100.0	30,025	7.9
Officers	92.0	2.7	0.4	5.0	100.0	6,465	4.1

[1]Includes warrant officers.

[2]Coast Guard as of January 1990.

Source: Women's Research and Education Institute, *Women in the Military 1980–1990*, 1990.

Table 6-15

Women accounted for 11 percent of the more than two million U.S. military personnel on active duty in fiscal year 1989. However, there were variations by service, notably between the Air Force (nearly 14 percent female enlisted personnel overall) and the Marine Corps (only five percent female enlisted personnel). Minority women—especially black women—were heavily represented among enlisted females in most of the services, but particularly among Army enlisted women (nearly 55 percent minority, 47 percent black). The Army and the Air Force had the highest proportions of minority women among their female officers—nearly 25 percent and 18 percent, respectively.

Table 6-16 • NUMBER OF WOMEN-OWNED FIRMS AND PERCENTAGE OF RECEIPTS GENERATED BY WOMEN-OWNED BUSINESSES, 1977 AND 1987

Industry	1977			1987		
	Number of Women-Owned Firms	Percentage of All Firms Owned by Women	Percentage of All Receipts Generated by Women-Owned Firms	Number of Women-Owned Firms	Percentage of All Firms Owned by Women	Percentage of All Receipts Generated by Women-Owned Firms
Construction	21,000	1.9	4.0	94,308	5.7	8.7
Manufacturing	19,000	6.6	9.4	93,960	21.7	13.6
Transportation and public utilities	12,000	2.9	5.7	79,768	13.5	14.3
Wholesale and retail trade	228,000	8.8	8.0	881,205	32.9	15.2
Finance, insurance, and real estate	66,000	4.7	3.2	437,360	35.6	14.4
Services	316,000	8.7	5.9	2,269,028	38.2	14.7
Other	40,000	10.2	5.7	259,158	22.1	11.7
Total, all industries	702,000	7.1	6.6	4,114,787	30.0	13.9

Source: U.S. Bureau of the Census, *Women-Owned Businesses 1977*, May 1980, Table E and *Women-Owned Businesses 1987*, August 1990, Tables 1 and 10.

Figure 6-11 • WOMEN-OWNED FIRMS AS A PERCENTAGE OF ALL BUSINESSES BY INDUSTRY, 1977 AND 1987

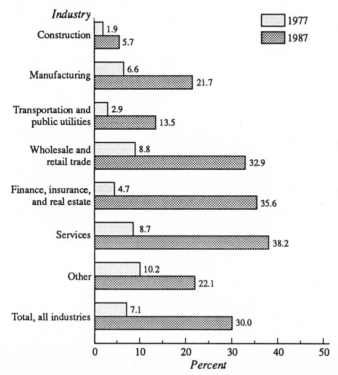

Source: U.S. Bureau of the Census, *Women-Owned Businesses 1977,* May 1980, Table E and *Women-Owned Businesses 1987,* August 1990, Tables 1 and 10.

Table 6-16 and Figure 6-11

The number of businesses owned by women in the United States soared between 1977 and 1987. While the greatest growth was in the services and finance, insurance, and real estate industries, in virtually every category women-owned companies at least doubled. As of 1987, women owned 30 percent of all businesses in the United States; their firms, however, accounted for just under 14 percent of all receipts generated by American companies in 1987. This was due to the type and size of businesses that women owned—90 percent were sole proprietorships with few or no employees and nearly four out of 10 had total receipts of less than $5,000.

Figure 6-12 • COMPOSITION OF BOARDS OF DIRECTORS OF FORTUNE 500 INDUSTRIAL AND SERVICE CORPORATIONS BY SEX AND RACE, 1989 (percent distribution)

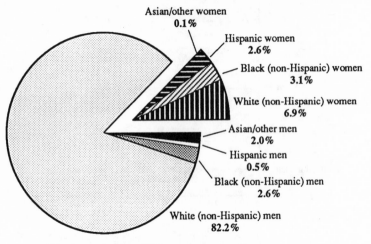

(Total corporations: 264)

Source: Heidrick and Struggles Communications Department, *The Changing Board*, 1990.

Figure 6-12

Directing America's biggest companies is still largely the preserve of white males. A 1989 survey of 264 "Fortune 500" companies found that women accounted for less than one in eight corporate board members, and nonwhite women for only about one in 17. Nevertheless, nonwhite females were better represented on these corporate boards than their male counterparts (one in 20).

Section 7: Earnings and Benefits

American workers may be paid not only with wages or salaries, but also with other benefits such as employer- or union-provided health insurance and pension coverage, and sometimes assistance with child care. However, as this section shows, both earnings and the liklihood of benefit coverage typically vary by gender, race, age, and part- or full-time work status. Benefit coverage also depends to a large degree on the size of the employer's workforce.

Notable Trends

- The female-male earnings ratio was the highest (90 percent) for younger women and men (ages 16 to 24) in 1990 (see Table 7–1).

Encouraging Trends

- In 1980, women earned 64 cents for every dollar earned by men; by 1990 this had increased to 72 cents (see Table 7–1).

- The proportion of workers paid at the minimum wage has declined since 1979. In 1989, seven percent of all female employees and four percent of all male employees earned the minimum wage ($3.35 per hour) (see Figure 7–3).

- The earnings gap closed slightly between women and men working in managerial and professional occupations. In 1990, females in these occupations earned 70 percent of what their male counterparts earned (see Table 7–3).

Discouraging Trends

- In 1990, black women workers were paid 62 cents for every dollar earned by white men (see Table 7–2).

- A work-disabled woman earned 84 percent of the wage of a woman with no disability in 1987; the comparable ratio for men was 81 percent (see Figure 7–4).

- The female-male wage gap narrowed in certain occupations (technical/sales/administrative support and service jobs) as much because of declines in men's salaries as of increases in women's wages (see Table 7–3).

- Women were more likely than men to work at minimum wage jobs in 1989 (see Table 7–5).

- Union membership declined among workers of both sexes and all races between 1983 and 1990 (see Table 7–6).

- In 1988, one out of eight Americans had no health insurance—this proportion was double (one out of four) among persons of Hispanic origin (see Table 7–7).

- The proportion of American workers with health insurance through either their employers or unions has decreased since 1980. In 1987, less than half of all female workers and just under two-thirds of all male workers had employer- or union-sponsored group health insurance (see Figure 7–6).

- Female workers were less likely than male workers to have employer- or union-sponsored pension plans in 1987, and between 1980 and 1987 the proportion of male workers with pension plans dropped six percentage points (see Table 7–9).

- A white man working in a managerial or professional occupation was the most likely and a Hispanic or black woman working as an operator, fabricator, or laborer was the least likely to have the option of a flexible schedule in 1989 (see Table 7–11 and Figure 7–7).

- The availability of maternity or paternity leave was not the norm for full-time workers in American firms in 1989 (see Tables 7–13 and 7–14).

Figure 7-1 • MEDIAN ANNUAL EARNINGS OF SELECTED YEAR-ROUND, FULL-TIME WORKERS AGE 16 AND OVER BY SEX, RACE, AND HISPANIC ORIGIN, SELECTED YEARS, 1969–1989 (in 1989 constant dollars)[1]

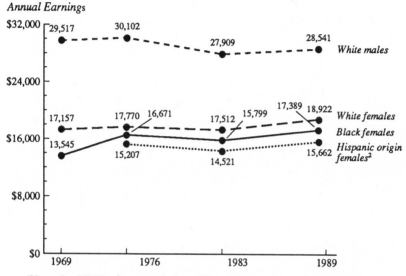

[1]Using the CPI-U inflator to calculate 1989 purchasing power of 1969, 1976, and 1983 earnings.

[2]Persons of Hispanic origin may be of any race. Data were not available for 1969.

Source: U.S. Bureau of the Census, unpublished data, 1989.

Figure 7-1

The average white woman who worked year round full time in 1989 had real (i.e., inflation-adjusted) annual earnings of $18,922, which was approximately 10 percent more than she made 20 years earlier. For a black woman, however, the net gain was considerable—her annual earnings in 1989 were 28 percent higher than in 1969. The gap between black and white women's earnings also narrowed: a typical black woman earned 92 cents for every dollar made by her white counterpart in 1989, up from 79 cents in 1969.

While white males earned far more than females, the ratio of women's to white men's annual earnings rose—in 1989, the ratio was 66 percent for white women, 61 percent for black women, and 55 percent for Hispanic women. The earnings gap narrowed not only because women's earnings increased but also because white men's earnings were slightly (three percent) lower in 1989 than in 1969.

Table 7-1 • MEDIAN WEEKLY EARNINGS OF FULL-TIME FEMALE WORKERS COMPARED TO FULL-TIME MALE WORKERS BY AGE AND RACE, 1980, 1989, AND 1990 (in percentages)

Age	All Races			White			Black		
	1980	1989[1]	1990	1980	1989[1]	1990	1980	1989[1]	1990
16–24	80.3	—	89.8	79.2	—	89.6	91.6	—	94.0
25–54	62.9	—	73.0	62.1	—	72.8	73.6	—	82.9
55 and over	60.4	—	65.0	59.5	—	62.8	71.9	—	79.5
Total, 16 and over	64.4	70.1	71.8	63.2	69.3	71.4	75.7	86.5	85.6

[1]Published data for the earnings ratio of female to male full-time workers by both age and race are not available for 1989. However, data for workers age 16 and over are provided to offer a basis of comparison with the preceding Figure 7-1.

Source: U.S. Bureau of Labor Statistics, *Handbook of Labor Statistics*, August 1989, Table 41 and unpublished data, 1990.

Table 7-2 • MEDIAN WEEKLY EARNINGS OF FULL-TIME WAGE AND SALARY WORKERS AGE 16 AND OVER BY SEX, AGE, AND RACE, 1980 AND 1990 (in 1990 constant dollars)[1]

| | All Races | | | | White | | | | Black | | | |
| | 1980 | | 1990 | | 1980 | | 1990 | | 1980 | | 1990 | |
Age	Women	Men	Women	Men	Women	Men	Women	Men	Women	Men	Women	Men
16–24	265	330	254	283	267	336	257	287	251	274	234	249
25–54	339	539	374	512	344	554	382	525	312	424	321	387
55 and over	320	530	342	526	325	546	348	554	276	384	303	381
Total, 16 and over	319	495	348	485	320	506	355	497	293	387	308	360

[1]Using the CPI-U inflator to calculate 1990 purchasing power of 1980 earnings.

Source: U.S. Bureau of Labor Statistics, Handbook of Labor Statistics, August 1989, Table 41 and unpublished data, 1990.

Tables 7-1 and 7-2

The earnings gap between men and women is narrower when it is calculated on the basis of the usual median weekly earnings of full-time workers than when it is calculated on the basis of the median annual earnings of full-time workers who work year round (as shown for 1969 to 1989 in Figure 7–1). (An analyst at the Bureau of Labor Statistics attributes this difference largely to the cumulative effect over a full year of more hours worked by full-time male workers than by full-time female workers.)

Nevertheless, the earnings gap has narrowed in recent years, whether it is measured on the basis of median annual earnings or median weekly earnings. Using the latter measure, the ratio of women's earnings to men's earnings rose from 64 to 72 percent between 1980 and 1990. Among the youngest workers (ages 16 to 24), the ratio was 90 percent in 1990, up from 80 percent in 1980. Among black workers (all ages), the ratio was 86 percent in 1990 versus 76 percent in 1980.

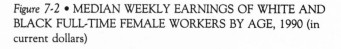

Figure 7-2 • MEDIAN WEEKLY EARNINGS OF WHITE AND
BLACK FULL-TIME FEMALE WORKERS BY AGE, 1990 (in
current dollars)

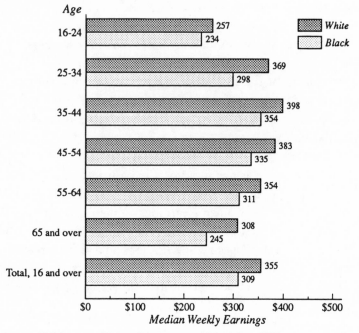

Source: U.S. Bureau of Labor Statistics, unpublished data, 1990.

Figure 7-2

In every age group, white full-time female workers had
higher median weekly earnings in 1990 than black full-time
female workers.

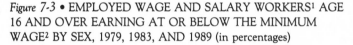

Figure 7-3 • EMPLOYED WAGE AND SALARY WORKERS[1] AGE 16 AND OVER EARNING AT OR BELOW THE MINIMUM WAGE[2] BY SEX, 1979, 1983, AND 1989 (in percentages)

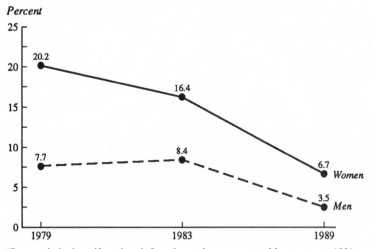

[1]Data exclude the self-employed. Sample weights were revised beginning in 1981.

[2]The minimum wage in 1979 current dollars was $2.90 per hour, the equivalent of $4.95 in 1989 constant dollars. In 1983, the current dollar minimum wage was $3.35, $4.17 in 1989 constant dollars. The minimum wage in 1989 was $3.35. On April 1, 1991, the minimum wage was raised to $4.25 per hour.

Source: U.S. Bureau of Labor Statistics, unpublished annual data, 1989.

Figure 7-3

Between 1979 and 1989, the proportion of women and men working at or below the minimum wage dropped sharply, by almost 14 percentage points for females and over four percentage points for males. In 1989, about seven percent of all employed women and less than four percent of all employed men worked for the minimum wage or below, earning less than $7,000 annually.

Figure 7-4 • MEAN EARNINGS OF YEAR-ROUND, FULL-TIME
WORKERS WITH AND WITHOUT WORK DISABILITIES[1] BY
SEX, 1980 AND 1987 (in 1987 constant dollars)[2]

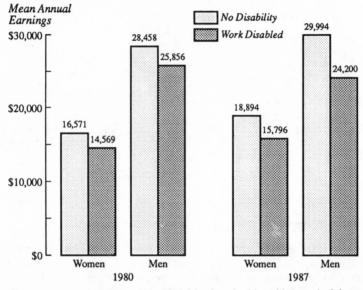

[1]Individuals are classified as work disabled if they have health problems or disabilities
that prevent them from working or that limit the kind or amount of work they can
do.

[2]Using the CPI-U inflator to calculate 1987 purchasing power of 1980 earnings.

Source: U.S. Bureau of the Census, *Labor Force Characteristics of Persons with a Work
Disability: 1981 to 1988,* July 1989, Table D.

Figure 7-4

Between 1980 and 1987, the real (i.e., inflation-adjusted)
average annual earnings of a work-disabled female employed
year round, full time increased by eight percent, while her
male counterpart's earnings declined by six percent. In
1987, a work-disabled woman employed year round, full
time earned, on average, 84 percent of what her counter-

part without a work disability earned; the comparable ratio for men was 81 percent. The most dramatic differences, however, occurred when comparing a work-disabled woman in 1987 to a work-disabled man—an $8,404 difference in annual earnings.

Table 7-3

Between 1983 and 1990, the female-male earnings ratio narrowed among full-time workers in four of the Labor Department's eight broad occupational categories. However, a comparison of median weekly earnings of full-time workers in 1990 with the earnings of their counterparts in 1983 (a recession year) suggests that a celebration may not be in order.

In only one of the occupational categories—managerial/professional—did men earn appreciably more in 1990 than their counterparts in 1983; in six categories they earned less. The earnings ratio closed slightly among managers and professionals because the females' earnings increased slightly more than the males' (nine percent versus eight percent).

In six of the eight occupational categories, men's earnings visibly declined. The narrowing of the earnings ratio in two of these, where women's earnings increased (technical/sales/administrative support and service), had as much to do with the drop in males' earnings as with the small increases in females' earnings. And among operators/fabricators/laborers, the ratio narrowed because earnings declined for both sexes but the men's dropped more than the women's.

The earnings gap actually widened between 1983 and

1990 in three occupational categories. In two of them (precision production/craft/repair and handlers/equipment cleaners/laborers), the reason was that earnings declined for both sexes and the women's dropped more than the men's.

Table 7-3 • MEDIAN WEEKLY EARNINGS OF FULL-TIME WAGE AND SALARY WORKERS AGE 16 AND OVER BY SEX AND OCCUPATION, 1983 AND 1990 (in 1990 constant dollars)[1]

Occupation	1983			1990		
	Female	Male	Female/Male Earnings Ratio	Female	Male	Female/Male Earnings Ratio
Managerial and professional specialty	469	677	69.3	511	731	69.9
Technical, sales, and administrative support	324	505	64.2	332	496	66.9
Service	227	335	67.8	230	320	71.9
Precision production, craft, and repair	336	508	66.1	316	488	64.8
Operators, fabricators, and laborers	268	404	66.3	262	378	69.3
Transportation and material moving	332	440	75.5	314	418	75.1
Handlers, equipment cleaners, and laborers	277	329	84.2	250	308	81.2
Farming, forestry, and fishing	222	263	84.4	216	263	82.1

[1]Using the CPI-U inflator to calculate 1990 purchasing power of 1983 earnings.

Source: U.S. Bureau of Labor Statistics, *Handbook of Labor Statistics*, August 1989, Table 43 and *Employment and Earnings*, January 1991, Table 56.

Table 7-4 • MEDIAN WEEKLY EARNINGS OF FULL-TIME WAGE AND SALARY WORKERS IN
SELECTED DETAILED OCCUPATIONS BY SEX, 1990 (in current dollars)

Occupation	Median Weekly Earnings		Female/Male Earnings Ratio
	Female	Male	
Total managerial and professional speciality	511	731	69.9
Engineers	736	822	89.5
Financial managers	558	837	66.7
Physicians	802	978	82.0
Total technical, sales, and administrative support	332	496	66.9
Computer programmers	573	691	82.9
Insurance sales	441	608	72.5
Secretaries, stenographers, and typists	341	387	88.1
Total service	230	320	71.9
Health aides, except nursing	281	314	89.5
Police and detectives	483	512	94.3
Waiters/waitresses	194	266	72.9

Total precision production, craft, and repair	316	488	64.8
Construction trades	394	480	82.1
Electrical and electronic equipment repair	499	576	86.6
Precision food[1]	239	374	63.9
Total operators, fabricators, and laborers	262	378	69.3
Assemblers	287	370	77.6
Production inspectors, checkers, and examiners	304	483	62.9
Textile sewing machine operators	211	255	82.7
Total transportation and material moving	314	418	75.1
Bus drivers	305	405	75.3
Total handlers, equipment cleaners, and laborers	250	308	81.2
Stock handlers and baggers	209	242	86.4
Laborers, except construction	258	320	80.6
Total farming, forestry, and fishing	216	263	82.1
Farm workers	202	234	86.3

[1]Includes butchers, bakers, and food batchmakers.

Source: U.S. Bureau of Labor Statistics, *Employment and Earnings*, January 1991, Table 56.

Table 7-4

Female-to-male earnings ratios varied considerably by occupation in 1990. The ratio was highest for police and detec-
tives, where females earned about 94 cents for every dollar of
their male counterparts, and lowest (63 cents) for production
inspectors, checkers, and examiners.

Table 7-5 • EMPLOYED WAGE AND SALARY WORKERS[1] AGE 16 AND OVER EARNING AT OR BELOW THE MINIMUM WAGE BY SEX AND OCCUPATION, 1989

Occupation	Women		Men	
	Total Number Employed (in thousands)	Percent Earning At or Below Minimum Wage	Total Number Employed (in thousands)	Percent Earning At or Below Minimum Wage
Managerial and professional specialty	4,196	1.6	2,132	1.2
Technicians and related support	1,173	1.1	952	1.1
Sales	4,334	7.6	1,714	5.6
Administrative support (including clerical)	9,141	2.1	2,373	2.7
Service	6,745	18.5	4,475	10.8
Precision production, craft, and repair	863	1.7	8,297	0.6
Operators, fabricators, and laborers	4,071	4.3	10,760	2.7
Farming, forestry, and fishing	178	9.0	983	9.3

[1]Data exclude the self-employed.

Source: U.S. Bureau of Labor Statistics, unpublished annual data, 1989.

Table 7-5

Workers in service occupations and in farming/forestry/ fishing were the most likely to be earning the minimum wage or less in 1989. (It should be noted that teens constitute a larger proportion of service workers than of any other occupational category and are more likely than adults to earn the minimum wage.) Although there were higher proportions of females than males earning the minimum wage in many occupations, the difference was most pronounced among service workers, where 19 percent of all females compared to 11 percent of all males earned the minimum wage or below.

Table 7-6 • EMPLOYED WAGE AND SALARY WORKERS AGE 16 AND OVER WITH UNION MEMBERSHIP OR UNION REPRESENTATION BY SEX, RACE, AND HISPANIC ORIGIN, 1983 AND 1990 (in percentages)

	All Races		White		Black		Hispanic Origin[1]	
	Women	Men	Women	Men	Women	Men	Women	Men
1983								
Union members[2]	14.6	24.7	13.5	24.0	22.7	31.7	16.6	24.1
Represented by unions[3]	18.0	27.7	16.7	26.9	27.4	36.1	20.1	27.0
Total employed (in thousands)	40,433	47,856	34,877	42,168	4,502	4,477	2,023	2,928
1990								
Union members[2]	12.6	19.3	11.7	18.8	18.0	24.4	12.5	16.3
Represented by unions[3]	14.9	21.4	14.0	20.8	21.2	27.5	14.2	18.0
Total employed (in thousands)	49,077	54,828	41,605	47,515	5,875	5,541	3,312	4,869

[1]Persons of Hispanic origin may be of any race.

[2]Refers to members of labor unions or employee associations similar to unions.

[3]Refers to union or employee association members plus workers who report no union affiliation but whose jobs are covered by employee association or union contracts.

Source: U.S. Bureau of Labor Statistics, *Employment and Earnings*, January 1985, Table 52 and *Employment and Earnings*, January 1991, Table 57.

Table 7-6

Historically, male workers have been more likely than female workers to belong to labor unions. While that remained the case in 1990, the proportions of both sexes who were members of unions decreased between 1983 and 1990. While the overall female wage and salary workforce grew faster than the male workforce, declining union membership was steeper among men (down five percentage points) than among women (down two percentage points). This combination of trends translated into an increase of nearly 300,000 in the number of women union members during a period when the number of male union members dropped by more than a million.

Union membership was most common among black men and women. In 1983, black women were more likely than white women to be union members, although the gap narrowed in 1990 because union membership dropped faster for black women (nearly five percentage points) than for white women (less than two percentage points).

Figure 7-5 • HEALTH INSURANCE COVERAGE BY SEX AND
TYPE OF INSURANCE, 1988 (in percentages)

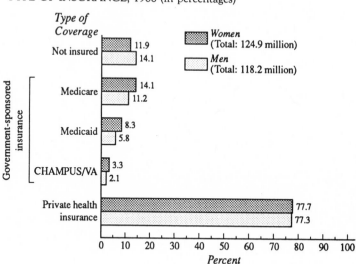

Source: U.S. Bureau of the Census, *Health Insurance Coverage: 1986–1988*, March 1990, Table 1.

Figure 7-5

In 1988, approximately 32 million Americans had no health insurance and men were slightly more likely than women to have no coverage, 14 percent compared to 12 percent. Of individuals with government-sponsored insurance, females were slightly more likely than males to have Medicare and Medicaid (due largely to higher proportions of old and poor women). Almost equal proportions of women and men had private health insurance coverage (over 77 percent), which was by far the predominant type of insurance.

Table 7-7 • HEALTH INSURANCE COVERAGE BY AGE, RACE, HISPANIC ORIGIN, AND TYPE OF INSURANCE, 1988 (in percentages)

Age	Percent with Government-Sponsored Health Insurance			Percent with Private Health Insurance	Total Percent Insured	Total Percent Not Insured	Total Number (in thousands)
	Medicare	Medicaid	CHAMPUS/VA				
Under 16	—	12.5	3.3	71.2	84.7	15.3	56,591
16–24	0.1	6.6	1.9	71.4	78.0	21.9	32,988
25–34	0.7	5.0	1.3	77.6	83.8	16.2	43,262
35–44	1.1	4.4	2.2	83.2	88.8	11.2	35,675
45–54	1.9	3.7	3.4	84.6	89.5	10.5	24,159
55–64	6.7	4.2	5.1	83.6	90.7	9.3	21,637
65 and over	98.0	8.3	3.0	79.0	99.7	0.3	28,782
Race							
All races	12.7	7.1	2.7	77.5	87.0	13.0	243,094
White	13.5	4.9	2.6	81.0	88.3	11.7	205,408
Black	9.2	20.6	3.0	55.3	79.8	20.2	29,775
Hispanic origin[1]	5.6	14.1	1.6	57.4	73.5	26.5	19,825

[1]Persons of Hispanic origin may be of any race.

Source: U.S. Bureau of the Census, *Health Insurance Coverage: 1986–1988*, March 1990, Table 1.

Table 7-7

In 1988, more than one in five Americans between the ages of 16 and 24 did not have health insurance coverage of any kind; the elderly, virtually all of whom (98 percent) were covered by Medicare, were the most likely to have coverage. The proportion of children under age 16 who were covered by Medicaid (13 percent) was higher than for any other age group, not surprising given the high poverty rate (approximately 20 percent—see Table 8–9) among children.

The lack of health insurance was particularly acute among Americans of Hispanic origin, more than one-quarter of whom had no coverage.

Table 7-8 and Figure 7-6

The proportion of American workers who have health insurance through their jobs has declined in recent years. By 1987, the latest year for which data were available, workers of both sexes were noticeably less likely to have employer- or union-sponsored health care coverage than in 1980. Further, workers who were insured were likely to be paying for more of the cost of coverage out of their own pockets.

Male workers have always been more likely than female workers to have health insurance through their jobs, primarily because many working wives were included in the coverage through their husbands' employment. The data suggest, however, that fewer dual-earner couples can count on getting coverage from one of the spouses' jobs—between 1980 and 1987, the proportions of workers of both sexes who had employer- or union-sponsored health insurance declined.

This drop in the proportion with coverage through their

jobs affected workers of every race and origin, but was by far
the steepest for Hispanic men (down nearly 17 percentage
points) and Hispanic women (down nearly seven percentage
points). It is no coincidence that, as shown in Table 7–7, the
proportion of Hispanic Americans who lack any health insurance at all is so high.

Table 7-8 • CIVILIAN WAGE AND SALARY WORKERS AGE 15 AND OVER WITH EMPLOYER- OR UNION-SPONSORED HEALTH INSURANCE COVERAGE BY SEX, SELECTED RACES, AND HISPANIC ORIGIN, 1980 AND 1987 (percent distribution)

Health Insurance Type	1980 Women White	1980 Women Black	1980 Women Hispanic Origin[1]	1980 Men White	1980 Men Black	1980 Men Hispanic Origin[1]	1987 Women White	1987 Women Black	1987 Women Hispanic Origin[1]	1987 Men White	1987 Men Black	1987 Men Hispanic Origin[1]
Employer/union paid total health plan cost	46.3	35.5	37.9	44.3	34.9	34.0	40.8	32.6	35.1	40.7	30.6	35.6
Employer/union paid partial health plan cost	48.9	57.8	56.7	51.3	59.4	60.0	54.2	60.9	58.8	54.5	64.1	58.5
Employer/union paid none of health plan cost	4.8	6.7	5.4	4.4	5.6	6.0	5.0	6.5	6.1	4.8	5.3	6.0
Total percent	100.0	100.0	100.0	100.0	100.0	100.0	100.0	100.0	100.0	100.0	100.0	100.0
Total number with group health coverage (in thousands)	21,620	2,955	1,126	36,852	3,376	2,099	22,639	3,300	1,466	35,616	3,345	2,336
Percent with group health coverage	51.2	54.5	47.8	71.7	61.5	63.2	47.7	50.7	41.1	65.4	54.0	46.6

[1]Persons of Hispanic origin may be of any race.

Source: U.S. Bureau of the Census, Characteristics of Households and Persons Receiving Selected Noncash Benefits: 1980, May 1982, Tables 4 and 17, and Receipt of Selected Noncash Benefits: 1987, unpublished report, 1988, Tables 4 and 17.

Figure 7-6 • CIVILIAN WAGE AND SALARY WORKERS AGE 15 AND OVER WITH EMPLOYER- OR UNION-SPONSORED HEALTH INSURANCE COVERAGE BY SEX, 1980 AND 1987 (in percentages)

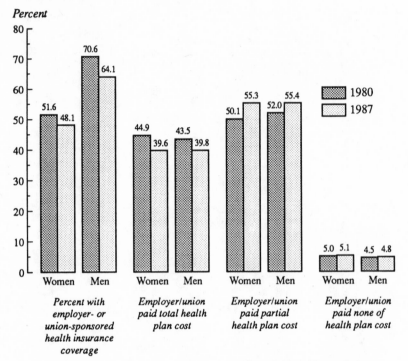

Source: U.S. Bureau of the Census, *Characteristics of Households and Persons Receiving Selected Noncash Benefits: 1980*, May 1982, Tables 4 and 17 and *Receipt of Selected Noncash Benefits: 1987*, unpublished report, 1988, Tables 4 and 17.

Table 7-9 • CIVILIAN WAGE AND SALARY WORKERS AGE 15 AND OVER WITH EMPLOYER- OR UNION-SPONSORED PENSION PLANS BY SEX, RACE, AND HISPANIC ORIGIN, 1980 AND 1987 (in percentages)

Race and Sex	1980	1987
All races		
Women	37.5	36.0
Men	51.1	45.1
White		
Women	37.4	35.6
Men	52.2	45.9
Black		
Women	38.9	38.2
Men	42.9	39.5
Hispanic origin[1]		
Women	30.2	28.2
Men	38.4	29.0

[1]Persons of Hispanic origin may be of any race.

Source: U.S. Bureau of the Census, *Characteristics of Households and Persons Receiving Selected Noncash Benefits: 1980*, May 1982, Tables 4 and 14 and *Receipt of Selected Noncash Benefits: 1987*, unpublished report, 1988, Tables 4 and 14.

Table 7-9

Having pension income in addition to Social Security is an important factor in ensuring economic security in old age, and in the 1970s Congress adopted reforms intended to make employer-provided pension plans more financially sound. Because they understood the connection between the higher rate of poverty and the much lower rate of pension recipiency among elderly women, Congress also enacted laws to make it possible for more female workers to qualify for pension coverage.

Nevertheless, not only are female workers much less likely than their male counterparts to be covered by pension plans through their jobs, but the proportion of all workers with employer- or union-sponsored pension plans decreased between 1980 and 1987. For example, in 1980, more than half of white male wage and salary workers had pension plans through their employment; by 1987, the proportion had dropped to below half (to 46 percent). Still, of all workers, white males were the most likely—and Hispanic females the least likely—to have employer- or union-sponsored pension plans.

Table 7-10 • CIVILIAN WAGE AND SALARY WORKERS AGE 15 AND OVER WITH SELECTED EMPLOYER- OR UNION-SPONSORED BENEFITS BY SEX AND EMPLOYMENT STATUS, 1987 (in percentages)

Benefit	Year	Women		Men	
		Part-Time	Full-Time	Part-Time	Full-Time
Employer/union-sponsored pension plan	1980	12.6	49.0	9.3	57.3
	1987	12.6	46.4	7.2	50.9
Employer/union-sponsored group health plan	1980	18.2	67.1	17.7	78.4
	1987	15.5	62.7	17.4	71.2
Both employer/union-sponsored pension and group health plans	1980	7.8	43.1	7.4	54.7
	1987	6.9	39.1	5.2	46.9
Total number of workers (in thousands)	1980	15,426	33,339	7,538	50,715
	1987	17,174	38,444	8,314	54,218

Source: U.S. Bureau of the Census, *Receipt of Selected Noncash Benefits: 1987*, unpublished report, 1988, Tables 4, 14, and 17.

Table 7-10

In 1987, as in 1980, full-time employees of both sexes were a great deal more likely than part-time employees to have health insurance and/or pension coverage through their jobs. Nevertheless, the proportions of full-time workers who had these benefits were lower in 1987 than they had been in 1980. The impact was most dramatic among men—even though the full-time male wage and salary workforce grew by several million over the period, the number of full-time male workers covered by employment-related health insurance dropped by over a million and the number with a pension plan dropped by over 1.5 million.

In most cases, the relatively small proportions of covered part-time workers also declined—part-time women workers with pension-plan coverage were the exception.

Table 7-11 • FULL-TIME WAGE AND SALARY WORKERS AGE 16 AND OVER ON FLEXIBLE WORK SCHEDULES BY OCCUPATION AND SEX, 1989 (in percentages)

Occupation	Women		Men	
	Total Number of Workers (in thousands)	*Percent on Flexible Schedules*	*Total Number of Workers (in thousands)*	*Percent on Flexible Schedules*
Managerial and professional specialty	10,455	15.0	12,358	21.2
Technical, sales, and administrative support	15,565	10.0	9,191	18.4
Service	4,277	8.3	4,282	8.2
Precision production, craft, and repair	806	7.1	10,161	6.4
Operators, fabricators, and laborers	3,847	3.5	11,020	6.3

Source: U.S. Bureau of Labor Statistics, unpublished data, 1989.

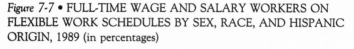

Figure 7-7 • FULL-TIME WAGE AND SALARY WORKERS ON
FLEXIBLE WORK SCHEDULES BY SEX, RACE, AND HISPANIC
ORIGIN, 1989 (in percentages)

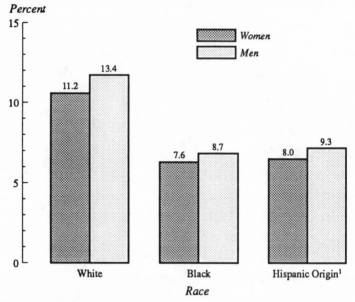

[1]Persons of Hispanic origin may be of any race.
Source: U.S. Bureau of Labor Statistics, unpublished data, 1989.

Table 7-11 and Figure 7-7

Examining America's full-time employees in five broad
occupational categories in 1989 reveals that a man in a managerial or professional occupation was the most likely to have
the option of a flexible work schedule. Conversely, a woman
operator/fabricator/laborer was the least likely to have this
benefit. Indeed, on the whole, men working full time were
more likely than women working full time to have flexible
work schedules.

Moreover, whites of both sexes were more likely than

blacks and Hispanics to have the option of flexible work schedules in 1989. This reflected the higher proportions of whites than of blacks or Hispanics among managerial/professional and technical/sales/administrative support workers— the large occupational categories most likely to offer flexible work schedules to full-time employees.

Table 7-12 • EMPLOYERS THAT PROVIDE BENEFITS AND/OR FLEXIBLE WORK SCHEDULES FOR CHILD CARE BY SECTOR, INDUSTRY, AND BENEFIT TYPE, 1987 (in percentages)

	Private Sector			
Benefit Offered	*Goods*[1]	*Services*[2]	*Total*	*Government*
Employer-sponsored day care	0.3	2.0	1.6	9.4
Assistance with child care expenses	1.9	3.5	3.1	2.9
Child care information or referral services	2.3	5.0	4.3	15.8
Counseling services	3.0	4.6	4.2	18.2
Flextime	31.3	47.5	43.6	37.5
Voluntary part-time work	22.4	39.4	35.3	26.7
Job sharing	9.0	16.9	15.0	23.5
Work at home	8.2	8.6	8.5	4.0
Flexible leave time	37.3	44.6	42.9	43.7
Total number of employers	272,000	856,000	1,128,000	74,000

[1]Includes mining, construction, and manufacturing industries.

[2]Includes transportation, communications, public utilities; wholesale and retail trade; finance, insurance, real estate; and other services.

Source: U.S. Bureau of the Census, *Statistical Abstract of the United States 1990,* January 1990, Table 680.

Figure 7-8 • EMPLOYERS PROVIDING BENEFITS AND/OR
FLEXIBLE WORK SCHEDULES FOR CHILD CARE BY FIRM
SIZE, 1987 (in percentages)

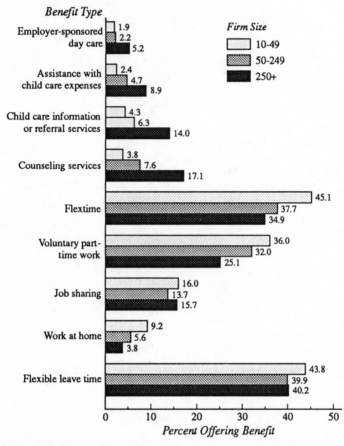

Source: U.S. Bureau of the Census, *Statistical Abstract of the United States 1990,*
January 1990, Table 680.

Table 7-12 and Figure 7-8

In 1987, slightly over a million private-sector firms, and 74,000 government organizations, had one or more policies to help their employees meet their child care needs. The most common policies involved giving employees flexible work schedules (flextime), and/or allowing them to go on part-time schedules; few (less than two percent) of the private-sector companies offered employer-sponsored day care, although nine percent of the government agencies did. Government employers were also more likely than private-sector employers to offer job sharing (24 percent versus 15 percent).

The smallest businesses (fewer than 50 employees) were more likely than larger firms to adopt approaches that involved workers' time in the workplace. The largest companies were the most likely to have policies that would involve direct expenditures by the employer, such as sponsoring day care centers or helping employees pay for child care.

Table 7-13 • AVAILABILITY OF PARENTAL LEAVE TO FULL-TIME EMPLOYEES OF MEDIUM- AND LARGE-SIZE FIRMS[1] BY OCCUPATION, 1989 (in percentages)

Occupation	Percent with Paid Leave Available		Percent with Unpaid Leave Available	
	Maternity	Paternity	Maternity	Paternity
Professional and administrative	4.0	2.0	39.0	20.0
Technical and clerical	2.0	1.0	37.0	17.0
Production and service	3.0	1.0	35.0	17.0
All employees	3.0	1.0	37.0	18.0

[1]With more than 100 employees.

Source: U.S. Bureau of Labor Statistics, "1989 Employee Benefits Address Family Concerns," *Monthly Labor Review,* June 1990, Table 1.

Table 7-14 • AVAILABILITY OF PARENTAL LEAVE TO
FULL-TIME EMPLOYEES OF SMALL-SIZE FIRMS[1] BY
OCCUPATION, 1990 (in percentages)

	Percent with Paid Leave Available		*Percent with Unpaid Leave Available*	
Occupation	*Maternity*	*Paternity*	*Maternity*	*Paternity*
Professional, technical, and related	3.0	—[2]	26.0	13.0
Clerical and sales	3.0	—[2]	20.0	8.0
Production and service	1.0	—[2]	12.0	5.0
All employees	2.0	—[2]	17.0	8.0

[1]With less than 100 employees.

[2]Less than 0.5 percent.

Source: U.S. Bureau of Labor Statistics, Press Release USDL 91-260, June 10, 1991, Table 1.

Tables 7-13 and 7-14

In 1989, maternity leave was not the norm for many full-time working women in American firms, although the chances were better for mothers in businesses with at least 100 employees than for those in smaller establishments. This was true for both paid and unpaid leave, although the proportion of workers with the availability of paid leave was small regardless of the size of the company.

No more than one in five full-time employees in medium- and large-size firms had the option of paternity leave and the proportions were much lower in small businesses. Paid paternity leave was very rare.

Table 7-15 • FULL-TIME EMPLOYEES PARTICIPATING IN SELECTED BENEFIT PROGRAMS BY SIZE OF FIRM, 1989 AND 1990 (in percentages)

Employee Benefit Program	Employed by Small Independent Private Firms,[1] 1990	Employed by Medium- and Large-Size Firms,[2] 1989
Illness and accident insurance	23.0	43.0
Long-term disability insurance	14.0	45.0
Medical care	66.0	92.0
Dental care	23.0	66.0
Life insurance	57.0	94.0
Flexible benefits plans	—[3]	9.0
Child care[4]	1.0	5.0

[1]Small independent establishments, such as local groceries, with less than 100 employees that are not part of a larger business enterprise.

[2]Firms with more than 100 employees.

[3]Less than 0.5 percent.

[4]Includes both on-site and near-site child care facilities, full or partial payment of child care expenses, and reimbursement accounts.

Source: U.S. Bureau of Labor Statistics, Press Release USDL 91-260, June 10, 1991, Table 3.

Table 7-15

The majority of full-time employees had medical and life insurance through their places of employment in 1989, although workers in firms with at least 100 employees were much more likely than their counterparts in small independent businesses to have these benefits. For example, more than 90 percent of full-time employees in medium- and large-size firms were covered by health insurance, compared to two-thirds of those in small businesses. Assistance with child care (arrangements as well as expenses) was available to few workers in companies of any size.

Section 8: Income and Assets

Several important measures of Americans' basic financial security are income, ownership of assets, and the value of those assets. As this section indicates, economic security depends to a great extent on marital status, race, and Hispanic origin.

Notable Trends

- In 1989, married-couple families with wives in the paid workforce had by far the highest incomes—nearly three times that of families headed by women with no spouse present (see Figure 8–1).

- For the first time, in 1989 the median annual income of female college graduates exceeded that of male high school graduates—by $100—due partly to a decline of 14 percent in the annual income of these men since 1979 (see Table 8–2).

- In 1990, married-couple families were the most likely and female-headed families were the least likely to be homeowners (see Table 8–5).

- Renters typically spend a considerably larger proportion of their incomes for housing than do owners. In 1987, the average elderly female renter who lived alone spent almost half of her income on housing, compared to the older woman homeowner who spent just 25 percent of her income on housing (see Table 8–6).

- Married couples are more likely than single women or men to own all types of assets—from cars to homes—and their assets tend to be far more valuable than those of single people. In 1988, the median net worth of married couples was four times greater than that of female householders (see Tables 8–7 and 8–8).

- White householders, whether married or single, have more valuable assets than nonwhites. For example, in 1988 the median net worth of white female householders was 29 times that of black female householders and 30 times that of Hispanic female householders (see Tables 8–7 and 8–8).

Discouraging Trends

- Although poverty rates for all Americans have decreased over the last 30 years, the face of poverty is much more youthful than it used to be. In 1989, one in five children was poor compared to just over one in 10 elderly people (see Table 8–9).

- Blacks and Hispanics of all ages had at least twice the poverty rate of whites in 1989 (see Table 8–9).

- In 1989, the proportion of elderly women (age 65 and older) living in poverty was nearly double that of elderly men (see Table 8–10).

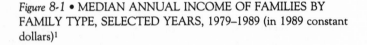

Figure 8-1 • MEDIAN ANNUAL INCOME OF FAMILIES BY
FAMILY TYPE, SELECTED YEARS, 1979–1989 (in 1989 constant
dollars)[1]

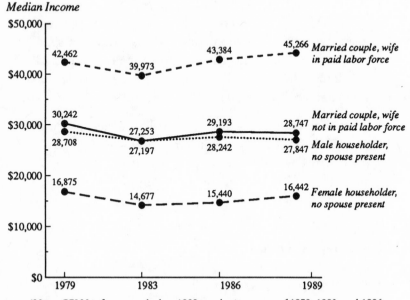

[1]Using CPI-U inflator to calculate 1989 purchasing power of 1979, 1983, and 1986
incomes.

Source: U.S. Bureau of the Census, *Money Income and Poverty Status in the United
States: 1980,* August 1981, Table 1; *Money Income and Poverty Status in the United
States: 1983,* August 1984, Table 1; *Money Income and Poverty Status 1986,* July 1987,
Table 1; and *Money Income and Poverty Status 1989,* September 1990, Table 7.

Table 8-1 • MEDIAN ANNUAL INCOME OF FAMILIES BY FAMILY TYPE, SELECTED RACES, AND HISPANIC ORIGIN, 1979 AND 1989 (in constant 1989 dollars)[1]

Family Type	1979			1989		
	White	Black	Hispanic Origin[2]	White	Black	Hispanic Origin[2]
Married couple	37,275	28,843	28,756	39,208	30,650	27,382
Wife in paid labor force	43,234	35,364	35,034	45,803	37,787	34,821
Wife not in paid labor force	31,092	19,818	22,349	29,689	18,727	20,717
Male householder, no wife present	30,231	21,335	24,879	30,487	18,395	25,176
Female householder, no husband present	19,560	11,795	11,339	18,946	11,630	11,745

[1]Using the CPI-U inflator to calculate 1989 purchasing power of 1979 incomes.

[2]Persons of Hispanic origin may be of any race.

Source: U.S. Bureau of the Census, Money Income of Families and Persons in the United States: 1979, November 1981, Table F and Money Income and Poverty Status in the United States: 1989, September 1990, Table 7.

Figure 8-1 and Table 8-1

Of all family types in 1989, married-couple families with wives in the paid labor force had by far the highest incomes— nearly triple that of the lowest-income families, those headed by women with no spouse present.

Regardless of race or Hispanic origin, having a wife in the labor force typically raised a married-couple family's income in 1989 and, not surprisingly, white couples were the most likely to have the highest incomes. White and black married couples saw their incomes increase between 1979 and 1989; Hispanic couples saw a decline. Conversely, while the incomes of both white and black families headed by women declined slightly over that period (by three and one percent, respectively), their Hispanic counterparts saw a modest increase (four percent).

Table 8-2 • MEDIAN INCOME OF YEAR-ROUND, FULL-TIME WORKERS AGE 25 AND OVER BY SEX AND EDUCATIONAL ATTAINMENT, 1979 AND 1989 (in constant 1989 dollars)[1]

	1979			1989		
	Median Income		Female/Male Income Ratio	Median Income		Female/Male Income Ratio
Educational Attainment	Female	Male		Female	Male	
0–8 years of elementary school	12,962	21,096	61.4	12,188	17,555	69.4
1–3 years of high school	14,530	25,967	56.0	13,923	21,065	66.1
High school graduates	17,917	30,870	58.0	17,528	26,609	65.9
1–3 years of college	20,236	33,027	61.3	21,631	31,308	69.1
College graduates	22,899	38,126	60.1	26,709	38,565	69.3
1 or more years of post-graduate work	28,470	44,111	64.5	32,050	46,842	68.4
All education levels	18,884	31,924	59.2	20,570	30,465	67.5

[1]Using the CPI-U inflator to calculate 1989 purchasing power of 1979 incomes.

Source: U.S. Bureau of the Census, *Money Income and Poverty Status in the United States: 1989*, September 1990, Table 12 and *Money Income and Poverty Status of Families and Persons in the United States: 1980*, August 1981, Table 9.

Table 8-2

Even among year-round, full-time workers with equal years of schooling, there was an income differential between females and males. Men had higher incomes in every educational category and such differences persisted between 1979 and 1989, although the gaps did narrow.

However, it is important to note that the narrowing was not necessarily because women's incomes were rising faster than the men's. In fact, the incomes of both male and female workers with high school educations or less decreased, and the gaps narrowed because men's incomes dropped more steeply than women's. For example, the median income of a male with one to three years of high school dropped by 19 percent compared to a four percent decline for women with comparable levels of education.

In 1989, it was no longer the case—as it had been in 1979—that the typical female college graduate who worked year round, full time had a lower income than the typical male high school graduate who worked year round, full time. The reason was not only that these women's incomes rose by nearly 17 percent but also that these men's incomes dropped, as noted above, by 14 percent.

Table 8-3 • SELECTED SOURCES OF INCOME FOR PERSONS AGES 15 TO 64 BY SEX, RACE, AND HISPANIC ORIGIN, 1988 (in percentages)

Source of Income	Women				Men			
	All Races	White	Black	Hispanic Origin[1]	All Races	White	Black	Hispanic Origin[1]
Wage or salary	75.8	76.1	74.8	73.2	84.8	84.9	84.6	88.0
Nonfarm self-employment	5.4	5.9	1.9	4.0	9.5	10.2	4.1	7.5
Unemployment compensation	2.9	2.7	3.7	3.1	4.6	4.6	5.4	4.6
Social Security benefits	6.2	6.1	7.4	3.8	4.7	4.6	6.5	3.5
Supplemental Security Income	1.7	1.3	4.6	2.1	1.3	1.0	3.4	1.2
Public assistance	5.0	3.2	16.4	10.9	1.1	0.8	3.1	1.4
Veterans benefits	0.5	0.4	0.6	0.2	1.6	1.7	1.9	0.6
Interest	60.5	64.9	30.4	38.4	57.5	60.7	30.7	32.0
Dividends	12.4	13.7	3.9	3.6	13.8	15.0	4.4	3.0
Rent or royalties	6.5	7.1	2.1	3.8	7.4	7.8	3.1	4.1
Pensions	1.9	1.9	1.6	0.8	4.5	4.8	3.0	2.1
Child support or alimony	5.2	5.3	5.5	5.1	0.3	0.3	0.3	0.3
Total number (in thousands)	73,865	62,434	8,957	5,015	74,565	64,482	7,638	5,902

[1]Persons of Hispanic origin may be of any race.

Source: U.S. Bureau of the Census, unpublished data, 1988.

Table 8-4 • SELECTED SOURCES OF INCOME FOR PERSONS AGE 65 AND OVER BY SEX, RACE, AND HISPANIC ORIGIN, 1988 (in percentages)

Source of Income	Women				Men			
	All Races	White	Black	Hispanic Origin[1]	All Races	White	Black	Hispanic Origin[1]
Wage or salary	10.0	10.0	10.4	8.3	17.1	17.1	15.5	16.4
Nonfarm self-employment	1.7	1.8	0.5	1.9	5.3	5.6	2.1	3.4
Unemployment compensation	0.3	0.3	0.2	0.6	0.2	0.3	—	—
Social Security benefits	92.6	93.2	89.7	79.5	90.6	91.2	88.8	82.3
Supplemental Security Income	7.0	5.1	24.8	25.7	3.1	2.5	7.0	11.8
Public assistance	0.5	0.3	1.9	1.7	0.2	0.1	1.3	0.2
Veterans benefits	1.8	1.8	1.9	0.4	6.8	6.8	6.4	6.6
Interest	65.9	70.2	23.8	35.4	69.2	73.5	26.9	41.8
Dividends	15.6	17.1	1.5	3.5	18.6	20.2	2.3	3.9
Rent or royalties	9.0	9.5	4.1	5.0	11.4	12.0	6.7	8.0
Pensions	19.4	20.1	13.4	12.2	46.5	48.2	33.7	29.1
Total number (in thousands)	16,728	15,059	1,423	517	12,019	10,765	972	440

[1]Persons of Hispanic origin may be of any race.

Source: U.S. Bureau of the Census, unpublished data, 1988.

Tables 8-3 and 8-4

In 1988, the majority of women and men ages 15 to 64 listed wages or salaries as sources of income, 76 percent and 85 percent, respectively. Interest was also a commonly cited source of income for both females and males, although whites were much more likely than blacks or Hispanics to have this type of income. Black and Hispanic women were much more likely than white women and all men to receive public assistance.

Not surprisingly, over 90 percent of elderly women and men (age 65 and over) had income from Social Security in 1988. However, proportionately fewer blacks and Hispanics received Social Security benefits than whites. Elderly men were more than twice as likely as elderly women to have pension income; however, whites were the most likely of their sex to have pensions. The proportions of elderly black and Hispanic women who received Supplemental Security Income were five times as high as the comparable proportion of white women, no doubt in part because they were more likely than white women to lack other resources.

Figure 8-2 • SELECTED SOURCES OF INCOME AND BENEFITS
RECEIVED BY WORK-DISABLED PERSONS AGES 16 TO 64 BY
SEX, 1988 (in percentages)

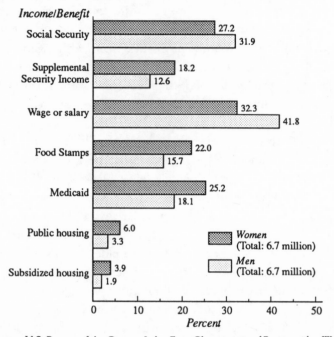

Source: U.S. Bureau of the Census, *Labor Force Characteristics of Persons with a Work
Disability: 1981–1988*, July 1989, Table 3.

Figure 8-2

A higher proportion of work-disabled men than work-
disabled women earned wage or salary income in 1988. Males
were also slightly more likely than females to list Social Security as a benefit. However, higher proportions of women than
men cited Medicaid, Supplemental Security Income, and
Food Stamps as sources of income.

Table 8-5 • RATES OF HOMEOWNERSHIP FOR FAMILIES BY
FAMILY TYPE, PRESENCE OF RELATED CHILDREN, RACE,
AND HISPANIC ORIGIN, MARCH 1990 (in thousands)

Family Type	Total Population	Homeowners	
		Number	Percent
MARRIED COUPLES			
All races[1]	52,317	40,773	77.4
With children	25,476	18,716	73.5
White[1]	46,981	37,506	79.8
With children	22,271	16,850	75.7
Black[1]	3,750	2,327	62.1
With children	2,179	1,252	57.5
Hispanic origin[1,2]	3,395	1,759	51.8
With children	2,309	1,092	47.3
FEMALE HOUSEHOLDER (no spouse present)			
All races[1]	10,890	4,749	43.6
With children	7,445	2,481	33.3
White[1]	7,306	3,718	50.9
With children	4,627	1,836	39.7
Black[1]	3,275	914	27.9
With children	2,624	588	22.4
Hispanic origin[1,2]	1,116	306	27.4
With children	848	181	21.3
MALE HOUSEHOLDER (no spouse present)			
All races[1]	2,884	1,620	56.2
With children	1,359	691	50.8
White[1]	2,303	1,364	59.2
With children	1,079	575	53.3
Black[1]	446	207	46.4
With children	228	89	39.0
Hispanic origin[1,2]	329	98	29.8
With children	157	46	29.3

[1]With and without children.

[2]Persons of Hispanic origin may be of any race.

Source: U.S. Bureau of the Census, Household and Family Characteristics: March 1990 and 1989, December 1990, Table 16.

Table 8-5

In 1990, a married-couple family, regardless of race or Hispanic origin, was by far the most likely of all family types to own a home, and a female-headed family was the least likely. A white family of any type was more likely than its black or Hispanic counterpart to own a home. Among families of each type, whether white, black, or Hispanic, the presence of children reduced the probability that a family owned its home. Hispanic and black women who headed families with children had the very lowest rates of homeownership— 21 and 22 percent, respectively.

Table 8-6 • RATIO OF MEDIAN HOUSING COSTS TO MEDIAN INCOME BY HOUSEHOLD TYPE, AGE OF HOUSEHOLDER, AND TENURE, 1987 (in percentages)

Household Type	Housing Costs as a Percentage of Median Income	
	Owners	Renters
Two- or more person households		
Married couples	14.2	22.7
65 and over	14.4	34.7
Female householders	18.8	43.1
65 and over	14.7	40.7
Male householders	16.6	31.4
65 and over	14.0	37.7
One-person households		
Female householders	23.6	40.9
65 and over	25.0	45.1
Male householders	15.6	25.4
65 and over	20.4	37.4

Source: U.S. Bureau of the Census and U.S. Department of Housing and Urban Development, *American Housing Survey for the United States in 1987*, December 1989, Tables 3-20, 3-21, 4-20, and 4-21.

Table 8-6

In 1987 renters spent a considerably larger proportion of their incomes for housing than did homeowners. A female householder, whether she owned or rented, paid more of her income for housing than did her male counterpart. Of all householders, married couples who owned their homes typically spent the lowest proportion of their incomes on housing (14 percent) and elderly female renters who lived alone spent the highest proportion (45 percent), although women renters heading two- or more person households were a close second (43 percent).

Tables 8-7 and 8-8

An important measure of a family's basic financial security is whether it owns assets, and how much those assets are worth. Married-couple families clearly have an advantage. In 1988, female householders lagged behind male householders and married couples in ownership of most types of assets—except for homes and regular (i.e., non-interest-bearing) checking accounts.

Moreover, married couples' assets were typically worth a great deal more than the assets of other types of households. However, there were enormous differences by race and Hispanic origin. For example, in 1988, the median net worth of white married couples was three and a half times that of black couples and about four times that of Hispanic couples. The net worth of white female householders was 29 times that of black female householders and 30 times that of Hispanic female householders. (It should be noted that whites were also considerably more likely than blacks and Hispanics to own—and thus to have equity in—homes [see Table 8–5]).

Table 8-7 • OWNERSHIP OF SELECTED ASSETS BY HOUSEHOLD TYPE, 1988 (in percentages)

Asset	Married-Couple Households	Male Householder	Female Householder
Interest-earning assets	79.9	65.0	63.1
Regular checking accounts	53.8	40.2	41.7
Stocks/mutual fund shares	26.4	18.1	14.6
Motor vehicles	96.2	83.1	68.0
Own home	77.0	43.9	47.7
Rental property	11.6	6.0	5.6
Other real estate	13.8	7.4	5.3
U.S. savings bonds	22.4	11.4	11.1
IRA or Keogh accounts	30.7	19.0	13.8

Source: U.S. Bureau of the Census, *Household Wealth and Asset Ownership 1988,* December 1990, Table 3.

Table 8-8 • MEDIAN NET WORTH OF HOUSEHOLDS BY HOUSEHOLD TYPE, RACE, AND HISPANIC ORIGIN, 1988 (in dollars)

Household Type	All Races	White	Black	Hispanic Origin[1]
All households	35,752	43,279	4,169	5,524
Married-couple households	57,134	62,386	17,635	15,691
Male householders	13,053	16,584	1,457	2,973
Female householders	13,571	22,099	757	736
Total number of households (in thousands)	91,554	79,169	10,278	5,916

[1]Persons of Hispanic origin may be of any race.

Source: U.S. Bureau of the Census, *Household Wealth and Asset Ownership 1988,* December 1990, Table L.

Table 8-9 • PERSONS LIVING IN POVERTY BY AGE, RACE, AND HISPANIC ORIGIN, SELECTED YEARS, 1959–1989 (in percentages)

Year	Race	Age Under 18	Age 18–64	Age 65 and Over
1959	White	—	—	33.1
	Black	—	—	62.5
	Hispanic origin[1]	—	—	—
	All races	27.3	17.0	35.2
1979	White	11.8	6.9	13.3
	Black	41.2	23.8	36.2
	Hispanic origin[1]	28.0	16.8	26.8
	All races	16.4	8.9	15.2
1983	White	17.5	10.0	11.7
	Black	46.7	29.2	36.0
	Hispanic origin[1]	38.1	22.5	22.1
	All races	22.3	12.4	13.8
1986	White	16.1	9.0	10.7
	Black	43.1	24.3	31.0
	Hispanic origin[1]	37.7	21.5	22.5
	All races	20.5	10.8	12.4
1989	White	14.8	8.3	9.6
	Black	43.7	23.3	30.8
	Hispanic origin[1]	36.2	20.9	20.6
	All races	19.6	10.2	11.4

[1]Persons of Hispanic origin may be of any race.

Source: U.S. Bureau of the Census, *Money Income and Poverty Status in the United States: 1989,* September 1990, Table 20.

Table 8-10 • PERSONS AGE 65 AND OVER LIVING IN POVERTY BY SEX, RACE, AND HISPANIC ORIGIN, SELECTED YEARS, 1979–1989 (in percentages)

	1979		1983		1986		1989	
Race	Women	Men	Women	Men	Women	Men	Women	Men
All races	17.9	11.0	17.0	10.0	15.2	8.5	14.0	7.8
White	15.8	9.5	14.7	8.2	13.3	6.9	11.8	6.6
Black	41.7	26.9	41.7	28.3	35.5	24.2	36.7	22.1
Hispanic origin[1]	29.0	22.8	23.7	22.4	25.2	18.8	22.4	18.6

[1]Persons of Hispanic origin may be of any race.

Source: U.S. Bureau of the Census, *Characteristics of the Population Below the Poverty Level: 1979*, December 1981, Table 3; *Characteristics of the Population Below the Poverty Level: 1983*, February 1985, Table 3; *Poverty Status in the United States: 1986*, June 1988, Table 7; and *Money Income and Poverty Status in the United States: 1989*, September 1990, Table 22.

Tables 8-9 and 8-10

The face of poverty is much more youthful than it used to be. In 1959, an elderly American (age 65 and over) was noticeably more likely than a child (under age 18) to be poor. As Table 8–9 illustrates, the poverty rates for both the young and the old were lower in 1989 than they were in 1959, but the drop was far steeper—and steadier—for the old than for the young.

Since at least 1979 black children have been at greatest risk of poverty. Nevertheless, in 1989, a child of any race was more likely to be poor than her counterpart just a decade earlier.

The 1989 poverty rate for the elderly was not much above the rate for the adult population ages 18 to 64 (11 percent compared to 10 percent), quite a change from 1959, when the rate for older Americans was twice as high as for other adults. Among the elderly, however, women had almost twice the poverty rate as men in 1989, and blacks and Hispanics of both sexes were much more likely than whites to live below the poverty line (see Table 8–10).

Table 8-11 • POVERTY RATES OF FAMILIES BY FAMILY TYPE, PRESENCE OF RELATED CHILDREN, SELECTED RACES, AND HISPANIC ORIGIN, 1989 (in percentages)

| Race | | *Percent in Poverty* | | |
	All Families	*Married-Couple Families*	*Male Household Head, No Wife Present*	*Female Household Head, No Husband Present*
White				
With children	11.8	6.5	15.0	36.1
With no children	3.9	3.5	5.0	7.0
Black				
With children	35.4	13.3	33.8	53.9
With no children	12.1	9.7	15.1	16.7
Hispanic origin[1]				
With children	29.8	19.6	26.8	57.9
With no children	9.6	8.8	7.0	14.6

[1]Persons of Hispanic origin may be of any race.

Source: U.S. Bureau of the Census, *Money Income and Poverty Status in the United States: 1989,* September 1990, Table 21.

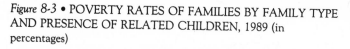

Figure 8-3 • POVERTY RATES OF FAMILIES BY FAMILY TYPE AND PRESENCE OF RELATED CHILDREN, 1989 (in percentages)

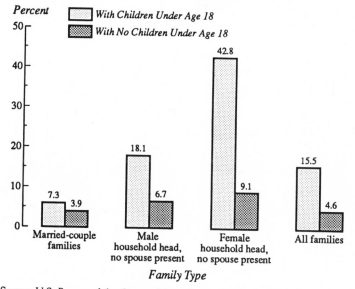

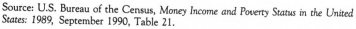

Source: U.S. Bureau of the Census, *Money Income and Poverty Status in the United States: 1989*, September 1990, Table 21.

Table 8-11 and Figure 8-3

A family of any type that includes children is more likely than a childless family to be poor. In particular, female-headed families have the greatest chance of living in poverty. Female-headed households with children in 1989 were six times as likely as married-couple families with children and more than twice as likely as male-headed households with children to be poor.

Poverty rates were higher for black and Hispanic families than for their white counterparts. In 1989, 35 percent of all black, 30 percent of all Hispanic, and 12 percent of all white families with children lived in poverty.

Section 9: Politics

Increasing numbers of women in America have been elected to public office, and today female politicians are no longer the anomalies they were 20 years ago. However, considering that over half of the U.S. population is female, women are significantly underrepresented among both elected officials and high-level appointed officials.

Encouraging Trends

- In 1991, almost one out of every five statewide elected officials and state legislators was female (see Table 9–1).

- Twenty percent of President Bush's Senate-confirmed appointments in 1991 were women (see Table 9–3).

- In 1971, one percent of all elected mayors were female. Since that year, the number has increased dramatically, and in 1991 women comprised 17 percent of all elected mayors (see Table 9–4).

Discouraging Trends

- In 1991, only six percent of all members of Congress were female (see Table 9–1).

- Fewer women and men are voting in national elections than was the case a generation ago, although higher proportions of women than of men voted in 1988 (see Table 9–5).

Table 9-1 • WOMEN IN ELECTIVE OFFICE, SELECTED YEARS, 1975–1991

	Percent Women				Number of Women
Elected Officeholders	1975	1981	1987	1991[1]	1991[1]
Members of Congress[2]	4	4	5	6	31
Statewide elected officials[3]	10	11	15	18	58
State legislators	8	12	16	18	1,359

[1]As of February 18, 1991.

[2]Includes the U.S. House of Representatives and the U.S. Senate. Includes one nonvoting delegate to the House from the District of Columbia elected in 1990.

[3]Does not include officials in appointed state cabinet-level positions, officials elected to executive posts by state legislatures, members of the judicial branch, or elected members of university boards of trustees or boards of education.

Source: Center for the American Woman and Politics, *Women in Elective Office 1991 Fact Sheet*, 1991.

Table 9-1

While the number of females in elective office on both the federal and state levels increased since 1975, women comprised only six percent of all members of Congress and less than one-fifth of statewide elected officials and members of state legislatures in 1991. However, the proportion of state legislators who were female more than doubled between 1975 and 1991.

Table 9-2 • FEDERAL JUDGES BY SEX AND RACE, 1990[1] (in percentages)

Judges	Number of Women	Percent Women	Percent Distribution by Race (Both Sexes)					
			White (Non-Hispanic)	Black (Non-Hispanic)	Hispanic	Asian	Native American	Total Percent
Supreme Court	1	11.1	88.9	11.1	0.0	0.0	0.0	100.0
Circuit courts[2]	18	11.3	90.6	6.3	2.5	0.6	0.0	100.0
District courts[3]	51	9.2	88.1	6.3	4.7	0.7	0.2	100.0
Bankruptcy courts	38	12.8	95.3	3.0	1.4	0.3	0.0	100.0
U.S. magistrates[4]	58	18.8	92.2	5.2	1.9	0.6	0.0	100.0
Total (all courts)	165	12.5	91.0	5.3	3.0	0.6	0.1	100.0

[1]As of September 1990.

[2]Includes the Temporary Emergency Court of Appeals.

[3]Includes the Territorial Courts; Claims Court; Court of International Trade; Special Court, Regional Rail Reorganization Act of 1973; and Judicial Panel on Multidistrict Litigation.

[4]Full-time magistrates only.

Source: Administrative Office of the United States Courts, *Annual Report on the Judiciary Equal Employment Opportunity Program*, 1990, Table 1.

Table 9-2

Federal Supreme Court, circuit court, and district court judges have lifetime appointments, while U.S. bankruptcy judges are appointed for 14 years and U.S. magistrate judges for eight years. In 1990, women comprised 13 percent of all federal judges, with magistrate judges having the highest percentage of females (19 percent) and district court the lowest (nine percent). Minority representation on all levels of the judiciary did not exceed 12 percent in 1990.

Table 9-3 • APPOINTMENT OF WOMEN TO SENATE-CONFIRMED POSITIONS, 1977–1991[1]

President	Total Number of Appointments	Number of Women Appointed	Percent Women
Jimmy Carter[2]	1,087	191	18
Ronald Reagan	2,349	277	12
George Bush	674	133	20

[1]As of May 30, 1991.

[2]Data for President Carter may not be exactly comparable to data for Presidents Reagan and Bush due to slight differences in scope of research.

Source: National Women's Political Caucus, *Factsheet on Women's Political Progress*, July 1991.

Table 9-3

The percentage of females appointed by U.S. presidents to Senate-confirmed positions has risen since 1977. Of the 674 appointments made by President Bush in two and a half years in office (as of May 30, 1991), 20 percent were women, compared to 12 percent under President Reagan (eight years) and 18 percent under President Carter (four years).

Table 9-4 • ELECTED WOMEN MAYORS, SELECTED YEARS, 1971–1991

Elected Mayors	1971	1977	1983	1989	1991[1]
Number of women	7	47	76	112	151
Percent women	1.0	6.2	8.7	12.7	17.1

[1]As of May 30, 1991.

Source: National Women's Political Caucus, *Factsheet on Women's Political Progress*, July 1991.

Table 9-4

Over the past 20 years, the number of women mayors has increased dramatically. In 1971, only one percent of all elected mayors were female—by 1991 this had risen to 17 percent.

Table 9-5 • PERSONS AGE 18 AND OVER REPORTED AS VOTING IN NATIONAL ELECTIONS BY SEX AND RACE, SELECTED YEARS, 1964–1988 (in percentages)

Race	1964[1]		1976		1980		1984		1988	
	Women	Men	Women	Men	Women	Men	Women	Men	Women	Men
White	68.2	73.4	60.5	61.5	60.9	60.9	62.0	60.8	59.8	58.3
Black	58.0	59.1	49.9	47.2	52.8	47.5	59.2	51.7	54.2	48.2
Hispanic origin[2]	—	—	30.1	33.9	30.4	29.2	33.1	32.1	30.1	27.4
All races	67.0	71.9	58.8	59.6	59.4	59.1	60.8	59.0	58.3	56.4

[1]Includes persons 19 and 20 years old in Alaska, 18 to 20 years old in Georgia and Kentucky, and 20 years old in Hawaii.

[2]Persons of Hispanic origin may be of any race.

Source: U.S. Bureau of the Census, *Voter Participation in the National Election November 1964*, October 1965, Table 1; *Voting and Registration in the Election of November 1976*, March 1978, Table 2; *Voting and Registration in the Election of November 1980*, April 1982, Table 2; *Voting and Registration in the Election of November 1984*, March 1986, Table 2; and *Voting and Registration in the Election of November 1988*, October 1989, Table 2.

Figure 9-1 • PERSONS AGE 18 AND OVER REPORTED AS
VOTING IN THE NATIONAL ELECTION BY SEX AND RACE,
1988 (in percentages)

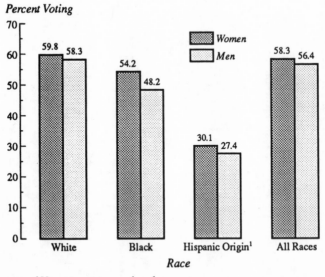

¹Persons of Hispanic origin may be of any race.

Source: U.S. Bureau of the Census, *Voting and Registration in the Election of November 1988*, October 1989, Table 2.

Table 9-5 and Figure 9-1

Although women were granted suffrage in 1920, they did not vote at the same rate as men until the mid-1970s. In 1980, the proportion of women reported as voting edged past that of men. In 1988, whites were the most likely and Hispanics the least likely to report voting in national elections, and higher proportions of females than males of all races reported voting.

Table 9-6 • PERSONS AGE 18 AND OVER REPORTED AS VOTING IN NATIONAL ELECTIONS BY SEX AND AGE, SELECTED YEARS, 1964–1988 (in percentages)

	1964		1976		1980		1984		1988	
Age	Women	Men	Women	Men	Women	Men	Women	Men	Women	Men
18–19	33.5[1]	—[2]	38.8	34.6	34.5	33.9	37.6	32.5	34.4	29.9
20–24	51.0[3]	51.7[3]	45.3	43.7	43.9	40.4	44.6	41.0	39.7	35.8
25–29	64.2[4]	65.2[4]	53.9	51.6	52.4	50.0	53.3	48.2	46.0	41.2
30–34	—[4]	—[4]	58.9	58.2	59.6	56.7	61.1	56.1	54.1	50.2
35–44	71.5	74.2	64.1	62.5	66.0	62.7	64.9	62.0	63.3	59.1
45–54	74.1	78.3	67.9	67.9	67.6	67.3	68.0	67.0	66.6	66.6
55–64	72.7	78.7	67.9	71.8	70.2	72.6	71.5	72.7	68.9	69.8
65–74	66.4	77.4	63.0	70.9	66.7	72.7	70.2	73.9	71.5	75.0
75 and over	49.4	66.4	50.1	62.9	52.9	65.7	57.2	68.3	57.5	70.2
Total, 18 and over	67.0[1]	71.9[1]	58.8	59.6	59.4	59.1	60.8	59.0	58.3	56.4

[1]Includes persons 19 and 20 years old in Alaska, 18 to 20 years old in Georgia and Kentucky, and 20 years old in Hawaii.

[2]Base is less than 150,000 men.

[3]Persons ages 21–24 reported as voting.

[4]Persons ages 25–34 reported as voting.

Source: U.S. Bureau of the Census, *Voter Participation in the National Election November 1964*, October 1965, Table 1; *Voting and Registration in the Election of November 1976*, March 1978, Table 1; *Voting and Registration in the Election of November 1980*, April 1982, Table 1; *Voting and Registration in the Election of November 1984*, March 1986, Table 1; and *Voting and Registration in the Election of November 1988*, October 1989, Table 1.

Table 9-6

In comparison to 1964, the percentage of both women and men who reported voting in national elections in 1988 decreased across all age groups except for women 65 years and older and men over age 75. Reported voting among these two groups rose during this time period, reflecting, perhaps, the increasing politicization of the elderly.

Figure 9-2 • PERSONS AGE 18 AND OVER REPORTED AS VOTING IN THE NATIONAL ELECTION BY SEX AND EDUCATIONAL ATTAINMENT, 1988 (in percentages)

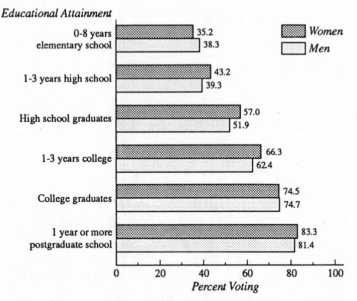

Source: U.S. Bureau of the Census, *Voting and Registration in the Election of November 1988*, October 1989, Table 7.

Table 9-7 • PERSONS AGE 18 AND OVER REPORTED AS VOTING IN NATIONAL ELECTIONS BY SEX AND EDUCATIONAL ATTAINMENT, SELECTED YEARS, 1964–1988 (in percentages)

Educational Attainment	1964[1]		1976		1980		1984		1988	
	Women	Men	Women	Men	Women	Men	Women	Men	Women	Men
0–8 years elementary school	53.7	64.0	40.0	48.5	39.6	45.8	41.3	44.7	35.2	38.3
1–3 years high school	62.6	68.8	46.6	47.9	45.7	45.5	45.7	42.9	43.2	39.3
High school graduates	75.2	77.3	61.1	57.0	60.6	56.5	61.1	55.5	57.0	51.9
1–3 years college	82.6	81.6	69.7	66.6	69.7	64.4	69.3	65.6	66.3	62.4
College graduates	88.2[2]	87.0[2]	80.0	77.3	78.9	77.8	77.9	76.5	74.5	74.7
1 year or more post-graduate school	—	—	82.1	81.7	82.5	82.0	84.4	80.3	83.3	81.4

[1]Data for 1964 are for persons age 21 and over.

[2]Includes persons with more than four years of college.

Source: U.S. Bureau of the Census, *Voter Participation in the National Election November 1964*, October 1965, Table 3; *Voting and Registration in the Election of November 1976*, March 1978, Table 10; *Voting and Registration in the Election of November 1980*, April 1982, Table 10; *Voter Participation in the Election of November 1984*, March 1986, Table 8; and *Voting and Registration in the Election of November 1988*, October 1989, Table 7.

Figure 9-2

As individuals achieve higher levels of education, they are more likely to report having voted in national elections. For example, in 1988, women who had completed some postgraduate study were more than twice as likely as women who did not continue past elementary school to report voting in national elections. Females with grade school educations were the only group who did not surpass (or at least equal) their male counterparts in voting participation. Interestingly, although voting declined among both women and men with relatively few years of schooling, the decline was much sharper among men than among women. For example, in the group who had not finished high school, the proportion of women with reported voting dropped by 19 percentage points between 1964 and 1988; the comparable drop for men was 30 percentage points.

Section 10: International Comparisons

For the first time, *The American Woman* includes a review of data on the status of women around the world. This section offers a basis of comparison between American women and women in selected industrialized and developing nations on health, family structure, employment, and politics.

Notable Trends

- Worldwide, women outlive men by approximately five years (see Figure 10–1).

- The infant mortality rate in the United States is higher than in most other industrialized nations (see Figure 10–2).

- In North America and Western Europe out-of-wedlock births have increased steadily since 1960 (see Table 10–1).

- Since 1960, most industrialized countries have seen rising divorce rates and declining marriage rates (see Table 10–2).

- In the 1980s, "economically active" women in industrialized countries tended to have jobs in the service sector, while women in developing nations were more likely to work in the agricultural sector (see Table 10–5).

- Around the world, in 1989, women were more likely than men to be unemployed (see Table 10–7).

- In 1985, the gap between the literacy rate of women and men was much wider in developing countries than in industrialized countries (see Table 10–8).

Figure 10-1 • LIFE EXPECTANCY AT BIRTH BY SEX, SELECTED COUNTRIES, 1989

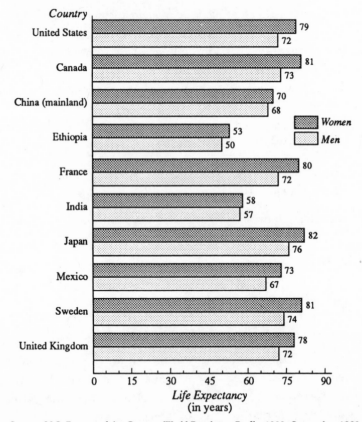

Source: U.S. Bureau of the Census, *World Population Profile: 1989*, September 1989, Table 8.

Figure 10-1

Worldwide, women outlive men by approximately five years. Although life expectancies in the United States were high on a global scale in 1989, 79 years for women and 72 years for men, they were lower than in several other industrialized countries including Canada, France, Japan, and Sweden. In developing countries, such as India and Ethiopia, life expectancies for both sexes did not exceed the age of 60.

Figure 10-2 • INFANT MORTALITY RATES, SELECTED
COUNTRIES, 1990

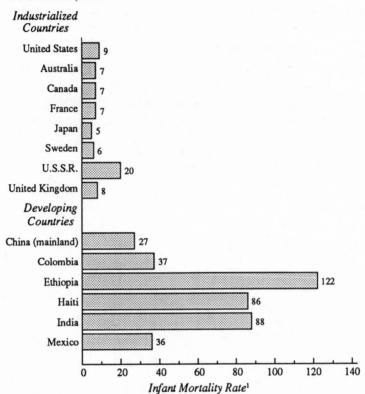

¹Number of infant deaths per 1,000 live births.

Source: United Nations Population Fund, *The State of World Population: 1991*, pp.
42–44.

Figure 10-2

Babies in industrialized countries have a much better
chance of surviving their first year than those in developing
countries. Of the developing nations shown in the figure,
Ethiopia had the highest infant mortality rate (IMR) at 122

infant deaths per 1,000 live births in 1990, while of the developed countries, Japan had the lowest IMR at five. Among these industrialized nations, the United States ranked the second highest in infant mortality, behind the Soviet Union.

Table 10-1 • BIRTHS TO UNMARRIED WOMEN AS A PERCENTAGE OF ALL LIVE BIRTHS, SELECTED COUNTRIES, SELECTED YEARS, 1960–1986

Country	1960	1970	1980	1986
United States	5.3	10.7	18.4	23.4
Canada	4.3	9.6	11.3	16.9
Denmark	7.8	11.0	33.2	43.9
France	6.1	6.8	11.4	21.9
Italy	2.4	2.2	4.3	5.6
Japan	1.2	0.9	0.8	1.0
Netherlands	1.3	2.1	4.1	8.8
Sweden	11.3	18.4	39.7	48.4
United Kingdom	5.2	8.0	11.5	21.0
West Germany	6.3	5.5	7.6	9.6

Source: U.S. Bureau of Labor Statistics, "The Changing Family in International Perspective," *Monthly Labor Review,* March 1990, Table 4.

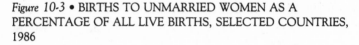

Figure 10-3 • BIRTHS TO UNMARRIED WOMEN AS A
PERCENTAGE OF ALL LIVE BIRTHS, SELECTED COUNTRIES,
1986

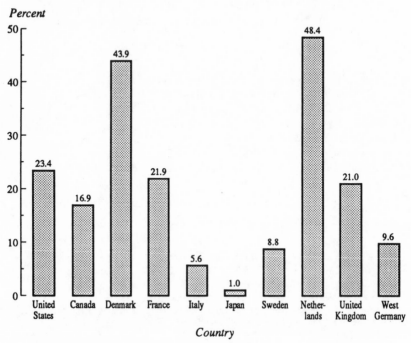

Source: U.S. Bureau of Labor Statistics, "The Changing Family in International
Perspective," *Monthly Labor Review,* March 1990, Table 4.

Table 10-1 and Figure 10-3

Since 1960, out-of-wedlock births have increased dramatically in most industrialized countries. In 1986, Sweden and
Denmark had the highest percentage of births to unmarried
women in the countries selected while the United States
ranked third; nearly one-quarter of all U.S. births were to
unmarried women. Japan was a notable exception—only one
percent of all births in 1986 were to unmarried women.

Figure 10-4 • CONTRACEPTIVE USE OF CURRENTLY
MARRIED WOMEN AGES 15 TO 44, SELECTED COUNTRIES,
MOST RECENT YEAR AVAILABLE[1] (in percentages)

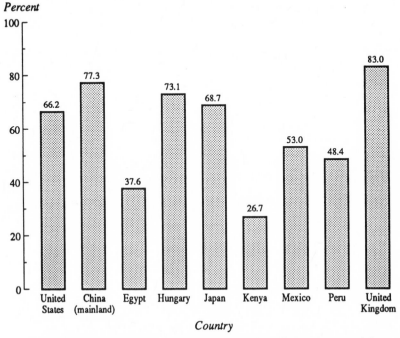

Percent

[1]United Kingdom, 1983; Japan, Hungary, and Peru, 1986; China, Mexico, and the
United States, 1987; Egypt, 1988; and Kenya, 1989.

Source: U.S. Bureau of the Census, *World Population Profile: 1989,* September 1989,
Table 9.

Figure 10-4

Of these selected countries, the United States ranked fifth
in the proportion of married women using contraceptives,
well behind countries such as China, where the government
attempts to limit family size to one child. Among these countries, contraceptive use by married women was highest in the
United Kingdom and lowest in Kenya.

Table 10-2 • MARRIAGE AND DIVORCE RATES, SELECTED COUNTRIES, SELECTED YEARS, 1960–1986

Country	Marriage Rate[1]				Divorce Rate[2]			
	1960	1970	1980	1986	1960	1970	1980	1986
United States	14.1	17.0	15.9	15.1	9.2	14.9	22.6	21.2
Canada	12.4	14.3	11.8	10.2	1.8	6.3	10.9	12.9
Denmark	12.2	11.5	7.9	9.0	5.9	7.6	11.2	12.8
France	11.3	12.4	9.7	7.3	2.9	3.3	6.3	8.5
Italy	11.7	11.3	8.7	7.5	—	1.3	.8	1.1
Japan	14.5	14.4	9.8	8.6	3.6	3.9	4.8	5.4
Netherlands	12.7	15.2	9.6	8.7	2.2	3.3	7.5	8.7
Sweden	10.2	8.2	7.1	7.2	5.0	6.8	11.4	11.7
United Kingdom	11.5	13.5	11.6	10.6	2.0	4.7	12.0	12.9
West Germany	13.9	11.5	8.9	8.7	3.6	5.1	6.1	8.3

[1]Rate is the number of marriages per 1,000 people ages 15–64.

[2]Rate is the number of divorces per 1,000 married women.

Source: U.S. Bureau of Labor Statistics, "The Changing Family in International Perspective," Monthly Labor Review, March 1990, Table 3.

Table 10-2

Divorce rates have risen steadily while marriage rates have declined in most industrialized countries since 1960. Although the American divorce rate (the number of divorces per 1,000 married women) declined slightly between 1980 and 1986, it was by far the highest among these industrialized nations. The United States also had the highest marriage rate, increasing to 15 marriages per 1,000 people during this time period.

Table 10-3 • HOUSEHOLD TYPES IN SELECTED COUNTRIES, 1960-61 AND MOST RECENT YEAR AVAILABLE (percent distribution)

Country and Year	Married-Couple Households[1]			Single-Parent Households	One-Person Households	Other Households[3]
	Total	With Children[2]	Without Children			
United States						
1960	74.3	44.2	30.1	4.4	13.1	8.2
1988	56.9	27.0	29.9	8.0	24.0	11.1
Canada						
1961	78.0[4]	50.8[4]	26.7[4]	3.8[4]	9.3	8.9[4]
1986	64.5	32.3	32.2	5.6	21.5	8.4
Japan						
1960	65.3	49.4	15.9	3.1	17.2	14.4
1985	67.4	39.2	28.2	2.5	20.8	9.3
France						
1968	70.1	43.6	26.5	4.2	20.3	5.4
1988	63.4	36.2	27.3	5.1	27.1	4.4

Sweden						
1960	66.4	35.7	30.6	3.5	20.2	9.9
1985	54.8	21.7	33.1	3.2	36.1	5.9
United Kingdom						
1961	73.7	37.8	36.0	2.3	11.9	12.1
1987	64.0	28.0	36.0	4.0	25.0	7.0

[1]May include unmarried cohabitating couples. Such couples are explicitly included under married couples in Canada (beginning in 1981) and France. For Sweden, beginning in 1980, all cohabitants are included as married couples. The 1960 data have not been adjusted for Sweden, but the number of unmarried cohabitants was insignificant. In other countries, some unmarried cohabitants are included as married couples, while some are classified under "other households," depending upon responses to surveys and censuses.

[2]Children are defined as unmarried children living at home according to the following age limits: under 18 years old in the United States, Canada, Japan, and United Kingdom, except that United Kingdom includes 16- and 17-year-olds only if they are in full-time education; under 25 years old in France; and under 16 years old in Sweden.

[3]Includes both family and nonfamily households not elsewhere classified. These households comprise, for example, siblings residing together, other households composed of relatives, or households made up of roommates. Some unmarried couples may also be included in the "other" group (see footnote 1).

[4]Estimated by the U.S. Bureau of Labor Statistics.

Source: U.S. Bureau of Labor Statistics, "The Changing Family in International Perspective," *Monthly Labor Review*, March 1990, Table 6.

Table 10-3

Married-couple families are the most common household type in industrialized countries, although single-person households have increased substantially since the early 1960s. Between 1960 and 1988, only in Japan, did the proportion of married-couple households increase—by two percentage points. During this time period, the proportion of all households that were headed by single parents nearly doubled in the United States and the United Kingdom while declining slightly in Japan and Sweden.

Figure 10-5 • ABORTION RATES FOR WOMEN AGES 15 TO 44, SELECTED COUNTRIES, 1975 AND 1987

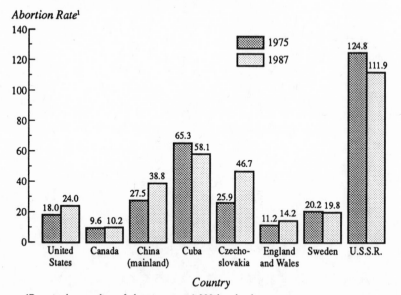

[1]Rate is the number of abortions per 1,000 live births.

Source: Alan Guttmacher Institute, *Induced Abortion: A World Review,* 1990 Supplement, Table 2 and Centers for Disease Control, *Abortion Surveillance, 1986–1987,* June 1990, Vol. 39, Table 1.

Figure 10-5

Between 1975 and 1987 abortion rates increased in some countries and decreased in others. Of the countries presented, Cuba experienced the greatest decline during this period, dropping from 65 abortions per 1,000 live births to 58 in 1987 (a decrease of 11 percent) and Czechoslovakia had the greatest increase (rising from 26 in 1975 to 47 in 1987, an increase of 80 percent).

Table 10-4 • WOMEN OBTAINING LEGAL ABORTIONS BY AGE, SELECTED COUNTRIES, 1987 (percent distribution)

	Age[1]					
Country	Under 19	20–24	25–29	30–34	35–39	40 and Over
United States	25.6	33.6	21.5	12.0	5.8	1.5
Canada	22.3	31.7	22.4	13.9	7.4	2.2
Czechoslovakia	7.7	23.5	24.3	23.4	15.5	5.5
England and Wales	24.9	31.5	20.0	12.1	8.1	3.3
Hungary	11.0	16.7	18.8	24.5	19.8	9.2
Japan	5.5	16.3	17.4	23.7	26.4	10.6
Sweden	17.1	26.9	19.3	15.4	13.8	7.5

[1]Women of unknown age having abortions are distributed pro rata.

Source: Alan Guttmacher Institute, Induced Abortion: A World Review, 1990 Supplement, Table 4 and Centers for Disease Control, Abortion Surveillance, 1986–1987, June 1990, Vol. 39, Table 18.

Table 10-4

In 1987, in the United States, Canada, and England and Wales, over half of all abortions were obtained by women under the age of 25. In contrast, in Hungary and in Japan, women over the age of 30 accounted for more than 50 percent of all abortions in 1987.

Figure 10-6 • ECONOMICALLY ACTIVE[1] POPULATION BY
SEX, SELECTED COUNTRIES, MOST RECENT YEAR
AVAILABLE[2] (in percentages)

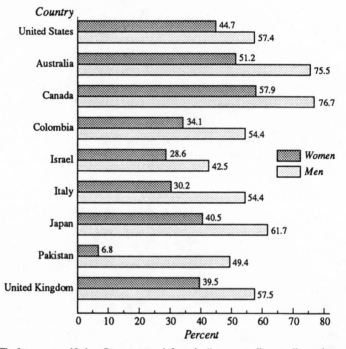

[1]The International Labor Organization defines the "economically active" population
as persons who furnish the supply of labor for the production of goods and services,
whether for the market, for barter, or for own consumption. However, by international standards, this does not normally include students, women occupied solely in
domestic duties, retired persons living entirely on their own, or persons wholly
dependent upon others.

[2]Data for the United Kingdom are for 1986. Data for the remaining countries are
for 1989.

Source: International Labor Organization, *Yearbook of Labor Statistics 1989–90*,
1990, Table 1.

Figure 10-6

In the 1980s, women in industrialized countries such as Canada had higher "economic activity" rates than women in developing nations such as Pakistan. (As defined by the International Labor Organization, "economically active" excludes women employed solely in "domestic duties" and is not comparable to the U.S. Department of Labor's labor force participation rate, which includes individuals working or looking for work.) By this measure women in Pakistan had the lowest economic activity rate of these selected countries because they were more apt to engage in agricultural and service work tied to their homes and families. Worldwide, more men than women were considered "economically active," with the greatest difference among the sexes found in Pakistan and the smallest difference found in the United States.

Tables 10-5 and 10-6

Since 1960 women's employment has shifted from the agricultural sector to the service sector. This is particularly true for women workers in industrialized nations, the majority of whom were employed in the service sector in 1980 (see Table 10–5).

In 1989, well over one-half of all economically active women were concentrated in three occupations: professional and technical, clerical, and service (see Table 10–6). Israel had an unusually high proportion of women employed in professional and technical occupations and Colombia had the highest percentage of women working in service occupations. Australia was the notable exception to this pattern with less than half of all economically active women working in these

three occupations. Nearly one-quarter of all Australian working women were employed in agricultural jobs with very small
proportions working in professional and technical jobs or
clerical occupations.

Table 10-5 • ECONOMICALLY ACTIVE[1] FEMALE POPULATION BY SECTOR, SELECTED COUNTRIES, 1960 AND 1980 (percent distribution)

Country	1960			1980		
	Agriculture	Industry	Service	Agriculture	Industry	Service
United States	2.1	24.0	74.0	1.7	19.2	79.2
Australia	3.8	25.8	70.4	5.1	18.0	77.0
Canada	4.6	19.9	75.5	3.1	16.2	80.8
Colombia	11.3	22.3	66.4	5.0	21.0	74.0
Israel	11.0	17.9	71.1	4.1	16.8	79.2
Italy	32.2	30.9	37.0	13.2	29.6	57.3
Japan	43.7	20.1	36.3	14.1	26.4	59.6
Pakistan	70.8	15.5	13.7	43.0	19.0	38.1
United Kingdom	1.3	36.1	62.6	1.4	22.7	76.0

[1]The International Labor Organization defines the "economically active" population as persons who furnish the supply of labor for the production of goods and services, whether for the market, for barter, or for own consumption. However, by international standards this does not normally include students, women occupied solely in domestic duties, retired persons living entirely on their own, or persons wholly dependent upon others.

Source: International Labor Organization, *Economically Active Population: 1950–2020*, 1990, Methodological Supplement, Annex B.

Table 10-6 • ECONOMICALLY ACTIVE[1] WOMEN BY OCCUPATION, SELECTED COUNTRIES, MOST RECENT YEAR AVAILABLE[2] (percent distribution)

Occupation	United States	Australia	Canada	Colombia	Israel	Italy	Japan	United Kingdom
Professional and technical	17.8	2.7	20.8	14.9	34.5	21.9	14.0	17.7
Administrative and managerial	10.9	12.3	11.1	1.1	2.4	25.0[3]	1.0	3.3
Clerical and related activities	28.7	7.2	32.4	23.3	31.4	—[3]	33.7	32.8
Sales	12.8	3.5	9.4	11.7	5.3	18.3[4]	12.6	9.2
Service	17.5	32.8	15.7	34.4	17.9	—[4]	10.7	23.0
Agriculture and related activities	0.6	24.0	1.1	0.4	0.5	8.5	0.6	0.6
Production, transport equipment, and laborers	11.8	17.5	9.5	14.3	8.0	26.4	27.4	13.4
Total percent	100.0	100.0	100.0	100.0	100.0	100.0	100.0	100.0
Total number (in thousands)	51,985	2,772	5,486	1,090	496	5,314	17,460	8,864

[1]Excludes members of the Armed Forces.

[2]Data for Italy and the United Kingdom are for 1981. Data for the remaining countries are for 1989.

[3]Categories for "administrative and managerial" and "clerical and related activities" are combined.

[4]Categories for "sales" and "service" are combined.

Source: International Labor Organization, Yearbook of Labor Statistics 1989–90, 1990, Tables 2B and 2C.

Table 10-7 • UNEMPLOYMENT RATES BY SEX, SELECTED COUNTRIES, 1980 AND 1989

Country	1980		1989	
	Women	*Men*	*Women*	*Men*
United States	7.4	6.8	5.3	5.1
Australia	7.9	5.1	6.9	5.7
Canada	8.4	6.9	7.9	7.3
Colombia	11.5	7.5	11.8	6.8
France	9.4	4.2	12.8	7.0
Italy	13.1	4.8	18.7	8.1
Japan	2.0	2.0	2.3	2.2
Sweden	1.6	1.3	1.6	1.6

Source: International Labor Organization, *Yearbook of Labor Statistics 1989–90*, 1990, Table 9A.

Table 10-7

Worldwide, women are more likely to be unemployed than men. In 1980 and in 1989, women had higher unemployment rates than men in all of the countries examined except for Sweden and Japan. Unemployment rates in the United States, Sweden, and Japan varied only slightly between the sexes, compared to Italy where women were more than twice as likely as men to be unemployed (Italian women were also less likely to work outside of the home than women in many other industrialized nations, see Figure 10–6).

Table 10-8 • LITERACY RATES[1] FOR PERSONS AGE 15 AND OVER BY SEX, SELECTED COUNTRIES, 1960 AND 1985 (in percentages)

Country	1960[2]		1985	
	Women	Men	Women	Men
United States	98	97	99	99
Bangladesh	9	33	25	48
Colombia	61	64	87	89
Ethiopia	4	8	5	11
France	96	97	99	99
Haiti	12	17	29	38
India	13	42	33	58
Japan	99	99	99	99
Mexico	61	70	84	89
Sweden	99	99	99	99

[1]Rate is the percent of the population who are able to read and write.

[2]Data for developing countries may represent a year in the late 1950s or early 1960s, depending upon availability.

Source: Ruth Sivard, Women . . . A World Survey, 1986, Table III.

Table 10-8

From 1960 to 1985, basic literacy (the ability to read and write) improved for both women and men around the world. In 1985, literacy rates were much higher in general and almost the same for both sexes in selected industrialized countries. It was a different story in developing nations. For example, in the United States almost 100 percent of both women and men could read and write, compared to only five percent of women and 11 percent of men in Ethiopia.

Table 10-9 • WOMEN HEADS OF STATE,[1] 1991

	Country	Year Assumed Office
Presidents		
Corazon C. Aquino	Philippines	1986
Violeta Barrios de Chamorro	Nicaragua	1990
Vigdis Finnbogadottir	Iceland	1980
Mary Robinson	Ireland	1990
Prime Ministers		
Gro Harlem Brundtland	Norway	1986
Mary Eugenia Charles	Dominica	1980
Edith Cresson	France	1991
Maria Liberia-Peters	Netherlands Antilles	1988
Khaleda Zia	Bangladesh	1991

[1]Excludes royalty.

Source: William E. Schmidt, "Who's in Charge Here? Chances Are It's a Woman," *The New York Times*, May 22, 1991.

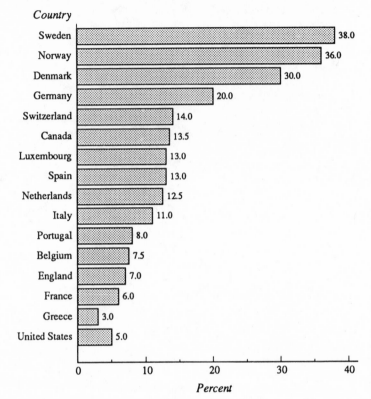

Figure 10-7 • WOMEN MEMBERS OF NATIONAL LEGISLATIVE BODIES, SELECTED COUNTRIES, MARCH 1990 (in percentages)

Source: The Fund for the Feminist Majority, "The Feminization of Power: An International Comparison," March 1991.

Table 10-9 and Figure 10-7

American women lag behind their European and Canadian counterparts when it comes to holding national political office. From France to the Philippines, since 1980 women have assumed high political posts around the world and in 1991, nine countries had female heads of state (presidents or prime ministers). In terms of female representation on national legislative bodies, the United States ranks almost last.

The Congressional Caucus for Women's Issues in the 102nd Congress

THE MEMBERS OF CONGRESS who belong to the bipartisan Congressional Caucus for Women's Issues are involved individually, as well as collectively, in efforts on behalf of women and their families. The 26 who constitute the Caucus's executive committee in the 102nd Congress represent 16 states and the District of Columbia. Twenty are Democrats, six are Republicans.

This section, which was prepared in the spring of 1991, begins with a report from Caucus cochairs Patricia Schroeder (D-CO) and Olympia Snowe (R-ME) on the Caucus's collective activities and concerns in the 102nd Congress. A brief profile of executive committee members, as well as their legislative agendas, follows the cochairs' report. All of the women and men who are members of the Caucus as of mid-June 1991 are listed alphabetically at the end of the section.

The Cochairs' Report . . .

The Honorable Patricia Schroeder and the Honorable Olympia J. Snowe: Women's concerns have moved to the forefront of the American agenda, with the Congressional Caucus for Women's Issues leading efforts to expand opportunities and achieve economic and health equity for women.

In the first session of the 102nd Congress, committees in both the House of Representatives and the Senate approved legislation that provides job protection for employees needing time off for family and medical emergencies, while the House passed legislation that protects women victims of employment discrimination. By the time *The American Woman* is published, it is hoped that both bills—the Family and Medical Leave Act and the Civil Rights Act of 1991—will have been enacted into law.

The Congressional Caucus for Women's Issues has focused on policies important to women and their families since its formation in 1977. The Caucus, a bipartisan organization dedicated to improving the status of American women, today boasts a membership of over 150, its highest ever. Twenty-six congresswomen form the executive committee, which sets the Caucus's priorities and goals.

Among the most compelling of the Caucus's activities is a new focus on women's health issues. That's because, simply put, American women are not treated equitably by our nation's health care system. Whether it be the lack of research on diseases afflicting women, the lack of inclusion of women in clinical research studies, or insufficient access to health care services, American women have been treated as second-class citizens when it comes to their health.

For example, the death rate from breast cancer has increased astronomically, up 24 percent from 1979 to 1986 alone, yet no one knows why. Women are the fastest growing group of those infected with AIDS, yet virtually no research has been done on women at risk of contracting the disease. And too many major clinical trials continue to use only men as their research subjects.

To remedy these and other inequities, the Caucus introduced the Women's Health Equity Act (WHEA), an omnibus package of 22 bills in the areas of research, services, and prevention. The package sets a broad agenda for addressing a number of important women's health issues including breast and ovarian cancer, osteoporosis, women and AIDS, contraception and infertility, health and social services for pregnant and parenting teens, prevention of infertility through improved screening and treatment for sexually transmitted diseases, and Medicaid coverage for mammography and pap smear screening.

Even though the first WHEA was introduced late in the 101st Congress, several of its measures became law. Additionally, others bills were passed by the Senate or were approved by committees in the House of Representatives. In the 102nd Congress, the Caucus is building on this success, and expects to see a number of these health measures enacted.

The Caucus is also continuing longstanding efforts on women's economic needs. The Economic Equity Act (EEA), an evolving package of legislation introduced in each Congress since 1981, has had notable and continued success throughout the years. In the 101st Congress, nine provisions of the EEA became law, including bills that increase the access of displaced homemakers to vocational education programs, provide child care services for residents of transitional housing, and enable battered immigrant women to escape from abusive relationships with their American husbands.

In the 102nd Congress, the EEA's focus is on expanding employment and education opportunities for women, as well as on promoting economic justice. Among the exciting new areas addressed by the EEA is greater access to nontraditional jobs for women. Not only will the EEA help women by increasing their chance at good-paying jobs, but it will benefit the nation as a whole by training women—who are already the majority of new entrants into the workforce—to be the highly skilled workers our economy so desperately needs.

The EEA also seeks to remedy inequities in pension and benefit programs. Women, who often take time off from work or work part time in order to care for family members, suffer for these caregiving roles through denial of benefits, lack of pension rights, and lower Social Security payments upon retirement. Several measures in the EEA would end these and other injustices in the current system.

Another serious problem on the Caucus's agenda is violence against women, both on the street and in the home. Sadly, this violence against women is on the rise, and its toll is dramatic. More women are injured by battering in their homes than are injured in car accidents, and three out of four women will be victims of violent crimes in their lifetimes. Major legislation has been introduced to address some of the problems faced by survivors of sexual abuse, and to try to stem the rising tide of violence against women.

American women, and the nation as a whole, have waited too long to resolve these problems. Daily life in the 1990s poses enough challenges without these inequities. Fortunately, the level of awareness about issues of importance to women has never been higher, and the opportunities for success have never been better. The Congressional Caucus for Women's Issues, working in a spirit of bipartisanship, will continue to take the lead in ensuring that Congress addresses the needs of the American woman.

The Executive Committee . . .

Representative Barbara Boxer (Democrat, 6th District, California) was first elected to Congress in 1982 and is serving her fifth term. She is on the House Armed Services Committee; the Government Operations Committee; and the Select Committee on Children, Youth and Families.

Congresswoman Boxer was born in Brooklyn, New York, in 1940 and began her career in politics serving on the Marin County Board of Supervisors, where she was elected the first woman President of the board. A former stockbroker and an award-winning journalist, Ms. Boxer earned her B.A. in economics from Brooklyn College. She is married and the mother of two adult children.

Barbara Boxer has been a consistent cosponsor of the Equal Rights Amendment and has introduced legislation to establish a Federal Council on Women. Rep. Boxer is also a cosponsor of the Freedom of Choice Act and is active on environmental issues.

Representative Barbara-Rose Collins (Democrat, 13th District, Michigan) was elected to the House in 1990. She serves on the Public Works and Transportation Committee; the Science, Space and Technology Committee; and the Select Committee on Children, Youth and Families.

Rep. Collins, born in Detroit in 1939, first entered public service as a member of the Detroit Region I Public School Board. She subsequently served in the Michigan House of

Representatives and on the Detroit City Council. A widow, she is the mother of two and the grandmother of three.

Barbara-Rose Collins is an outspoken advocate of black men and her legislative priorities include reducing crime, drug use, and joblessness.

Representative Cardiss Collins (Democrat, 7th District, Illinois) was first elected in June 1973 to fill the seat left vacant by the death of her husband. She currently serves on the Energy and Commerce Committee, the Government Operations Committee, and the Select Committee on Narcotics Abuse and Control. The longest-serving black woman in Congress, Rep. Collins was also the first woman elected to the House from a Midwestern district, and the first woman and first black to hold a Democratic leadership position in the House.

Born in 1931 in St. Louis, Missouri, Representative Collins earned her B.A. from Northwestern University. Her career in politics began when she became a Democratic Party committeewoman in Detroit, Michigan.

Cardiss Collins's legislative agenda for the 102nd Congress includes comprehensive federal child care and improving access for people of color in the communications arena.

Representative Rosa DeLauro (Democrat, 3rd District, Connecticut) is serving her first term in Congress. She is assigned to the Committees on Public Works and Transportation, Government Operations, and the Select Committee on Aging.

Rep. DeLauro was born in New Haven, Connecticut, in 1943 and has been in public service for much of her lifetime. She was the first woman to serve as Executive Assistant to the Mayor of New Haven and was Chief of Staff to Senator Christopher Dodd prior to her election to Congress. DeLauro received her B.A. from Marymount College and her M.A. from

Columbia University. She is married and has three grown children.

Rosa DeLauro's legislative goals include tax relief for middle-income taxpayers and pursuing a workable national health care insurance program.

Representative Joan Kelly Horn (Democrat, 2nd District, Missouri) was elected to the House in 1990. She serves on the Public Works and Transportation Committee; the Science, Space and Technology Committee; and the Select Committee on Children, Youth and Families.

Born in St. Louis in 1936, Congresswoman Horn is married, has six adult children and eight grandchildren. She earned both her B.A. and M.A. degrees in political science from the University of Missouri in St. Louis. Before her election to Congress, Rep. Horn was president of a research and planning firm and she is a former faculty member of the University of Missouri.

Ms. Horn is a co-sponsor of the Family Medical Leave Act and the Women's Health Equity Act, and she also supports increased funding for the Head Start program and the special supplemental food program for women, infants, and children (WIC).

Representative Nancy L. Johnson (Republican, 6th District, Connecticut) was elected to Congress in 1983. In 1988, she became the first Republican woman to be named to the House Ways and Means Committee, where she continues to serve. She is also a member of the House Committee on Standards of Official Conduct (Ethics).

Rep. Johnson was born in Chicago, Illinois, in 1935. She received her B.A. from Radcliffe and served as a civic leader and adjunct professor prior to her political career. Before her election to Congress, Nancy Johnson was a three-term Connecticut state senator. She is married and the mother of three children.

Congresswoman Johnson is a proponent of reforming federal trade policies and improving child day care and health care. She is also active on issues of welfare reform and environmental protection.

Representative Marcy Kaptur (Democrat, 9th District, Ohio) was elected to Congress in 1983. She is a member of the House Appropriations Committee and is treasurer of the Congressional Caucus for Women's Issues.

Rep. Kaptur was born in 1946 Toledo, Ohio, and earned her B.A. from the University of Wisconsin and her M.A. in urban planning from the University of Michigan. She was an urban planner for 15 years before seeking congressional office and served as an urban advisor to President Carter.

Recent legislation sponsored by Congresswoman Kaptur addresses such issues as child care in public housing, environmental protection, and new GI education benefits.

Senator Nancy Landon Kassebaum (Republican, Kansas) was first elected to the United States Senate in 1978. She is currently on the Committees on Foreign Relations; Labor and Human Resources; Banking, Housing and Urban Affairs; and the Select Committee on Indian Affairs.

Born in Topeka, Kansas, in 1932, Nancy Kassebaum is the daughter of Alfred M. Landon, former governor of Kansas and Republican presidential nominee. Senator Kassebaum earned her B.A. from the University of Kansas and her M.A. in diplomatic history from the University of Michigan. A former radio executive, Ms. Kassebaum entered politics as a member of the Maize, Kansas School Board. She is the mother of four children.

As ranking Republican on the Senate Subcommittee on

Education, Senator Kassebaum is working on strengthening the status of women and families, and advocates the coordination of government services for children and families.

Representative Barbara B. Kennelly (Democrat, 1st District, Connecticut) has been in Congress since 1982. She currently serves on the House Ways and Means Committee and is the first woman to sit on the Permanent Select Committee on Intelligence.

Born in 1936 and raised in Hartford, Connecticut, Rep. Kennelly earned her B.A. from Trinity College in Washington, D.C., and her M.A. from Trinity College in Hartford. She is married to James J. Kennelly, former Connecticut state representative and Speaker of the House, and has four children. Prior to her congressional election, Barbara Kennelly served as Secretary of State in Connecticut and as a member of the Hartford Court of Common Council.

Congresswoman Kennelly's legislative priorities include child support enforcement, welfare reform, and long-term care insurance.

Representative Marilyn Lloyd (Democrat, 3rd District, Tennessee) became the first woman from Tennessee elected by popular vote to the House of Representatives in 1974. She is on the Science, Space and Technology Committee; the House Armed Services Committee; and the Select Committee on Aging.

Rep. Lloyd was born in Fort Smith, Arkansas, in 1929, and is the mother of four children. Prior to her election to Congress, Marilyn Lloyd was the owner and manager of a radio station.

Ms. Lloyd recently worked to reintroduce the Breast Cancer Screening Safety Act and to establish mammogram quality standards.

Representative Jill Long (Democrat, 4th District, Indiana) was first elected to Congress in a special election on March 28, 1989. She serves on the Committee on Agriculture, the Committee on Veterans' Affairs, and the Select Committee on Hunger.

Rep. Long was born in Warsaw, Indiana, in 1952. She was first elected to public office in 1983, when she won a seat on the Valparaiso City Council. Before entering politics, Congresswoman Long was an assistant professor of business administration at Valparaiso University, where she earned her B.A., and an adjunct professor of marketing at Indiana University, where she earned both her M.B.A. and Ph.D. degrees.

Congresswoman Long supports the Family and Medical Leave bill, providing job-protected family leave to workers, and is committed to improving the workplace environment and its impact on the American family.

Representative Nita M. Lowey (Democrat, 20th District, New York) was first elected to the House of Representatives in 1988. She serves on the Committee on Education and Labor and on the Committee on Merchant Marine and Fisheries.

Rep. Lowey was born in the Bronx, New York, in 1937 and received her B.A. from Mt. Holyoke College. She served in the New York Department of State for 12 years and was one of the founders of the New York State Association of Women Office Holders. She is married and the mother of three children.

Nita Lowey's legislative efforts include improving child nutrition programs, expanding affordable child care, environmental protection, and quality health care.

Representative Jan Meyers (Republican, 3rd District, Kansas), elected to Congress in 1984, currently sits on the

Foreign Affairs Committee, the Committee on Small Business, and the Select Committee on Aging.

Born in Lincoln, Nebraska, in 1928, Ms. Meyers earned a B.A. in communications at the University of Nebraska. She served five years on the Overland Park City Council and 12 years in the Kansas Senate prior to her election to the House of Representatives. She is married and has two children.

Rep. Meyers's legislative priorities include family health care, child care, and improving low-income housing for families.

Senator Barbara A. Mikulski (Democrat, Maryland), elected to the United States Senate in 1986, was the first Democratic woman to serve in both houses of Congress and was the first woman to win a statewide election in Maryland. She sits on the Senate Appropriations Committee, the Labor and Human Resources Committee, and the Small Business Committee.

Senator Mikulski began her career in public service as a Baltimore social worker and entered politics with her election to the Baltimore City Council. Born in Baltimore in 1936, Barbara Mikulski earned her B.A. from Mount St. Agnes College and received her M.S.W. degree from the University of Maryland.

The upcoming legislative agenda for Senator Mikulski includes an emphasizes women's health needs and ensuring that women and families are provided equal opportunities.

Representative Patsy T. Mink (Democrat, 2nd District, Hawaii), who was first elected to Congress in 1964 and served until 1977, returned to the House in September of 1990 after winning the special election to complete the unexpired term of Congressman Daniel Akaka. Mink then won re-election in November of 1990 to a full two year term. Representative

Mink sits on the Education and Labor Committee as well as on the Government Operations Committee.

Congresswoman Mink was born in 1927 in Paia, Hawaii, and has been in public service for more than 35 years. After earning a B.A. from the University of Hawaii and a Doctor of Law from the University of Chicago Law School, Patsy Mink went on to serve in Hawaii's House of Representatives and later in the state Senate. Representative Mink was appointed Assistant Secretary of State (OES) under the Carter Administration. Prior to her most recent election to Congress, Representative Mink served on the Honolulu City Council and as Chair of the Council for 2 years. She is married and has one daughter.

Rep. Mink advocates improvements in the American educational system and is a supporter of the Family and Medical Leave Act.

Representative Susan Molinari (Republican, 14th District, New York) came to Congress in a special 1990 election to fill the vacant seat left by her father, Guy V. Molinari. She serves on the Committees on Public Works and Transportation and Education and Labor.

Born on Staten Island, New York, in 1958, Congresswoman Molinari earned both her B.A. and M.A. degrees from the State University Center at Albany. She became the youngest person ever elected to the New York City Council in 1985, where she served before entering the House of Representatives.

Rep. Molinari is an outspoken advocate of environmental protection and a supporter of the Family and Medical Leave Act and the Women's Equal Opportunity Act.

Representative Constance A. Morella (Republican, 8th District, Maryland) was first elected to the House in 1986, where she now serves on the Science, Space and Technology Committee; the Post Office and Civil Service Committee; and the Select Committee on Aging. She also chairs the Arms Control and Foreign Policy Caucus, and is vice-chair of the Clearinghouse on the Future.

Rep. Morella was born in Somerville, Massachusetts, in 1931. She received her A.B. from Boston University and her M.A. from American University. She served for eight years in the Maryland General Assembly. Prior to entering politics, Rep. Morella was a professor of English at Montgomery College. She is married and has raised nine children.

Constance Morella's legislative agenda includes efforts to address the growing AIDS epidemic among women, domestic violence, and professional equity for women.

Representative Eleanor Holmes Norton (Democrat, District of Columbia Delegate) is serving her first term as non-voting delegate. She is the first woman elected to represent the District of Columbia in the House of Representatives. Representative Norton serves on the District of Columbia Committee, the Post Office and Civil Service Committee, and the Public Works and Transportation Committee.

Congresswoman Norton was born in the District of Columbia in 1937. She earned her B.A. degree from Antioch College and her M.A. and a law degree from Yale University. Prior to her recent election, Eleanor Norton was a law professor at Georgetown University. She has two children.

Representative Norton's legislative agenda focuses on economic and political independence for the District of Columbia, and she is a supporter of the Civil Rights Act of 1991.

Representative Mary Rose Oakar (Democrat, 20th District, Ohio) was first elected to Congress in 1976. She serves on the Banking, Finance and Urban Affairs Committee; the Committee on House Administration; the Post Office and Civil Service Committee; and the Select Committee on Aging. She was the first Democratic woman from Ohio elected to Congress.

Born in 1940 in Cleveland, Ohio, Rep. Oakar earned a B.A. from Ursuline College and an M.A. from John Carroll University. She served as a Cleveland City Councilwoman before her election to the House of Representatives.

In the 102nd Congress, Ms. Oakar's legislative focus includes reform of health benefits for federal employees, support of breast cancer and Alzheimer's disease research, and ending discrimination against women in the Social Security system.

Representative Elizabeth J. Patterson (Democrat, 4th District, South Carolina) was first elected to Congress in 1986. She is currently serving on the Veterans' Affairs Committee; the Select Committee on Hunger; and the Banking, Finance and Urban Affairs Committee.

Rep. Patterson was born into a political family in 1939 in Columbia, South Carolina. Her father, Olin D. Johnston, served as both a U.S. Senator and as governor of South Carolina. Congresswoman Patterson is a graduate of Columbia College, is married, and has three children. She began her political career as a member of the Spartanburg County Council, and went on to serve in the South Carolina state Senate before her election to Congress.

Elizabeth Patterson actively works for federal budget reform and reduction of the U.S. trade deficit.

Representative Nancy Pelosi (Democrat, 5th District, California) was elected to Congress in 1987. She serves on the House Appropriations Committee and the Committee on Standards of Official Conduct (Ethics).

Born in 1940 in Baltimore, Maryland, Rep. Pelosi comes from a family with a tradition of public service. Her father, Thomas D'Alesandro, Jr., served in Congress for 10 years and both he and her brother were mayors of Baltimore. Congresswoman Pelosi earned her B.A. from Trinity College and later served as state chair of the California Democratic Party. She and her husband reside in San Francisco and have five children.

Legislatively, Rep. Pelosi is concerned with human rights, promotion of the Women's Health Equity Act, and environmental protection.

Representative Patricia Schroeder (Democrat, 1st District, Colorado) was elected to the House of Representatives in 1972 and is the most senior woman in Congress. She serves on the House Armed Services Committee; the Judiciary Committee; the Post Office and Civil Service Committee; and the Select Committee on Children, Youth and Families, of which she is the chairwoman. Congresswoman Schroeder is also co-chair of the Congressional Caucus for Women's Issues.

Born in Portland, Oregon, in 1940, Rep. Schroeder earned her B.A. from the University of Minnesota and her J.D. from Harvard University. She was a practicing attorney and university lecturer before her election to the House. She is married and has two children.

Patricia Schroeder's top priorities include family issues, women's health, and defense burdensharing. In the future, she plans to focus on workplace reform geared toward the family, and to ease tax burdens on middle-class families.

Representative Louise M. Slaughter (Democrat, 30th District, New York) was elected to the House of Representatives in 1986. She serves on the House Budget Committee, the Select Committee on Aging, and is the only woman currently serving on the House Rules Committee.

Rep. Slaughter was born in Harlan County, Kentucky, in 1929 and received both her B.S. and M.S. degrees from the University of Kentucky. She entered the Monroe County Legislature in New York in 1975 and went on to serve in the New York State Assembly before her bid for Congress. She is married and the mother of three children.

Congresswoman Slaughter's major legislative priorities for this Congress include educating homeless children, increasing funding for Head Start and child immunization, and enacting the Family and Medical Leave Act, which would provide workers with job-protected family leave policies.

Representative Olympia Snowe (Republican, 2nd District, Maine) is serving her seventh term in Congress. In her first term, she was the youngest Republican woman ever elected to the House of Representatives. She serves on the House Committee on Foreign Affairs, the Joint Economic Committee, and the Select Committee on Aging. Olympia Snowe is co-chair of the Congressional Caucus for Women's Issues and also serves as an Assistant Republican Party Whip.

Rep. Snowe was born in Augusta, Maine, in 1947 and received her B.A. from the University of Maine. She began her political career in 1973 when she was first elected to the Maine House to fill the seat vacated by her late husband. Ms. Snowe is married to Governor John R. McKernan, Jr.

Rep. Snowe's agenda for women focuses on ensuring that women are included in medical research by establishing an Office of Research on Women's Health at the National Institutes of Health, providing resources for osteoporosis research, and addressing the health and economic needs of women in developing countries around the world.

Representative Jolene Unsoeld (Democrat, 3rd District, Washington) was elected to the House of Representatives in 1988. She serves on the Education and Labor Committee, the Merchant Marine and Fisheries Committee, and the House Select Committee on Aging.

Rep. Unsoeld was born in Corvallis, Oregon, in 1931 and attended Oregon State University. Before her election to Congress, Ms. Unsoeld was a citizen lobbyist, a member of the Washington State Legislature and the first woman to climb the direct North Face of the Grand Teton mountain. She is a widow and has three children.

Congresswoman Unsoeld is a supporter of family and medical leave legislation, environmental protection, and reproductive freedom for women.

Representative Maxine Waters (Democrat, 29th District, California) was elected to Congress in 1990. She serves on the Committee on Banking, Finance and Urban Affairs and the Committee on Veterans' Affairs.

Born in St. Louis, Missouri, in 1938, Rep. Waters earned a B.A. in sociology from California State University. Prior to her election to Congress, Ms. Waters served in the California State Assembly for nearly 15 years, where she became the first woman to be elected to chair the Assembly Democratic Caucus. She is married and is the mother of two children.

In the 102nd Congress, Maxine Waters's legislative priorities are women, children, and the American family.

Congressional Caucus for Women's Issues

Neil Abercrombie (D-HI)

Gary L. Ackerman (D-NY)

Michael A. Andrews (D-TX)

Robert Andrews (D-NJ)

Beryl Anthony, Jr. (D-AR)

Les Aspin (D-WI)

Chester G. Atkins (D-MA)

Les AuCoin (D-OR)

Anthony C. Beilenson (D-CA)

Howard L. Berman (D-CA)

David E. Bonior (D-MI)

Robert A. Borski (D-PA)

*Barbara Boxer (D-CA)

George E. Brown, Jr. (D-CA)

John Bryant (D-TX)

Ben Nighthorse Campbell (D-CO)

Tom Campbell (R-CA)

Benjamin L. Cardin (D-MD)

Thomas R. Carper (D-DE)

Rod Chandler (R-WA)

William Clay (D-MO)

Ronald D. Coleman (D-TX)

*Barbara-Rose Collins (D-MI)

*Cardiss Collins (D-IL)

Gary Condit (D-CA)

John Conyers, Jr. (D-MI)

Jerry F. Costello (D-IL)

Peter A. DeFazio (D-OR)

*Rosa DeLauro (D-CT)

Ronald V. Dellums (D-CA)

Norman D. Dicks (D-WA)

John D. Dingell (D-MI)

Julian C. Dixon (D-CA)

Calvin Dooley (D-CA)

Thomas J. Downey (D-NY)

Richard J. Durbin (D-IL)

Bernard J. Dwyer (D-NJ)

Dennis E. Eckart (D-OH)

Don Edwards (D-CA)

Ben Erdreich (D-AL)

Lane Evans (D-IL)

Dante B. Fascell (D-FL)

Vic Fazio (D-CA)

Hamilton Fish, Jr. (R-NY)

Floyd Flake (D-NY)

Thomas M. Foglietta (D-PA)

Thomas S. Foley, Speaker of the House (D-WA)

Barney Frank (D-MA)

Martin Frost (D-TX)

Jaime B. Fuster (Del-D-PR)

Sam Gejdenson (D-CT)

Richard A. Gephardt (D-MO)

Benjamin A. Gilman (R-NY)

William H. Gray, III (D-PA)

Bill Green (R-NY)

Frank J. Guarini (D-NJ)

Steven Gunderson (R-WI)

Charles A. Hayes (D-IL)

George J. Hochbruecker (D-NY)

*Joan Kelly Horn (D-MO)

Frank Horton (R-NY)

Steny H. Hoyer (D-MD)

*Nancy L. Johnson (R-CT)

Harry Johnston (D-FL)

Jim Jontz (D-IN)

*Marcy Kaptur (D-OH)

*Nancy Landon Kassebaum (Sen-R-KS)

Joseph P. Kennedy, II (D-MA)

*Barbara B. Kennelly (D-CT)

Dale E. Kildee (D-MI)
Gerald D. Kleczka (D-WI)
Mike Kopetski (D-OR)
John J. LaFalce (D-NY)
Tom Lantos (D-CA)
Jim Leach (R-IA)
William Lehman (D-FL)
Sander M. Levin (D-MI)
Mel Levine (D-CA)
John Lewis (D-GA)
William O. Lipinski (D-IL)
*Marilyn Lloyd (D-TN)
*Jill L. Long (D-IN)
*Nita M. Lowey (D-NY)
Frank McCloskey (D-IN)
Jim McDermott (D-WA)
Matthew F. McHugh (D-NY)
Thomas C. McMillen (D-MD)
Ronald K. Machtley (R-RI)
Edward J. Markey (D-MA)
Matthew G. Martinez (D-CA)
Robert T. Matsui (D-CA)
*Jan Meyers (R-KS)
Kweisi Mfume (D-MD)
*Barbara Mikulski (Sen-D-MD)
George Miller (D-CA)
John Miller (R-WA)
Norman Y. Mineta (D-CA)
*Patsy Mink (D-HI)
John Joseph Moakley (D-MA)
*Susan Molinari (R-NY)
Jim Moody (D-WI)
James Moran (D-VA)
*Constance A. Morella (R-MD)
Sid Morrison (R-WA)
Robert J. Mrazek (D-NY)
Richard E. Neal (D-MA)
Stephen L. Neal (D-NC)

*Eleanor Holmes Norton (Del-D-DC)
Henry J. Nowak (D-NY)
*Mary Rose Oakar (D-OH)
James L. Oberstar (D-MN)
Major R. Owens (D-NY)
Wayne Owens (D-UT)
*Elizabeth Patterson (D-SC)
Donald M. Payne (D-NJ)
*Nancy Pelosi (D-CA)
Jim Ramstad (R-MN)
Charles B. Rangel (D-NY)
John F. Reed (D-RI)
Bill Richardson (D-NM)
Robert A. Roe (D-NJ)
Charles Rose (D-NC)
Martin Olav Sabo (D-MN)
Bernard Sanders (I-VT)
George E. Sangmeister (D-IL)
Thomas C. Sawyer (D-OH)
James H. Scheuer (D-NY)
*Patricia Schroeder (D-CO)
Jose E. Serrano (D-NY)
Christopher Shays (R-CT)
Gerry Sikorski (D-MN)
David E. Skaggs (D-CO)
*Louise Slaughter (D-NY)
Lawrence J. Smith (D-FL)
*Olympia J. Snowe (R-ME)
Harley O. Staggers, Jr. (D-WV)
Louis Stokes (D-OH)
Gerry E. Studds (D-MA)
Dick Swett (D-NH)
Al Swift (D-WA)
Mike Synar (D-OK)
Edolphus Towns (D-NY)
Morris K. Udall (D-AZ)
*Jolene Unsoeld (D-WA)

Bruce F. Vento (D-MN)
Peter J. Visclosky (D-IN)
Craig A. Washington (D-TX)
*Maxine Waters (D-CA)
Henry A. Waxman (D-CA)
Ted Weiss (D-NY)

Alan Wheat (D-MO)
Pat Williams (D-MT)
Howard Wolpe (D-MI)
Ron Wyden (D-OR)
Sidney R. Yates (D-IL)

*Executive committee member.

References

Introduction

Kurth, Peter. *American Cassandra*. Boston, MA: Little, Brown, and Co., 1990.

O N E Changing the Rules and the Roles: Five Women in Public Office

Boyarsky, Bill. Personal conversation with author, October 22, 1990.

Kennedy, Michael J. "The Cowboy and the Good Ol' Girl." *Los Angeles Times Magazine*, October 21, 1990.

McNeely, Dave. *Austin American Statesman*, March 25, 1990.

Northcott, Kaye. *Ft. Worth Star-Telegram*, March 12, 1990.

Richards, Ann, with Peter Knobler. *Straight From the Heart*. NY: Simon and Schuster, 1989.

The Hartford Courant. February 15, 1991.

The Texas Poll Report 7. No. 4, November 1990.

Woolf, Virginia. *A Room of One's Own*. NY: Harcourt, Brace, and World, 1929.

T H R E E Do Women Office Holders Make a Difference?

Associated Press. March 17, 1982.

Burns, Nancy Elizabeth, and Paul Schumaker. "Gender Differences in Attitudes about the Role of Local Government." *Social Science Quarterly* 68 (March 1987): 138–147.

Carroll, Susan J., and Wendy S. Strimling. *Women's Routes to Elective Office: A Comparison with Men's*. New Brunswick, NJ: Center for the American Woman and Politics, Eagleton Institute of Politics, Rutgers University, 1983.

Center for the American Woman and Politics (CAWP). *Women in Elective Office 1991 Fact Sheet*. New Brunswick, NJ: CAWP, Eagleton Institute of Politics, Rutgers University, 1991.

Freeman, Jo. *The Politics of Women's Liberation: A Case Study of an Emerging Social Movement and Its Relation to the Policy Process*. New York: David McKay Co., 1979.

Havens, Catherine, and Lynne M. Healy. "The Impact of Women in Appointive Public Office: Cabinet Level Appointees in One State." In *The Impact of Women in Public Office*. New Brunswick, NJ: Center for the American Woman and Politics, Eagleton Institute of Politics, Rutgers University, 1991.

Johnson, Marilyn, and Susan J. Carroll. "Profile of Women Holding Office II." In *Women and Public Office: A Bibliographic Directory and Statistical Analysis*. 2d ed., compiled by the Center for the American Woman and Politics. Metuchen, NJ: Scarecrow Press, 1978.

Klein, Ethel. *Gender Politics*. Cambridge, MA: Harvard University Press, 1984.

Mandel, Ruth B. "Outside/Inside: The Continuing Tradition of U.S. Women's Political Leadership." Paper prepared for *Meeting the Challenge: Women as Leaders, The Radcliffe Conferences*, Cambridge, MA, May 1989.

Martin, Elaine. "Judicial Gender and Judicial Choices." In *The Impact of Women in Public Office*. New Brunswick, NJ: Center for the American Woman and Politics, Eagleton Institute of Politics, Rutgers University, 1991.

Merritt, Sharyne. "Sex Differences in Role Behavior and Policy Orientations of Suburban Officeholders: The Effect of Women's Employment." In *Women in Local Politics*, edited by Debra W. Stewart. Metuchen, NJ: Scarecrow Press, 1980.

Mezey, Susan Gluck. "Women and Representation: The Case of Hawaii." *Journal of Politics* 40 (1978): 369–385.

Rix, Sara E., ed. *The American Woman 1988–89: A Status Report*. NY: W.W. Norton and Company, 1988.

Shalala, Donna E. Speech delivered at the Round Table Conference on Minorities and Women, sponsored by the International City Management Association, Washington, DC, June 1979.

Shanahan, Eileen. "Women Organize for Political Power." *The New York Times*, July 11, 1971.

Stanwick, Kathy, and Katherine E. Kleeman. *Women Make a Difference*. New Brunswick, NJ: Center for the American Woman and Politics, Eagleton Institute of Politics, Rutgers University, 1983.

Tolchin, Susan J. *Women in Congress*. Washington, DC: U.S. House of Representatives, Report No. 94-1732, 1976.

Welch, Susan, and Sue Thomas. "Do Women in Public Office Make a Difference?" In *The Impact of Women in Public Office*. New Brunswick, NJ: Center for the American Woman and Politics, Eagleton Institute of Politics, Rutgers University, 1991.

Section 1: Population

National Center for Health Statistics. "Advance Report of Final Natality Statistics, 1988." *Monthly Vital Statistics Report*. Vol. 39, No. 4, Supplement. Hyattsville, MD: U.S. Department of Health and Human Services, August 15, 1990.

_____. "Advance Report of Final Mortality Statistics, 1988." *Monthly Vital Statistics Report*. Vol. 39, No. 7, Supplement. Hyattsville, MD: U.S. Department of Health and Human Services, November 28, 1990.

U.S. Bureau of the Census. Current Population Reports, Series P-25, No. 917. *Preliminary Estimates of the Population of the United States by Age, Sex, and Race: 1970 to 1981*. Washington, DC: U.S. Government Printing Office, July 1982.

_____. *General Population Characteristics: United States Summary*. No. PC80-1-B1. Washington, DC: U.S. Government Printing Office, May 1983.

_____. Current Population Reports, Series P-25, No. 1018. *Projections of the Population by Age, Sex, and Race: 1988–2080*. Washington, DC: U.S. Government Printing Office, January 1989.

_____. Current Population Reports, Series P-25, No. 1057. *U.S. Population Estimates by Age, Sex, Race, and Hispanic Origin: 1989*. Washington, DC: U.S. Government Printing Office, March 1990.

U.S. Department of Commerce. Press Release CB91–215. Washington, DC: U.S. Department of Commerce, June 12, 1991.

Section 2: Health

Alan Guttmacher Institute. *Abortion and Women's Health*. Washington, DC: Alan Guttmacher Institute, 1990.

Centers for Disease Control. *HIV/AIDS Surveillance*. Atlanta, GA: U.S. Department of Health and Human Services, January 1987.

_____. *HIV/AIDS Surveillance*. Atlanta, GA: U.S. Department of Health and Human Services, January 1988.

_____. *HIV/AIDS Surveillance*. Atlanta, GA: U.S. Department of Health and Human Services, January 1989.

_____. *HIV/AIDS Surveillance*. Atlanta, GA: U.S. Department of Health and Human Services, January 1990.

_____. *CDC Surveillance Summaries*. June 1990. MMWR 1990; 39 (No. SS-2).

_____. *HIV/AIDS Surveillance*. Atlanta, GA: U.S. Department of Health and Human Services, January 1991.

_____. *HIV/AIDS Surveillance*. Atlanta, GA: U.S. Department of Health and Human Services, March 1991.

National Cancer Institute. *Cancer Statistics Review 1973–1988*. Bethesda, MD: National Institutes of Health, 1991.

National Center for Health Statistics. "Breast Cancer Risk Factors and Screening: United States, 1987." *Vital and Health Statistics Bulletin*. Hyattsville, MD: U.S. Department of Health and Human Services, January 1990.

_____. *Contraceptive Use in the United States: 1973–88*. Advance Data, No. 182. Hyattsville, MD: U.S. Department of Health and Human Services, March 20, 1990.

_____. "Advance Report of Final Natality Statistics, 1988." *Monthly Vital Statistics Report*. Vol. 39, No. 4, Supplement. Hyattsville, MD: U.S. Department of Health and Human Services, August 15, 1990.

_____. "Advance Report of Final Mortality Statistics, 1988." *Monthly Vital Statistics Report*. Vol. 39, No. 7, Supplement. Hyattsville, MD: U.S. Department of Health and Human Services, November 28, 1990.

U.S. Bureau of the Census. *Statistical Abstract of the United States 1990*. Washington, DC: U.S. Government Printing Office, January 1990.

_____. Current Population Reports, Series P-23, No. 165. "Maternity Leave Arrangements: 1961–85." *Work and Family Patterns of American Women*. Washington, DC: U.S. Government Printing Office, March 1990.

U.S. House of Representatives. Select Committee on Children, Youth, and Families. *U.S. Children and Their Families: Current Conditions and Recent Trends, 1989*. Washington, DC: U.S. Government Printing Office, November 1989.

Section 3: Family and Household Structure

U.S. Bureau of the Census. Current Population Reports, Series P-20, No. 218. *Household and Family Characteristics: 1970*. Washington, DC: U.S. Government Printing Office, March 1971.

_____. Current Population Reports, Series P-60, No. 127. *Money Income and Poverty Status of Families and Persons in the United States: 1980*. Washington, DC: U.S. Government Printing Office, August 1981.

_____. Current Population Reports, Series P-23, No. 162. *Studies in Marriage and the Family*. Washington, DC: U.S. Government Printing Office, June 1989.

_____. Current Population Reports, Series P-60, No. 168. *Money Income and Poverty Status in the United States: 1989*. Washington, DC: U.S. Government Printing Office, September 1990.

_____. Current Population Reports, Series P-20, No. 447. *Household and Family Characteristics: March 1990 and 1989*. Washington, DC: U.S. Government Printing Office, December 1990.

_____. Current Population Reports, Series P-20, No. 450. *Marital Status and Living Arrangements: March 1990*. Washington, DC: U.S. Government Printing Office, May 1991.

Section 4: Child Care and Support

U.S. Bureau of the Census. Current Population Reports, Series P-23, No. 127. *Child Care Arrangements of Working Mothers: June 1982*. Washington, DC: U.S. Government Printing Office, November 1983.

_____. Current Population Reports, Series P-23, No. 167. *Child Support and Alimony: 1987*. Washington, DC: U.S. Government Printing Office, June 1990.

_____. Current Population Reports, Series P-70, No. 20. *Who's Minding the Kids?* Washington, DC: U.S. Government Printing Office, July 1990.

U.S. Bureau of Labor Statistics. *Handbook of Labor Statistics*. Washington, DC: U.S. Government Printing Office, August 1989.

Section 5: Education

American Council on Education. *1989–90 Fact Book on Higher Education*. NY: Macmillan Publishing Company, 1989.

Cooperative Institutional Research Program. *The American Freshman: Twenty Year Trends*. Los Angeles: Higher Education Research Institute, January 1987.

_____. *The American Freshman 1987*. Los Angeles: Higher Education Research Institute, December 1987.

_____. *The American Freshman 1989*. Los Angeles: Higher Education Research Institute, December 1989.

"The Future of Academic Salaries: Will the 1990s Be a Bust Like the 1970s or a Boom Like the 1980s?" *Academe* 77 (March-April 1991): 9–33.

National Center for Education Statistics. *Digest of Education Statistics 1989*. Washington, DC: U.S. Department of Education, December 1989.

_____. *The Condition of Education 1990*. Washington, DC: U.S. Department of Education, 1990.

_____. *Digest of Education Statistics 1990*. Washington, DC: U.S. Department of Education, February 1991.

Touchton, Judith G., and Lynne Davis. *Fact Book on Women in Higher Education 1990*. NY: Macmillan Publishing Company, 1991.

U.S. Bureau of the Census. *Statistical Abstract of the United States 1990*. Washington, DC: U.S. Government Printing Office, January 1990.

U.S. Department of Health, Education and Welfare. Office for Civil Rights. *Data on Earned Degrees Conferred by Institutions of Higher Education by Race, Ethnicity and Sex, Academic Year 1976–1977*. Photocopy.

Section 6: Employment

Heidrick and Struggles Communications Department. *The Changing Board*. Chicago: Heidrick and Struggles, 1990.

U.S. Bureau of the Census. *Women-Owned Businesses 1977*. Washington, DC: U.S. Government Printing Office, May 1980.

_____. Current Population Reports, Series P-23, No. 160. *Labor Force Characteristics of Persons with a Work Disability: 1981 to 1988*. Washington, DC: U.S. Government Printing Office, July 1989.

_____. *Women-Owned Businesses 1987*. Washington, DC: U.S. Government Printing Office, August 1990.

U.S. Bureau of Labor Statistics. *Employment and Earnings*. Washington, DC: U.S. Government Printing Office, January 1984.

_____. "Occupational Employment Statistics for 1972–82." *Employment and Earnings*. Washington, DC: U.S. Government Printing Office, January 1984.

_____. *Labor Force Statistics Derived from the Current Population Survey*. BLS Bulletin 237. Washington, DC: U.S. Government Printing Office, August 1988.

_____. *Handbook of Labor Statistics*. Washington, DC: U.S. Government Printing Office, August 1989.

_____. "Industry Output and Employment: A Slower Trend for the Nineties." *Monthly Labor Review* 112, No. 11 (November 1989): 25–41.

_____. "New Labor Force Projections, Spanning 1988 to 2000." *Monthly Labor Review* 112, No. 11 (November 1989): 3–12.

_____. "Projections of Occupational Employment, 1988–2000." *Monthly Labor Review* 112, No. 11 (November 1989): 42–65.

_____. "Multiple Jobholding Up Sharply in the 1980's." *Monthly Labor Review* 113, No. 7 (July 1990): 3–9.

_____. *Employment and Earnings*. Washington, DC: U.S. Government Printing Office, January 1991.

U.S. Office of Personnel Management. *Affirmative Employment Statistics*. Washington, DC: U.S. Government Printing Office, 1982.

_____. *Affirmative Employment Statistics*. Washington, DC: U.S. Government Printing Office, 1988.

Women's Research and Education Institute (WREI). *Women in the Military 1980–1990*. Washington, DC: Women's Research and Education Institute, June 1990.

Section 7: Earnings and Benefits

U.S. Bureau of the Census. Current Population Reports, Series P-60, No. 131. *Characteristics of Households and Persons Receiving Noncash Benefits: 1980*. Washington, DC: U.S. Government Printing Office, May 1982.

_____. *Receipt of Noncash Benefits: 1987*. Report from the March 1988 Current Population Survey. Photocopy.

_____. Current Population Reports, Series P-23, No. 160. *Labor Force Characteristics of Persons with a Work Disability: 1981 to 1988*. Washington, DC: U.S. Government Printing Office, July 1989.

_____. *Statistical Abstract of the United States 1990*. Washington, DC: U.S. Government Printing Office, January 1990.

_____. Current Population Reports, Series P-70, No. 17. *Health Insurance Coverage: 1986–88*. Washington, DC: U.S. Government Printing Office, March 1990.

U.S. Bureau of Labor Statistics. *Employment and Earnings*. Washington, DC: U.S. Government Printing Office, January 1985.

_____. *Handbook of Labor Statistics*. Washington, DC: U.S. Government Printing Office, August 1989.

_____. "1989 Employee Benefits Address Family Concerns." *Monthly Labor Review* 113, No. 6 (June 1990): 61–63.

_____. *Employment and Earnings*. Washington, DC: U.S. Government Printing Office, January 1991.

_____. Press Release USDL 91–260, June 10, 1991.

Section 8: Income and Assets

U.S. Bureau of the Census. Current Population Reports, Series P-60, No. 127. *Money Income and Poverty Status of Families and Persons in the United States: 1980*. Washington, DC: U.S. Government Printing Office, August 1981.

_____. Current Population Reports, Series P-60, No. 129. *Money Income of Families and Persons in the United States: 1979*. Washington, DC: U.S. Government Printing Office, November 1981.

_____. Current Population Reports, Series P-60, No. 130. *Characteristics of the Population Below the Poverty Line: 1979*. Washington, DC: U.S. Government Printing Office, December 1981.

_____. Current Population Reports, Series P-60, No. 145. *Money Income and Poverty Status of Families and Persons in the United States: 1983*. Washington, DC: U.S. Government Printing Office, August 1984.

_____. Current Population Reports, Series P-60, No. 147. *Characteristics of the Population Below the Poverty Level: 1983*. Washington, DC: U.S. Government Printing Office, February 1985.

_____. Current Population Reports, Series P-60, No. 157. *Money Income and Poverty Status of Families and Persons in the United States: 1986*. Washington, DC: U.S. Government Printing Office, July 1987.

_____. Current Population Reports, Series P-60, No. 160. *Poverty in the United States 1986*. Washington, DC: U.S. Government Printing Office, June 1988.

_____. Current Population Reports, Series P-23, No. 160. *Labor Force Characteristics of Persons with a Work Disability: 1981 to 1988.* Washington, DC: U.S. Government Printing Office, July 1989.

_____. Current Population Reports, Series P-60, No. 168. *Money Income and Poverty Status in the United States: 1989.* Washington, DC: U.S. Government Printing Office, September 1990.

_____. Current Population Reports, Series P-20, No. 450. *Household and Family Characteristics: March 1990 and 1989.* Washington, DC: U.S. Government Printing Office, December 1990.

_____. Current Population Reports, Series P-70, No. 22. *Household Wealth and Asset Ownership 1988.* Washington, DC: U.S. Government Printing Office, December 1990.

U.S. Bureau of the Census and U.S. Department of Housing and Urban Development. *American Housing Survey for the United States in 1987.* Washington, DC: U.S. Government Printing Office, December 1989.

U.S. Bureau of Labor Statistics. *Handbook of Labor Statistics.* Washington, DC: U.S. Government Printing Office, August 1989.

_____. *Employment and Earnings.* Washington, DC: U.S. Government Printing Office, January 1991.

Section 9: Politics

Administrative Office of the United States Courts. *Annual Report on the Judiciary Equal Employment Opportunity Program.* Washington, DC: Administrative Office of the United States Courts, September 30, 1990.

Center for the American Woman and Politics (CAWP). *Women in Elective Office 1991 Fact Sheet.* New Brunswick, NJ: CAWP, Eagleton Institute of Politics, Rutgers University, 1991.

National Women's Political Caucus (NWCP). *Factsheet on Women's Political Progress.* Preliminary Data. Washington, DC: American Council of Life Insurance and the NWPC, July 1991.

U.S. Bureau of the Census. Current Population Reports, Series P-20, No. 143. *Voter Participation in the National Election of November 1964.* Washington, DC: U.S. Government Printing Office, October 1965.

_____. Current Population Reports, Series P-20, No. 322. *Voting and Registration in the Election of November 1976.* Washington, DC: U.S. Government Printing Office, March 1978.

_____. Current Population Reports, Series P-20, No. 370. *Voting and Registration in the Election of November 1980.* Washington, DC: U.S. Government Printing Office, April 1982.

_____. Current Population Reports, Series P-20, No. 405. *Voting and Registration in the Election of November 1984.* Washington, DC: U.S. Government Printing Office, March 1986.

_____. Current Population Reports, Series P-20, No. 440. *Voting and Registration in the Election of November 1988*. Washington, DC: U.S. Government Printing Office, October 1989.

Section 10: International Comparisons

Alan Guttmacher Institute. *Induced Abortion: A World Review: 1990 Supplement*. NY: Alan Guttmacher Institute, June 1990.

Centers for Disease Control. *Abortion Surveillance: 1986–87*. Atlanta, GA: U.S. Department of Health and Human Services, June 1990.

Fund for the Feminist Majority, The. *The Feminization of Power: An International Comparison*. Arlington, VA: The Fund for the Feminist Majority, March 1991.

International Labor Organization. *Economically Active Population: 1950–2020. Methodological Supplement*. Geneva, Switzerland: International Labor Organization, 1990.

_____. *Yearbook of Labor Statistics: 1989–90*. ed. Geneva, Switzerland: International Labor Organization, 1990.

Schmidt, William. "Who's in Charge Here? Chances Are it's a Woman." *The New York Times*. May 22, 1991.

Sivard, Ruth. *Women . . . A World Survey*. Washington, DC: World Priorities, Inc., 1985.

United Nations Department of Public Information. *Women in Politics*. NY: United Nations Publishing Service, 1990.

United Nations Population Fund. *The State of World Population: 1991*. NY: United Nations Population Fund, 1991.

U.S. Bureau of the Census. *World Population Profile: 1989*. Washington, DC: U.S. Government Printing Office, September 1989.

_____. *Statistical Abstract of the United States 1990*. Washington, DC: U.S. Government Printing Office, January 1990.

U.S. Bureau of Labor Statistics. *Handbook of Labor Statistics*. Washington, DC: U.S. Government Printing Office, August 1989.

_____. "The Changing Family in International Perspective." *Monthly Labor Review* 113, No. 3 (March 1990): 41–56.

Notes on the Contributors

Vincent J. Breglio is president and co-founder of Research/ Strategy/Management, Inc., a Washington, D.C.-based consulting firm formed in 1983. Dr. Breglio has been the executive director of the National Republican Senatorial Committee and was co-founder and president of Decision/Making/Information. He also served as director of polling for the Bush-Quayle 1988 presidential campaign and has conducted numerous public opinion surveys on subjects including the environment, abortion, gun control, and foreign affairs.

Debra L. Dodson is senior research associate at the Center for the American Woman and Politics (CAWP) and an assistant research professor at the Eagleton Institute of Politics at Rutgers University. Her work focuses on reproductive issues, women in politics, and political parties. She has directed research at CAWP on the role of the abortion issue in states elections and is currently investigating the impact of women in public office.

Betty Parsons Dooley has been director of the Women's Research and Education Institute since 1977. An early Texas feminist, she was active in state politics before moving to Washington, D.C. In 1964, she was a candidate for the U.S. House of Representatives from the 16th congressional district of Texas. She served for several years as director of the Health Security Action Council, an advocacy organization that worked for comprehensive national health insurance.

Celinda C. Lake is vice-president of Greenberg-Lake, The Analysis Group, Inc., a national polling firm, and has been widely recognized as an expert on the election of women candidates. She is the author of *Public Opinion Polling: A Manual for Public Interest Groups*, which was published in 1986. In 1984, she was chief analyst on the polling team at Peter Hart Research, Inc., for the Mondale-Ferraro campaign and has also served as political director for the Women's Campaign Fund prior to joining Greenberg-Lake.

Ruth B. Mandel is a professor at the Eagleton Institute of Politics at Rutgers University and is the director of Eagleton's Center for the American Woman and Politics (CAWP). She writes and speaks widely about women as political candidates, women in office, women's political networks, and the "gender gap." Her book, *In the Running: The New Woman Candidate* (Beacon Press, 1983), describes women's experiences campaigning for political office.

Celia Morris is the author of *Fanny Wright: Rebel in America* (Harvard Press, 1984) and of an upcoming book on the Texas and California gubernatorial races, *Storming the Statehouse*, to be published in April 1992 by Scribner's. In 1984 she was given the Woman of the Year award by the Texas Women's Political Caucus for her work in a voter registration program, "Texas Women for the 80s," which she designed and directed.

Irene Natividad is president of Natividad & Associates, a public affairs consulting firm in Washington, D.C., and has been named director of the 1992 Global Summit of Women. Ms. Natividad served two terms as president of the National Women's Political Caucus—the first Asian American to ever head a national political organization. She is on numerous boards and her efforts on behalf of women in politics have earned her many honors and awards, including the 1989 Woman of Distinction Award from the National Conference for College Women Student Leaders and the Women Making History Award from the Congressional Caucus for Women's Issues.

About the Women's Research and Education Institute

BETTY PARSONS DOOLEY, *Executive Director*
PAULA RIES, *Director of Research*
ANNE J. STONE, *Research Associate*
ALISON C. DINEEN, *Fellowship Program Director*
TERRY A. WALKER, *Office Manager*
NANCY L. PEPLINSKY, *Research Assistant*

THE WOMEN'S RESEARCH AND EDUCATION INSTITUTE (WREI) is a non-profit (501[c][3]) organization located in Washington, D.C. Established in 1977, WREI provides information, research, and policy analysis to the bipartisan Congressional Caucus for Women's Issues, as well as to other members of Congress. Over the years, WREI's reputation as a source of reliable data and clear thinking about the status of American women has traveled far beyond the nation's Capitol.

- WREI's resources are among the nation's best, and include research and policy centers throughout the country where scholars are conducting cutting-edge research on a host of issues concerning women.

- WREI puts vital information on key issues affecting women into the hands of policymakers in the form of reports and fact sheets that are prepared by WREI staff or outside scholars.

- WREI urges researchers to consider the public policy implications of their work and fosters the exchange of ideas and expertise between researchers and policymakers.

- WREI promotes the informed scrutiny of policies regarding their effect on women, and encourages the development of policy options that recognize the circumstances of today's women and their families.

- WREI identifies and trains new leaders through its Congressional Fellowships on Women and Public Policy. Established in 1980, this program enhances the research capacity of congressional offices, especially with respect to legislation's implications for women, and has given scores of promising women hands-on experience in the federal legislative process.

- WREI is a national information source and clearinghouse. Reporters, researchers, public officials, government agencies, advocacy organizations, and others contact WREI for information relating to women.

Board of Directors

Jean Stapleton, *President*
Dorothy Gregg, *Vice President*
Dorothy Height, *Secretary*
Esther Coopersmith, *Treasurer*
Lindy Boggs
Martina L. Bradford
Sharon Pratt Dixon
Evelyn Dubrow
Margaret M. Heckler
Joann Heffernan Heisen

Matina Horner
Juanita Kreps
Helen Stevenson Meyner
Alma Rangel
Annette Strauss
Celia G. Torres
Paquita Vivó
Diane E. Watson

Index

Page numbers in *italics* refer to illustrations.

About the Editors

PAULA RIES is director of research at the Women's Research and Education Institute (WREI), where she specializes in policy research and analysis. Her primary research interests are the implications of educational and employment policies for women. She holds a Ph.D. from the University of California, Los Angeles.

Before coming to WREI, Dr. Ries was a research analyst at the Higher Education Research Institute where she worked on a variety of research projects related to education at the institutional, state, and national levels, including a study of college alumni, an analysis of the efficacy of statewide job training providers, and an assessment of states' policies toward independent colleges and universities.

ANNE J. STONE is research associate at WREI, where she has authored and coauthored policy analyses on various subjects, including the federal budget, employment issues for women, and tax reform legislation. She has also worked on the three previous editions of *The American Woman*, coauthoring a chapter on women and affordable housing. Prior to coming to WREI, Ms. Stone served on the Washington staff of then-U.S. Representative Elizabeth Holtzman.